T0288236

The Main Event

Wilbur S. Shepperson Series in Nevada History

The Main Event

*Boxing in Nevada
from the Mining Camps
to the Las Vegas Strip*

Richard O. Davies

University of Nevada Press Reno & Las Vegas

Wilbur S. Shepperson Series in Nevada History

Series Editor: Michael S. Green

This publication is made possible in part by a
grant from Nevada Humanities, a state program
of the National Endowment for the Humanities.

University of Nevada Press, Reno, Nevada 89557 USA
Copyright © 2014 by University of Nevada Press
All rights reserved
Manufactured in the United States of America
Design by Kathleen Szawiola

Portions of chapter 4, "Nevada Loses Its Boxing Mojo," appear in
Mariann Vaczi, ed., *Playing Fields: Power, Practice, and Passion in Sports*
(Reno: Center for Basque Studies, 2014).

Library of Congress Cataloging-in-Publication Data
Davies, Richard O., 1937–
The main event : boxing in Nevada from the mining camps to
the Las Vegas strip / Richard O. Davies.
pages cm. — (Shepperson series in Nevada history)
Includes index.
ISBN 978-0-87417-928-6 (hardback)—
ISBN 978-0-87417-938-5 (e-book)
1. Boxing—Nevada—History. 2. Boxers (Sports)—Nevada—History.
3. Nevada—Social life and customs. I. Title.
GV1125.D38 2014
796.8309793—dc23   2013043529

The paper used in this book meets the requirements of American
National Standard for Information Sciences—Permanence of Paper
for Printed Library Materials, ANSI/NISO Z39.48-1992 (R2002).
Binding materials were selected for strength and durability.

First Printing
23 22 21 20 19 18 17 16 15 14
5 4 3 2 1

Boxing is a rough, dangerous, and thrilling sport, the most basic and natural and uncomplicated of athletic competitions and—at its best—one of the purest of art forms.

—Red Smith, 1962,
New York Herald Tribune columnist

Contents

Illustrations follow page 116

Preface

When I moved to Reno in 1980 to assume a senior administrative position at the University of Nevada, one of the first items to come across my desk was a contractual matter concerning boxing coach Jimmy Olivas. A couple of questions quickly popped into my mind: *A boxing coach? Why do we have a boxing coach?* Much to my surprise, the answer was that the university had established an intercollegiate boxing team as early as 1927 and that the Wolf Pack team had long been popular with local sports fans and students. I had previously served on three public university faculties over a span of twenty years and none had a boxing team, and to the best of my knowledge the manly art was not even part of the physical education programs. Although I had always kept up with intercollegiate athletics, boxing on campus was not a subject with which I was familiar. But as I soon learned, boxing was deeply ingrained in the culture of the state of Nevada, and it was only natural that the university sponsor a team.

The pages that follow attempt to define the special niche that boxing has long enjoyed in my adopted state. Although there are many books describing famous fights and individual boxers, there has never been an attempt to connect the sport to the broader themes of the history and culture of the state. From crude bare-knuckle bouts in mining camps of the nineteenth century to the championship bouts that have been an important part of the lure of contemporary Las Vegas, prizefighting has played a significant role in the construction of Nevada's popular culture, and in particular its economic development strategy. This book is an attempt to fill that void. Nevada's boxing subculture did not exist in a vacuum, but early on was reflective of the men who worked in the mines where life was hazardous. Thus, those few men who willingly entered a ring to face an opponent determined to inflict serious punishment were naturally admired. At a time when Nevada was losing population and needed to encourage affluent visitors, it was only natural that boxing was used to promote tourism.

The tradition of the Big Fight, born in rough-hewn frontier outposts like Goldfield, Ely, Tonopah, and Carson City at the dawn of the twentieth century, would be reprised decades later in Las Vegas, where more than two hundred championship fights have been staged to attract sports fans, especially "high-roller" gamblers, to the lavish casinos that line the world-famous Strip.

Throughout most of the twentieth century, Nevada was widely considered a moral outlier, its libertarian outlook regarding the ambiguities of human behavior producing a wave of sermons, political speeches, and newspaper editorials from across the land denouncing the "Sin State," "America's Disgrace," or worse. Although much of the moralistic condemnation stemmed in response to the state's easy divorce laws, legal brothels, and wide-open casino gambling, it was the passage in 1897 of legislation that made Nevada the first state in the Union to legalize the widely condemned blood sport of boxing that first attracted widespread national criticism. A bill permitting "glove contests" was passed by state legislators and signed by the governor at the behest of businessmen anxious to lure affluent members of the sporting community to Nevada to stimulate a weak economy, but specifically to permit the long-anticipated, and repeatedly postponed, heavyweight championship fight between Gentleman Jim Corbett and challenger Bob Fitzsimmons to take place in the tiny state capital of Carson City (population three thousand). Ironically, one hundred years later, Nevada hosted another controversial championship bout in which Mike Tyson infamously bit off a chunk of Evander Holyfield's ear before a live crowd of sixteen thousand and a worldwide television audience of millions.

This project has enabled me to blend my continuing research interest in American sports history to the history of the state in which I have lived for more than three decades. I am indebted to Joanne O'Hare, director of the University of Nevada Press, and acquisitions editor Matt Becker for inviting me to undertake this project. It has proved to be a delightful and rewarding endeavor that I otherwise would never have contemplated.

I am indebted to many friends and colleagues who have generously assisted me in locating sources and by critiquing draft chapters. Phillip Earl shared with me his extensive knowledge of Nevada history and saved me many hours of digging through newspapers with his personal index files to early newspapers. The staff at the Nevada Historical Society cheerfully responded to my many requests, and former Nevada state archivist Guy Rocha provided expert guidance regarding arcane legislative matters. *Reno Gazette Journal* feature writer Guy Clifton generously shared his files on the years that Jack Dempsey spent in Nevada.

Several friends and colleagues have generously read some or all of the chapters of this book and provided many helpful suggestions: Dee Kille, Andrew McGregor, Frank Mitchell, and Thomas E. Smith. I am especially grateful for the detailed attention paid to the manuscript by my friend Michael Green, whose vast knowledge of Nevada history never ceases to amaze. Two anonymous readers provided useful commentaries that steered me away from potential problems and toward a more focused narrative. My friend and golfing partner Robert Q. Martin has rescued me from many a near disaster of lost files and other self-inflicted predicaments and generally kept my Apple computer functioning. I also thank the following for their help along the way: Alicia Barber, Jenni Baryol, Scott Casper, Neal Cobb, Allen Davis, Mackenzie Hoy, Marc Johnson, Richard Kirkendall, Tommy Lane, Luther Mack, Mike Martino, Ethan Opdahl, Colleen Rosencrantz, Jane Tors, Jannet Vreland, Claudene Wharton, and Yancy Young. Throughout my long career as a university professor and administrator, my wife, Sharon, has been supportive of my research, teaching, and administrative endeavors. Once again, I gratefully acknowledge her support and encouragement that have been a constant throughout our life together.

The Main Event

The Prelims

*I saw how different boxers are from other athletes. They are at
significant physical risk. The courage to box is beyond anything
I can understand.* —Howard Schatz, sports photographer,
At the Fights (2012)

On the evening of September 23, 1926, more than 120,000 spectators
jammed into Philadelphia's Sesquicentennial Stadium to watch Jack
Dempsey defend his heavyweight-boxing crown against the stylish
Gene Tunney. The *New York Times* reported that the enormous throng
included some 2,000 millionaires, many of whom were decked out in
formal wear and accompanied by women in elegant evening dresses.
The iconoclastic journalist H. L. Mencken was moved to write that
the attendees were "well-dressed, good-humored and almost distinguished." Indeed they were. Sitting at ringside were such political figures as Secretary of the Treasury Andrew Mellon, financiers Charles
Schwab and W. Averill Harriman, publishing giants William Randolph
Hearst and Joseph Pulitzer, and many sports and motion picture stars,
including Babe Ruth, John McGraw, Charlie Chaplin, and Tom Mix.[1]
That this enormous crowd included so many of the rich, famous, and
powerful vividly confirmed that major changes had occurred in the
public perception of prizefighting. Just one decade earlier, law enforcement officials would have not permitted the event to take place in the
City of Brotherly Love, arresting the major participants if necessary.
Reflecting a stunning reversal in public opinion, several state legisla-
tures had legalized prizefighting and created commissions to oversee
the sport. The popularity of prizefighting was evidenced in the public

acclaim for the charismatic Dempsey, who had been made a heavy favorite by professional gamblers. Dempsey's vast popularity during the 1920s attested to the dramatic change in public perception that occurred with the blood sport of prizefighting, prompting historian Randy Roberts to conclude that the charismatic Dempsey was an "appropriate symbol" for the decade of the Roaring Twenties.[2]

Detailed coverage of the fight dominated the nation's newspapers the next day. The *New York Times* splayed a large headline across the front page proclaiming that Tunney, who professed to be a "scientific" boxer rather than a slugger like Dempsey, had won a surprisingly easy unanimous decision. The *Times,* once a leading crusader against the blood sport, dedicated seven pages to the event. The fight was promoted by George Lewis "Tex" Rickard, the maverick entrepreneur who enjoyed celebrity status during the 1920s as a promoter of prizefights and served as general manager of the recently opened third iteration of Madison Square Garden, the nation's largest indoor sports and entertainment venue.

On that early-autumn evening in Philadelphia, prizefighting emerged fully from its dubious past into the mainstream of American life. Only after the Great War did the sport emerge from the shadows into widespread public acceptance, in part because the US Army had incorporated boxing into its training regimen for recruits being prepared to do battle in the trenches of France. Rickard was no novice when it came to staging prizefights because he had honed his promotional skills in the sparsely populated state of Nevada during the first decade of the new century. The affable Tex made no record of the thoughts that may have gone through his mind on that glorious evening as he surveyed the grand scene as Tunney flummoxed Dempsey with his deft footwork and stinging counterpunches. It is likely that at some point Rickard reflected back upon his sensational promotions in Goldfield and Reno that helped establish a strong boxing tradition in Nevada.

After a roller-coaster ride of good and bad luck as a gambler and saloon owner in the gold-crazed Yukon Territory, Rickard had been inexorably drawn to the gold mining boom that had erupted amid the sagebrush and rock-strewn hillsides of Esmeralda County in 1905. The heart of this boom was the rapidly growing mining camp of Goldfield, located some one hundred miles north of the tiny railroad settlement of as yet unincorporated Las Vegas. There the thirty-five-year-old

Rickard opened a popular saloon that catered to hard-rock miners and mining executives alike. In 1906 Rickard assumed the leadership of a group of local businessmen who wanted to promote a championship fight between the lightweight champion Joe Gans, the first African American champion, and the infamous brawler and master of low blows and other nefarious ring tactics Oscar "Battling" Nelson. Their purpose was not simply out of love of the sport, but rather a crass effort to attract wealthy men to the town in hopes of selling to them substantial amounts of highly speculative stock in the several score of mining companies springing up around Goldfield.

Most Americans had never heard of Goldfield and considered the announcement to be a prank. The skepticism turned to curiosity when the unknown Rickard announced a purse of thirty thousand dollars for the fight, the largest ever offered up to that time. Rickard grabbed the nation's attention with his stunning announcement. He attracted even more publicity when he stacked fifteen hundred twenty-dollar gold pieces in the window of a local bank to demonstrate that the unprecedented purse was authentic. Rickard immediately became a featured story line coming out of Goldfield, garnering as much newspaper coverage as the two fighters.

Enthusiastic locals were probably overly optimistic when they estimated that fifteen thousand persons flooded into the isolated mining camp for the Labor Day weekend; the newly constructed wooden arena seated only seven thousand, but it was filled to capacity. By all estimates, the promotion was wildly successful: spectators were treated to a three-hour bout that went forty-two rounds, the town's many saloons sold vast amounts of beer and whiskey, the town's corps of prostitutes conducted a land-office business, and several hundreds of thousands of dollars of mining stocks were unloaded upon gullible out-of-state visitors. Four years later, Rickard drew national attention to Nevada when he once again pitted a black champion against a white challenger in an epic bout that for several days made the small city of Reno the center of the nation's attention. When the flamboyant black heavyweight champion Jack Johnson handily defeated the "Great White Hope," Jim Jefferies, before a packed stadium of twenty-two thousand spectators, he did so under the intense scrutiny of an America obsessed with the crude underlying racial implications that Rickard shamelessly exploited in promoting the fight.

The fact that prizefighting remained illegal in much of the United States at this time contributed to the intense scrutiny that Nevada received during the days surrounding these promotions. Throughout the nineteenth century, all across the United States prizefighting existed outside the law, condemned by leaders of society and criminalized by state governments. Despite the hostility of law enforcement officials (or perhaps because of it), prizefighting was avidly followed in large part due to the extensive coverage provided by big-city newspapers and, especially, the popular "Bible of the Barber Shop," the *National Police Gazette*. Its flamboyant publisher, Richard Kyle Fox, correctly sensed that his predominantly male readership across the country would buy the weekly newspaper that he printed on garish pink newsprint in order to read about the exploits of leading pugilists. It was Fox, more than anyone, who made the "Boston Strong Man," John L. Sullivan, the nation's first idolized sports figure.

Despite its illegality, prizefighting existed along the margins of American life throughout the nineteenth century. In the rural frontier regions of Virginia, Tennessee, and Kentucky, a crude and cruel form of one-on-one combat called "rough-and-tumble" was popular. The sport had no perceptible rules; slugging and wrestling holds were permitted, but so too were gouging of sensitive body parts, including the extraction of eyeballs by long fingernails that were sharpened and reinforced by wax. Not only did rough-and-tumble provide a convenient way to settle personal disputes, but scheduled matches became an attraction at county fairs. Far from the mountains of Appalachia, across the United States, bare-knuckle prizefighting became a popular amusement among working-class males. As the sport grew in popularity, especially in urban centers that attracted large numbers of immigrants, a close relationship developed between prizefighters and their handlers with machine politicians, saloon owners, bookmakers, and gamblers.[3]

Prizefighting sparked a backlash, especially from influential Protestant ministers and prudish community leaders. Victorian reformers aggressively targeted prizefighting because it encouraged behaviors they abhorred. The brutal nature of bare-knuckle fighting itself provided ample justification for the enforcement of laws prohibiting its practice, but reformers were equally concerned about the behaviors it stimulated: rowdy crowds, copious consumption of alcohol, and gambling. These contests were conducted with few rules and no government oversight; the welfare of the fighters was of little concern to promoters or spectators. Two contestants, stripped to the waist, "came to scratch" at a line drawn in the middle of a ring in the dirt or sawdust on the barroom floor and proceeded to slug away until one man was unable to continue. These were "fights to the finish." There were no limits on the number of rounds, no judges to score the contest, and seldom was a referee appointed to control the action. A round ended when a contestant was knocked or thrown to the ground, after which he had thirty seconds to start a new round by "coming to scratch." Under these rules, a bout could last but a few minutes, but upon occasion an hour or more. Fights of twenty rounds or more were not unusual. The winner usually collected the entire purse along with the side bets he had made on himself.[4]

That the great majority of the pugilists were uneducated and impoverished young men who came largely from suspect immigrant groups—Irish, and German in particular—only added to the suspicions of Victorian critics. These reform-minded middle- and upper-middle-class men and women understood that prizefighting was closely tied to saloon keepers who enjoyed profitable connections with corrupt politicians and their notorious machines. These well-intentioned Victorian reformers, however, did not understand that from the perspective of a strong young man, prizefighting afforded an avenue by which he might escape the bleak prospects he faced as a member of the urban underclass.

During the final decades of the nineteenth century, public opposition to prizefighting slowly began to wane. In 1867 John Douglas, the Marquis of Queensberry, codified and published a list of informal rules for boxing that had been floating around London. The "Queensberry rules for the sport of boxing" changed the way the sport was conducted in England and America, producing a grudging reassessment of the merits of the sport. Prominent among the new rules were the use of padded gloves, the abolition of wrestling maneuvers, the ten-second knockout (KO), the use of a referee, and three-minute rounds interspersed with one-minute rest periods.[5] The new rules provided no more than a patina of civilized behavior upon a sport that remained brutal and dangerous, but prizefighting enthusiasts exploited them to move the sport into the mainstream of modern American sports.

Because the Queensberry rules softened the arguments against the sport, it encouraged some local law enforcement officials to permit bouts judiciously described as "scientific exhibitions." Urban athletic clubs that catered to an affluent male membership offered instructional programs that taught the "manly art of self-defense," and they also staged bouts matching accomplished amateurs as well as professional fighters—as "scientific exhibitions," of course. Ardent advocates of the new gospel of "muscular Christianity" such as Theodore Roosevelt, who himself learned to box as a teenager under the guidance of a coach hired by his father, extolled the virtues of boxing under Queensberry rules. Roosevelt continued to box in college, and even as president he famously sparred occasionally, a recreation that led to his losing the sight in one eye as a result of damage incurred in a White House sparring match with a navy champion.[6]

In 1890 the city council of New Orleans voted to permit private clubs to sponsor bouts fought under the Queensberry rules, with the reassuring proviso that no alcohol be served to spectators. On September 7, 1892, ten thousand spectators, including several hundred ladies, filled a local arena for the first heavyweight championship bout conducted under the Queensberry rules. Newspapers across the country featured reports on the upcoming fight between the wildly popular champion John L. Sullivan and the handsome challenger (and popular stage actor) James J. Corbett. As the day of the fight approached, thousands of visitors arrived in the Crescent City, packing hotels, restaurants, and taverns. The *Times Democrat* happily reported that "streets were filled with visitors of all classes, from the millionaire to the baker to the fakir. Politicians, lawyers, merchants and gamblers elbowed each other in all public places on comparatively equal terms."[7]

Those who managed to secure a ticket were not disappointed, because under bright electric lights and with city political and business leaders seated prominently at ringside, Corbett dominated the bout against the aging champion, knocking him out in the twentieth round with a crushing blow to the jaw that caused him to "fall like an ox." The transition of boxing from a renegade activity to mainstream spectacle had begun. It changed the image of a rogue sport in which bouts where furtively held at clandestine locations on river barges and islands and in isolated wooded areas into a popular commercialized entertainment extravaganza. The symbolic nature of this transformation was evident that night in New Orleans: Sullivan had earned his reputation as a bare-knuckle brawler practicing his craft in secret locations to avoid the sheriff, but his career ended with his wearing padded gloves in a bout sanctioned by city government and watched by an audience of ten thousand.

The example of New Orleans did not go unnoticed. It especially resonated in the state capital of Carson City, Nevada, at a time when the state's business and political leaders were pondering how to combat the deep and persistent recession that had devastated the state's economy. In February 1897 the state legislature voted to permit what were termed "glove contests." The immediate intent was to attract thousands of tourists to Nevada to watch a championship prizefight between Corbett and challenger Bob Fitzsimmons. Within six weeks after the well-oiled wheels of Nevada government had cranked out the nation's first state law legalizing prizefighting, a makeshift wooden outdoor arena was erected a few blocks from the state capitol, and the fight was on. It occurred, fittingly for the Irish American champion Gentleman Jim Corbett, on St. Patrick's Day. Promoted by a Texas gambler and prominent sporting man, Daniel Stuart, the long-anticipated meeting between the two pugilists produced a flurry of national publicity—much of it negative—for the Silver State.

Unlike the leading citizens in other states, relatively few Nevada leaders viewed boxing as a social evil. The legislature faced only token opposition from church-affiliated groups, and the bill sped through both houses of the legislature and received Governor Reinhold Sadler's signature. Passage of the bill was relatively easy because prizefighting had been a popular leisure activity in the rugged mining camps sprinkled across the vast landscape of the western United States. Nevada was no exception. In ramshackle mining towns, the work was hard and often dangerous. Serious injury and death were not uncommon in the mine shafts burrowed deep below the earth's surface. It was only natural that miners gravitated toward recreations that reflected the dangerous work they did underground. Bare-knuckle prizefighting, a violent blood sport that required fighters to deliver and receive brutal blows and risk injury, was universally popular across the mining frontier regions of western America.[8]

For those attracted to these spectacles, prizefighters exemplified the rugged traits of masculinity that were highly regarded on the mining frontier. To be a prizefighter required a willingness to enter the ring alone, to be hit in the face and torso, to swallow one's own blood, and to get up from the floor in a mental fog brought on by a nasty punch to absorb yet more punishment, all in the hopes of earning a few dollars. Writer Joyce Carol Oates has written eloquently about the violence that has always been essential to the unique appeal of boxing: "I have never thought of it as a sport. There is nothing fundamentally playful about it; nothing that seems to belong to daylight, to pleasure." She writes that the possibility of serious injury or even death is always lurking in the background and that participants receive physical punishment that most human beings could never endure: "Baseball, football, basketball—these quintessentially American pastimes are recognizably sports because they involve play: they are games. One *plays* football, one doesn't *play* boxing."[9] Prizefighting, with its special requirements of masculinity—strength, courage, and resilience—aptly reflected the difficult and often dangerous life in Nevada mining towns. Nearly a century later, prizefighting returned to Nevada in spectacular fashion. On special weekends when a Big Fight attracted high rollers from around the globe and frenetic mobs packed the sidewalks and casinos up and down the Strip, and with millions watching the action on television, Las Vegas became the boxing capital of America.

Round 1

Fistic Carnival in Carson City

Mr. Stuart has never swerved from his purpose, though con-
fronted with what to an ordinary individual would seem to be
insurmountable obstacles.
                    —Official Fight Program, March 17, 1897

It was a bleak time when the Nevada Legislature convened for its biennial session in late-January 1897. The mining economy had been devastated by depletion of high-quality ore on the Comstock, and new mineral explorations were discouraged by federal policy that had demonetized silver. Additionally, surpluses of beef on national commodity markets had severely depressed the prices Nevada ranchers received for their cattle. The state's population had tailed off to fewer than fifty thousand, and reports out of the nation's capital carried the troubling news that powerful men in Washington were contemplating merging Nevada with Utah or even ignominiously returning Nevada to territorial status. Desperate times produce desperate measures, and so a group of legislators and Governor Reinhold Sadler opted to rescind the state's antiprizefighting law to permit a heavyweight championship fight to take place in Carson City. In return for the promise of an economic stimulus, they were willing to accept the scorn that progressive-minded reformers would heap upon the state. They were equally unmoved by the ethical considerations regarding the blood sport that had led to its abolition across the United States.

Nevada's political leaders were also aware of the raging battle that had unfolded during the previous eighteen months over a proposed heavyweight championship fight between the popular James J. Corbett and a scrawny but resilient challenger by way of New Zealand, Robert Prometheus Fitzsimmons. If nothing else, the fight would settle the argument as to which man was actually the reigning champion. In November 1895 Corbett unofficially "resigned" his title and named journeyman fighter Irishman Peter Maher as his replacement; this was a not-so-subtle dig at Fitzsimmons, with whom he had been waging a heated war of words. "Ruby Robert" had defeated Maher handily three years earlier.

In February 1896 Fitzsimmons once more defeated Maher in a bout held on a sand spit located in the middle of the Rio Grande—was it in Texas or in Mexico?—and was generally recognized as the new champion in this, the most unorganized of sports. Corbett's fans demurred and insisted their man was still the champ. If nothing else, they wanted a meeting of the two that would settle this squabble in a boxing ring rather than in press releases. The controversy intensified the desire that the two men settle the issue the way real men should—with their fists.

Actually, an effort to hold the bout had begun in 1895, but at every turn the promoter was outmaneuvered by the determined antiboxing crowd, creating a series of bizarre events that became fodder for journalists and sparks incredulity more than a century later. In one corner was the sporting set that wanted to see what they anticipated would be a closely contested brawl, but in the other corner stood a national coalition of high-minded progressive reformers who viewed prizefighting as a barbaric spectacle that dimmed the nation's claim to be an enlightened democracy. Ever since the fight had first been proposed in the spring of 1895, the opponents had won every round by mobilizing religious and reform groups that pressured public officials to enforce existing—but often ignored—laws prohibiting exhibitions of the blood sport. Those determined souls uncomfortably recognized that public opinion, which had at one time been strongly on their side, was inexorably shifting away from their position due to growing interest in prizefighting. In particular, the widespread popularity of legendary bare-knuckle champion John L. Sullivan had stimulated a perceptible increase in public interest, and his promised presence at the proposed fight in Carson City added a greater sense of legitimacy.

When a prominent Texan who had being trying, without success, to promote the match that "sporting men" everywhere wanted to see first approached Nevada officials in late 1896 about the possibility of locating the fight in Nevada, he received an enthusiastic affirmative response. His long quest to identify an acceptable location where he would not be threatened with arrest or even bodily harm was finally over.

Nevada's First Prizefight Promoter

Dan Stuart was obviously a man who would not be easily denied. But by the time he visited Nevada's powers that be, his patience was running out. For nearly two years, he had been repeatedly frustrated by authorities in three states, two territories, and one foreign country, and in the process had spent a considerable amount of his own money that he desperately wanted to recoup. Stuart had arrived in Dallas in 1872 from his native New York at the age of twenty-six and established himself as a promising young man who had plenty of zip. He became a respected Dallas businessman with investments in cattle and cotton, but he was best known as a sporting man who had a reputation for making large bets. According to one Dallas source, Stuart was "looked upon as a man who will under all circumstances fulfill any promise which he has ever made."[1] That is, he paid his gambling debts. Stuart also operated saloons, pool halls, and a theater in Dallas and became active in national gambling and sporting activities.

Stuart had become president of the Jacksonville-based Florida Athletic Club that had promoted the Corbett–Charlie Mitchell championship fight in 1894. Based upon that relationship, he announced in the spring of 1895 that he intended to promote a "finish fight" between Corbett and Fitzsimmons. (A "finish fight," typical for the era, would have no round limit and end only when one man was counted out or was unable to continue.) It was a match that fight fans around the country were eagerly anticipating. With the Dallas economy mired in the depression set off by the panic of 1893, Stuart readily received support and investments from Dallas businessmen and politicians when he described how the fight would perk up the town's languid economy. A shrewd gambler who knew how to figure the odds of any proposition, Stuart was known to wager on most anything: baseball, the horses, dice, cards, and, of course, prizefights. At the time, it seemed like a sure thing.

Sometime in early 1895, Stuart decided that the odds of making a big killing were very good if he could put the two leading fighters of the day into the same Texas ring. He was entering new territory, having never promoted a major fight in his life. Thus, on May 21, he changed the course of boxing history when he fired off a telegram to the managers of the two battlers: "Corbett and Fitzsimmons, New York. Will be in New York before June 1, ready to talk business." Both men and their handlers were initially skeptical, because no one had heard of the Texan. But he arrived bearing a certified check for forty-one thousand dollars, more than enough to convince both camps that he was someone with whom they could do business. Stuart confidently announced that the fight would be staged in conjunction with the Texas State Fair in October, and both fighters agreed to his terms and announced plans for establishing training camps in Galveston and Asbury Park. The certified check that Stuart brandished, the *New Orleans Picayune* reported, had swept away bids from rival promoters and impressed everyone that Stuart was "a sporting man of plenty of money and grit."[2]

Moving quickly upon his return to Dallas, and thinking big in stereotypical Texas mode, Stuart unveiled plans to construct an enormous outdoor wooden arena that would accommodate fifty-two thousand spectators (including a nineteenth-century version of luxury boxes that he would rent to high rollers for two hundred dollars). He predicted that wealthy sportsmen would flock to Dallas via chartered trains, pay full freight at the city's hotels, and spend freely at local restaurants and bars. He even revealed plans to house visitors unable to book a hotel room in a cluster of Pullman cars that would resemble a small city. Stuart was also a man ahead of his times. He had figured out an angle that promised to make him money even if ticket sales lagged behind projections. He cut a lucrative deal with pioneer filmmaker Enoch J. Rector to capture the fight on his newfangled Edison camera called a Kinetoscope and market the film to motion picture theaters across the country.

A stout man of considerable girth who dressed in the latest men's fashions, Stuart parted his black hair down the middle and sported a formidable handlebar mustache. The *New Orleans Picayune* described the dapper Stuart as a leading citizen of Dallas, "the wealthiest sports man in Texas," and improbably as "a very modest and retiring sort of man," who was "adverse to being talked about or flattered."[3] Perhaps, but he was also possessed of an indefatigable determination once he set his mind to something. His ability to stay the course would be sorely tested, however, because it would take him the best part of three years attempting to outfox and evade outraged preachers, nervous politicians, and armed state and federal law enforcement officers, as well as the conniving handlers of the two elusive pugilists, before what he euphemistically called a "fistic carnival" could occur.

When he announced his plans, Stuart was assured by supporters that the fight could be held in Dallas because of a vaguely written statute passed by the state legislature in 1889 that curiously authorized "prizefights, bullfights, and other dangerous contests" if a five-hundred-dollar "occupation tax" was paid to the state. However, the reliability of that statute's status was in doubt because in 1891, progressive governor James S. Hogg had signed into law legislation that he had urged upon the legislature that made promoting or participating in a prizefight a felony. Given the elusive wording of the two statutes, no one actually knew whether the 1891 law superseded the previous one, but four hundred businessmen—the backbone of the Dallas business community—pledged enthusiastic support when Stuart plunked down his five hundred dollars to the tax collector and started construction of the arena that would hold seven thousand more persons than the total population of Dallas. Upon his triumphant return from New York, Stuart had authorized a budget of fifty thousand dollars for construction, and one hundred workmen were soon busily erecting the enormous wooden structure on a large lot located just a quarter of a mile from the fairgrounds. On August 8 Stuart began sale of tickets and happily reported that sales were brisk. Some eighteen thousand were sold in a few days.[4]

All across the country, betting pools were established, but prescient bookmakers offered odds on not only Fitzsimmons or Corbett, but also ominously whether Stuart would actually succeed in putting on the fight or if it would be stopped by a growing band of hostile Texas preachers (Stuart was made an early three-to-one favorite).

Stuart apparently did not accurately anticipate the ferocity that a group of unbridled Methodist ministers could muster. Nor had he anticipated that his various investment activities had created a serious enemy in the young and moralistic Texas governor, Charles A. Culberson. In June a hastily created statewide ministerial association objected to the fight as if Western civilization itself were imperiled.

The ensuing campaign was marked by sensationalized charges concerning the debasement of the moral standards of the Lone Star State, and state legislators heard the message loud and clear. The first press release issued by the spokesman for the Dallas Pastors' Association, the Reverend E. L. Spraggins, condemned prizefighting as "brutalizing to an unspeakable degree" and predicted that the event "will concentrate in our midst a horde of gamblers, thieves, pickpockets, thugs and harlots." Soon "indignation meetings" sprang up across the state, and grassroots pressure from churches descended upon anxious legislators and the governor, who did not need prompting to spoil Dan Stuart's party. Resolutions declared the fight a "violent threat to all the interests of order and virtue as well as of Christianity," and one novel missive even declared that the fight would reduce Texas to a moral stature below Mexico, an assertion based upon the premise that bullfights were more humane than prizefights because the bull was ultimately destined for a butcher shop anyway.

The mayor of Dallas, Colonel Frank P. Holland, naturally looked at the practical side of things, duly noting that if all tickets were sold, more than $1,225,000 would flow into Stuart's coffers and thereby have a salutary effect upon the local economy. As for the moral issue, he argued, Stuart was not promoting an event that would threaten the moral climate of Dallas and the Lone Star State, but rather was offering up for public edification "an athletic exhibition, the greatest physical culture exhibition, the most scientific boxing contest in the world."[5]

While the two sides waged an escalating war of words, Fitzsimmons and Corbett arrived in Texas to begin serious training. Meanwhile, Stuart and the ministers slugged it out. One Dallas judge ruled that the 1889 law was in effect and that the fight could go on, but Governor Culberson decided that the economic returns were outweighed by the rising chorus of opposition he was receiving from voters and their churches around the state. With the huge wooden "colleseum" (as one Dallas newspaper called it) now rising off the ground, Culberson called a special session of the legislature for October 1 in order to prevent an "affront to the moral sense and enlightened progress of Texas." He backed a bill that ended any doubt about prizefighting's status in Texas. It unambiguously made prizefighting a felony and stipulated substantial fines and serious jail time for offenders. In just three hours, both houses of the legislature passed the bill and the "good Christian governor" readily signed it into law. Stuart thereupon confirmed that he was "law-abiding" and ordered work stopped on the arena. In his next breath, he said that the fight would still be held somewhere that local officials appreciated the financial bounty he anticipated. That place would definitely be outside the state of Texas. Dan Stuart was already out some $25,000 of his own money as well as that of his investors.

Stuart had been knocked to his knees by the swift blow delivered from Austin. But he was far from being down for the count.

Hot Springs and El Paso

The furious battle that had engulfed Texas now moved on to promising new venues. Stuart first indicated that he had his sights set on the tourist town of Hot Springs, Arkansas, and that the fight would take place on November 11. He ordered the half-assembled arena be dismantled and the lumber shipped to Hot Springs. But not so fast! Jim Corbett arrived in Little Rock ready to do battle, but was arrested on order of Governor James P. Clarke and charged with conspiracy to do bodily harm to one Robert Fitzsimmons, who had not yet arrived in the state. A local judge, however, ordered Corbett released after finding that the fight could be held because "a contest with gloves . . . is not dangerous to human life," as compared to football, baseball, and, curiously, horse racing. Conversely, in Little Rock, Sheriff Robert Houpt announced that he was under orders from the governor to shoot both fighters if they appeared in the ring. With the managers of both fighters now maneuvering ceaselessly for any financial advantage, and with Houpt publicly bearing a .45 on his hip, Fitzsimmons announced he had no desire to test the governor's order.

Frustrated but still determined, Stuart now cast his eyes toward the distant Southwest. Businessmen in El Paso had previously attempted to lure Stuart and his prizefighters to their frontier outpost, but the new state law had ended that possibility. Anticipating that they could still cash in if the fight were staged across the border in Juárez in conjunction with a series of bullfights, they invited Stuart to consider holding the fight in February 1896. They were undeterred when Mexican president-for-life, Porfirio Díaz, vowed to send in the army to prevent his country's good name from being sullied by a prizefight. Unhappy with the prospects that the fight would be held, and desirous of pursuing his increasingly lucrative acting career, Corbett left for the East Coast for an acting gig and agreed to forfeit his title.

Stuart substituted in his place the seasoned journeyman Peter Maher, a native of Ireland who had already logged more than fifty prizefights into his record (several of which were ended prematurely by law enforcement intervention). The intentions of Stuart and prominent El Paso businessmen that a Maher-Fitzsimmons match be held in Juárez to determine the new heavyweight champion were scuttled when the governor of Chihuahua, Miguel Ahumada, mobilized his militia and deployed them along the banks of the Rio Grande under orders to "open fire" if the prizefighters should attempt to cross.

With the threat of armed resistance from Chihuahua, rumors quickly spread that Stuart was now considering the territories of New Mexico and Arizona. This prompted the New Mexico territorial delegate to the US Congress, Thomas Benton Catron, to urge that the national legislature make prizefighting a felony in the western territories, punishable by five years in prison. Dispensing with public hearings and debate, Congress enacted the so-called Catron Anti-Prizefighting Bill with alacrity, and it was signed into law on February 5 by President Grover Cleveland. In Tucson the territorial governor of Arizona, Louis C. Hughes, already reviled by many locals for his fervent crusades against alcohol and prostitution and in favor of votes for women, put the territorial militia on alert after receiving rumors that Stuart was shipping his stacks of lumber to Yuma on the main line of the Southern Pacific. Hughes sternly announced that his troopers would shoot to kill should Stuart's entourage enter Arizona Territory.[6]

Judge Roy Bean to the Rescue

The indefatigable Stuart, however, was determined that fight fans who had come to El Paso would see Maher and Fitzsimmons meet in a ring, somewhere. A squadron of Texas Rangers, dispatched to El Paso by the resolute Governor Culberson, went on high alert when rumors began to circulate that Stuart was up to something. And indeed he was. In the early-morning hours of February 20, a ten-car passenger train pulled out of El Paso heading eastward on the Southern Pacific, carrying the prizefighters and their entourages, referee George Siler, an estimated 230 fight fans, security director Bat Masterson, filmmaker

Enoch Rector with his cumbersome Kinetoscope, and, curiously, General Woodford Mabry of the Texas Rangers and twenty-six of his best men. Destination unknown.

Once under way the word began to spread from car to car that they were heading for Langtry, Texas, a watering stop for the Southern Pacific close by the Mexican border, some 375 miles distant from El Paso. There the law rested firmly in the hands of Judge Roy Bean, who owned the ramshackle Jersey Lilly saloon. He famously dispensed frontier justice upon local lawbreakers from behind the bar along with whiskey at ten cents a shot.

America's most famous justice of the peace "west of the Pecos" was not about to violate the Texas antiprizefighting law, however, and he casually informed General Mabry that the fight would be held "down the street and down the bluff." A trail led two hundred feet down into a canyon and across five hundred yards of deep sand and mud to the Rio Grande, where a recently constructed pontoon bridge extended out onto a small sandbar island that constituted the northernmost tip of the Mexican state of Coahuila. Any possibility that the governor of the state of Coahuila might send troops to enforce President Díaz's edict was negated by the site's location far from any Mexican outpost. Peering down from the canyon ridge, General Mabry saw a boxing ring encircled by a canvas fence to prevent those without tickets from viewing the ensuing battle. A small hut had been erected to accommodate Enoch Rector and his Kinetoscope and provide the pugilists with dressing rooms. Those with tickets had to pass by the steely eye of Bat Masterson, who was in charge of security.

Thus, at 4:35 p.m. on February 21, with a few hundred fans clustered around the ring, referee Siler called Maher and Fitzsimmons to the center of the ring for instructions, which included his pronouncement that they were not to hit below the belt and that the winner would be the new heavyweight champion of the world. Enoch Rector was not pleased, however, because the sky was overcast and a mist had formed that rendered his state-of-the-art Kinetoscope inoperable. High on the rim, watching the action for free across the international border, stood General Mabry and his Rangers, along with several hundred other freeloaders. Given that Stuart had initially planned on fifty-two thousand to watch the first iteration of this championship fight, he could not have been pleased, but he was a man of his word: he had promised a championship fight, and he had delivered. This would be the last so-called championship prizefight to be held in a remote location to avoid the long arm of the law.[7]

It had taken Stuart nine months to get to this point, and the fight lasted for all of ninety-five seconds. The world heavyweight championship fight began with Maher hurling roundhouse punches at the savvy Fitzsimmons, but he left himself unprotected while throwing a wild overhand and was met with a solid right hand that connected with the Irishman's reputed glass jaw. Maher plummeted backward, his head bouncing loudly off the canvas-covered wood floor. Fitzsimmons later recalled that Maher "fell flat on his back in a stiff sort of way like a man in a trance . . . out cold and his eyes wide open." The Irishman futilely attempted to rise and then collapsed as Siler counted to ten. The fight that had fascinated the nation for months on end had ended almost before it began. Stuart had lost untold thousands of dollars, but he paid the winning purse of twenty thousand dollars to Martin Julian, Fitzsimmons's manager. News that the crown the popular Jim Corbett had held since 1892 now was worn by a man he despised quickly leaked out of Langtry. That evening in Chicago at the Haymarket Theater, as he stepped to the front of the stage to accept the applause of the audience after another stirring performance as lead in *The Naval Cadet,* Corbett announced that Julian had sent him a telegram with the news. To the cheers of the theatergoers, Corbett announced he was ready to "lick Fitzsimmons" as soon as a fight could be arranged.[8]

The next day, the *New York World* plastered Dan Stuart's picture on its front page, announcing that he was the clever man who had "outwitted the Mexicans, the Texas Rangers, the Mexican Rurales [former bandits now members of the rural militia], the Arizona militia and a half-dozen Governors who were united against him."[9]

Stuart had already decided that he had to look farther west if he was to recoup the money he had lost. He once again set out to put Corbett and Fitzsimmons together in the same ring.

"Nevada's Disgrace"

Dan Stuart found a warm welcome from the leading citizens of Carson City, Nevada, a small town that snuggled up against the majestic Sierra Nevada. It had a population of nearly three thousand and served as the capital of the sparsely populated state. Nevada's leaders had long been pondering how they could reverse the downward spiral in which the state's economy was ensnared. Many agreed that hosting a championship boxing match was a good idea. It would attract extensive publicity and high rollers willing to spend good money. But the legality of such a prizefight was problematic, and legislative action was deemed prudent. According to the fight program, in December 1896 Stuart dispatched his "right hand man," W. K. Wheeler, from Dallas "to do some missionary work, providing his emissary with essential lobbying funds."[10] Apparently liberally dispensing those "essential lobbying funds" to persons of influence, Wheeler had soon lined up his ducks with the assistance of prominent Carson City attorney Charles A. Jones, who drafted a bill to be introduced in the legislature. Jones, along with assembly member Al Livingston, owner of a local bar and head of the State Fair and Agricultural Association, worked behind the scenes to line up support for the bill. Editorials endorsing the plan appeared in the Carson City and Reno newspapers. Livingston said that he and his associates intended to "legalize boxing and remove from them [sic] any unpleasant qualities."[11]

To close the deal, Stuart arrived in Nevada before the legislature convened for its biennial session and made a good impression upon the local power structure, announcing his plans to build a seventeen-thousand-seat wooden amphitheater on the east edge of town at the racetrack with lumber provided by the Carson and Tahoe Flume and Lumber Company. (The arena was erected on what today is the sheriff's office, located at the corner of Musser and Pratt Streets.) On January 29 Governor Reinhold Sadler signed into law a bill that had moved at warp speed through the legislature (passing the assembly 20–9 and the senate 9–6). According to Sadler's spokesman, "The Governor takes the ground that scientific contests with gloves are less demoralizing to society and less dangerous to life and limb than football games."[12] The local Women's Christian Temperance Union (WCTU) and a few ministers had voiced their impassioned opposition, but their protests were ignored.

The relatively new Queensberry rules had created the illusion that boxing was now much more humane and safe, leading many to suggest that the sport now was about enhancing physical culture and developing "scientific" technique. Bare-knuckle matches, in comparison, were considered uncivilized and brutal. Advocates of the manly art contended that the use of five-ounce padded gloves and three-minute rounds separated by a minute of rest created a more enlightened sport that encouraged good sportsmanship and skill. Nevada was definitely a different place than Texas or Arkansas, because those Nevada citizens who were moved to contact their legislators about the legislation overwhelmingly supported the law, some pointedly noting that students at the University of Nevada had begun playing the controversial new game of football, which they said was inherently more dangerous than boxing with padded gloves.

The new statute permitted "glove contests" to be held if a fee of one thousand dollars was paid to the state and the participants passed a physical examination. The Silver State—already the brunt of criticism emanating from beyond its borders for its toleration of casino-style gambling and brothels—was targeted from across the nation by outraged critics. "Nevada's Disgrace" became the operative slogan of protest.

In reality, the criticism was of little consequence to those legislators who voted for legalization. A prizefight would not harm any citizen, and it did not pose a threat to public health. Nevadans were, in fact, outliers in a country that was dominated by Victorian sensibilities. Their leaders were always on the lookout for a new angle to stimulate economic growth. The state would soon become a flaming symbol for lax morality when lawyers across the country discovered that ever since territorial days, Nevada had permitted "quickie" divorces that required only a six-month residency period and sent their clients to Reno. The divorce trade became a bonanza for Reno lawyers by 1910. Tellingly, on the same day that the all-male legislature legalized prizefighting, it rejected a proposal to grant women the right to vote.

Both fighters set up training camps outside of town, Fitzsimmons at Cook's Ranch, Corbett at Shaw's Springs. They had readily agreed to the bout because Stuart had pledged a fifteen-thousand-dollar purse for the winner, with nine thousand dollars going to the loser. As was the norm during this era, it was expected that both fighters and their handlers would seek to enhance their earnings by placing side bets on the fight. Reporters from major newspapers arrived weeks before the fight to report the "daily dope" from the training camps; even the announced referee, fifty-year-old sportswriter for the *Chicago Tribune* George Siler, reported daily for six newspapers, sparking criticism that he was jeopardizing his neutrality. Word out of the Corbett camp was not encouraging. The popular "Gentleman Jim" had recently turned thirty years of age, and he had not fought a serious bout in three years, as he concentrated upon his acting career. Some concerns about his conditioning floated among insiders. Reporters were surprised that a novice sparring partner had been able to land solid punches to Corbett's abdomen to the point that he was rumored to be suffering from a stomach injury. The young sparring partner turned out to be a stout farmer from Southern California, James Jeffries, who would capture the heavyweight title in 1899. Hearst newspaper writer W. W. Naughton fired off a report on these ominous developments, concluding that in the wiry Fitzsimmons, he faced a dangerous foe: "Corbett can't be champion any more unless he goes in and punches Fitzsimmons, for that gentleman unpunched, can stay in the ring as long as Corbett. Also Corbett cannot punch without going into Fitzsimmons's range, and when he is there he may receive a blow that will end his career."[13]

The contrast between the two fighters became the major story line for reporters. Corbett was handsome and charismatic, with an impressive résumé that went beyond the ring. He had won the title in 1892 in the first gloved championship fight when he knocked out defending champion John L. Sullivan. That historic bout had signaled the beginning of a shift in public opinion toward tolerating prizefighting because it had demonstrated that there was big money to be made by promoting the right sort of prizefight. By requiring the adoption of Queensberry rules, the New Orleans city ordinance had given prizefighting a veneer of respectability and created a false impression that the sport had been made less dangerous.

Corbett was born and raised in an Irish neighborhood of San Francisco and became a popular boxing instructor at an elite private gymnasium, the Olympic Club. In 1891, after putting on many sparring exhibitions and easily defeating local challengers, he agreed to a bout with the boxing instructor from across the city at the rival Golden Gate Athletic Club. Peter Jackson, the "Black Prince," was born in the West Indies and began his boxing career in 1882 in Australia. He moved to the United States, determined to earn big paydays, but was stunned when he learned that Sullivan would not enter a ring against a black opponent. He was warmly received in San Francisco, where his talent was appreciated. Jackson readily agreed to meet Corbett when a local promoter put up a purse of ten thousand dollars (with eighty-five hundred dollars for the winner). In October 1891 the two men battled for sixty-one rounds before the referee, observing that the two completely exhausted fighters were unable to continue, called the fight a draw. It was Corbett's strong showing against Jackson that earned him his shot at Sullivan, who stoutly refused to rescind his pledge not to enter the ring with a black man.[14]

Corbett's reputation was based upon the published record that he had won scores of fights, but many of those were controlled sparring exhibitions. In fact, after defeating Sullivan he used his title to enhance his acting career. He definitely was not eager to defend his title, but in 1894 he easily dispatched Englishman Charlie Mitchell in Jacksonville, Florida, by a third-round knockout. Under the guidance of his manager, William Brady, who handled both fighters and actors, Corbett became a big draw on the legitimate theater circuit. After defeating Sullivan, he launched a long tour as the star in *Gentleman Jack* and later was the male headliner in the popular four-act comedy *The Naval Cadet.* Audiences in the United States and England praised his acting skills, and women were drawn to the handsome young man who carried his 183 pounds on a solid six-foot-one frame. He was often called "Pompadour Jim" because of his stylish black haircut that framed his photogenic face. While on tour Corbett earned substantial sums, sparring in staged "exhibitions" against local challengers, sometimes on the same stage and on the same day he played the leading man.

According to the unofficial rules of the day, a reigning champion had to accept a legitimate challenge within six months or forfeit his title. Thus, a challenge from "Ruby Robert" Fitzsimmons in 1895 had set in motion the bizarre set of events orchestrated by Dan Stuart. By this time the two men had already become bitter enemies due to a few altercations when their paths crossed; most famously, they almost came to blows in the lobby of a Philadelphia hotel. Both fighters engaged in an ongoing verbal jousting that grew increasingly acrimonious. Essentially, they engaged in a nineteenth-century version of trash talking, each accusing the other that he was afraid to decide the issue in the ring. When Stuart was unable to find an acceptable venue in Texas and Arkansas, Corbett opted to forfeit his title to return to the theater for an ensured payday.[15]

Fitzsimmons lacked both the sensual appeal and the charisma of

Corbett. His scrawny physique did not define him as an imposing challenger. He claimed to weigh 167 pounds, but he probably weighed less. His wiry six-foot frame rested upon shockingly thin "bandy" legs; one writer described him as a "fighter on stilts." His unimpressive physique, however, belied a sinewy upper body that had been forged as a teenage blacksmith that enabled him to unleash powerful punches. His most promising feature was a blanched skin covered with bright freckles and a bland countenance set off by a receding auburn hairline. Born in Cornwall in 1863, he moved at the age of nine to New Zealand with his parents and began bare-knuckle fighting as a teenager. He enjoyed considerable success and won the middleweight championships of New Zealand and Australia.

Fitzsimmons came to the United States in 1889 in search of bigger paydays, and two years later he won the world middleweight title by knocking out the popular American champion, Jack "the Nonpareil" Dempsey, in New Orleans. (At this stage in the development of boxing, only two weight classifications were recognized: middleweight and heavyweight.) Unlike Corbett, the "Freckled Wonder" fought frequently against all comers, having developed a reputation for his savvy counterpunching style that featured short but rapidly delivered blows to the torso that carried devastating power. His hidden advantage over Corbett was the knowledge and experience gleaned in more than fifty legitimate bouts and that his frequent bouts kept him in tip-top condition.

Stuart set the title match for late morning on March 17, 1897: St. Patrick's Day. In the weeks leading up to the much-anticipated event, one hundred workmen earned a generous five dollars a day hammering together an arena optimistically designed for seventeen thousand spectators. The octagon-shaped arena had thirty-five rows of plank seating, with a series of boxes set along ringside. To protect the fighters from possible rain or snow, a canvas canopy was placed high over the ring. Nevadans were not pleased when referee-designate George Siler released an article that said he was in the tiny state capital because "Dan Stuart quietly and diplomatically turned to the bankrupted Commonwealth of Nevada, with a total population of less than 60,000 and a hopeless insolvency." That "insolvency" was the reason, he said, "the Sage Hen State opened wide its arms and embraced Stuart and his enterprise." About ten days before the fight, the covey of reporters who had arrived in Carson City to cover the fight happily reported on an impromptu confrontation when the two fighters, outside the town on a dirt road doing their roadwork, by chance encountered one another. Their respective dogs (apparently pit bulls from some contemporary photographs) got into a snarling fight and had to be pried apart. Fitzsimmons graciously offered his hand to Corbett, who refused to accept the handshake, and both men thereupon exchanged threats and unprintable words. The next day Fitzsimmons told the press that "I will fight a square fight, an honorable fight, but there shall be no mercy, no quarter, no tenderness. I will fight him to the bitter end and conclude this issue and wipe out his insults." Several days before the fight, he predicted, "I'll win with a left somewhere in the body. It ain't so easy to 'it him in the chin." This was, of course, his trusty "solar plexus punch" that he had honed in many previous fights. It proved to be a prescient comment.[16]

Meanwhile, Stuart came down with a terrible illness, presumably pneumonia, that kept him in bed for seventeen days. For a time doctors feared he might not survive his high fever, but he slowly recovered with the assistance of a compound of quinine and morphine. Several celebrities were drawn to the event. From his sickbed, Stuart announced that the famous gunfighter Bat Masterson—"a prince of a sporting man"—had been employed to head up security that would include fifty Pinkerton detectives and local law enforcement officers. Masterson thereupon announced that he intended to seize any firearm carried to the arena by spectators. John L. Sullivan, aging and seriously overweight, arrived in town, announcing to loud guffaws that he would come out of retirement (again) and challenge the winner. No one took him seriously. Wyatt Earp, gunfighter, lawman, saloon owner, and sometime fight referee, became a fixture in local taverns in the days leading up to the fight. Earp himself was embroiled in a current boxing controversy, because the previous month in San Francisco he had handed a badly beaten Tom Sharkey a victory when he (to the disbelief of nearly all spectators) disqualified Fitzsimmons for disabling his opponent with a low blow. Fitzsimmons's manager, Martin Julian, publicly accused Earp of defrauding his man out of the ten-thousand-dollar purse because Earp had reportedly bet a large sum on Sharkey. (The issue ended up in a local court, whereupon, despite strong testimony

presented to confirm Julian's charges, the judge ruled in favor of the
famed gunman who had prevailed at the O. K. Corral.)[17]

Much of the big money came in from Corbett's San Francisco fans
who had arrived en masse in several charter trains. In local bars and
in betting poolrooms across the country, the odds stabilized, with Corbett a prohibitive favorite at ten to six and a half.

Gender Issues at Ringside

Despite his severe illness, Stuart had to deal with a contentious
issue that was new to prizefighting. Although women had just been
denied the right to vote in Nevada, some of Nevada's finest ladies were
demanding the right to break down a gender barrier and watch two
men stripped to the waist and wearing short pants do harm to each
other. Considering the reality that ticket sales were languishing, and in
the face of the shrill demands of the local WCTU that he protect femi-
nine sensibilities by denying women admission, Stuart opted to stand
up for equal rights—and profits—by granting women the right to purchase tickets. He duly noted that his attorney had informed him that
the legislation enabling the fight was mute on the subject of female
spectators. Stuart also stated that he had been informed that "some of
the most prominent men in the State" had indicated they wished to be
accompanied to the contest by their wives and that women had been
spotted in the crowds watching the two fighters during training sessions. His decision, however, clearly indicated that a male sanctuary
was about to be breached. The day before the fight, with a heavy, wet
snow falling, Stuart conducted a large group of invited women on a
tour of the arena.[18]

Stuart insisted, however, that only ladies escorted by gentlemen
would be admitted, and he set aside a section for them where they
would be shielded from gawking male fans by a canvas barrier. Estimates by attendees suggested that fewer than one hundred women
actually watched the fight. Such precautions, however, did not persuade the rotund John L. from voicing his objections to a tavern full of
reporters. "I am not in favor of having ladies at the fight," he bellowed.
"It is natural that they should admire fighters. Naturally they think
more of a man who can fight than of any other man, because if men
did not fight we should all be slaves and the English or somebody else

would rule us. George Washington was a fighter, and no man was more admired by the ladies than he was. But ladies ought not to see fights."[19]

Rows and Rows of Empty Seats

Stuart's dreams of selling seventeen thousand tickets were far from realized. During the week leading up to the fight, heavy, wet snows—not unusual for that time of the year in western Nevada—cascaded in from California over the Sierra Nevada. The snow quickly turned to slush, resulting in the unpaved streets becoming a muddy morass. The skies cleared the morning of the fight, producing an enticing panorama of snow-covered mountains and a crystal-clear blue sky. Stuart anticipated a payday of three hundred thousand dollars, but vast expanses of the wooden bleachers were empty when referee Siler called the men to the center of the ring for his instructions at 12:07 p.m. Both fighters had entered the ring wearing heavy robes to protect against the cold air that slid down from the nearby mountains. Fitzsimmons was wearing pea-green shorts; Corbett's very short shorts were a festive red, white, and blue. The official temperature was a chilly forty degrees. The size of the crowd, based upon guesstimates by those in attendance, ranged from four to six thousand. The anticipated influx of legions of big-spending sportsmen had not materialized, although all Reno and Carson hotels were reported filled and even some local residents who had opposed the fight discovered the financial benefits by renting out rooms.

One of the enduring criticisms of prizefighting was that the sport catered to the worst elements of society. To some observers, the audience did not reflect that stereotype, because many of Nevada's leading citizens were on hand, including prominent businessmen and political figures who took their seats near ringside. Steep ticket prices, however, tended to dictate a relatively affluent crowd and kept attendance from even coming close to filling half of the arena. Row after row of empty planks were captured by photographers during the fight. Even the least expensive five-dollar standing-room-only area atop the arena was only partially filled. Ticket prices for seats on the planks sold for twenty and thirty dollars, with seats in the ringside boxes priced at forty dollars. Governor Sadler and his son watched from a special box provided by a grateful Dan Stuart. The crowd reflected a unique western ambience. Out-of-state reporters were struck by the large numbers of Paiute and Washoe Indians who mingled easily with Chinese and Mexicans alongside the predominantly white crowd outside the arena. A prominent three-term retired US senator from Kansas, John J. Ingalls, was among the spectators, and he wrote that he observed a diverse crowd that included "average American citizens: miners, merchants, farmers, cowboys, ranchmen, lawyers," along with "some toughs and crooks." Local newsman Alf Doten was less charitable, writing that the crowd included a goodly number of "pugs, gamblers, newspaper reporters, scrubs, whores, and sons of bitches in plenty." Journalist Thomas T. Williams was even less charitable when describing the small coterie of women who attended the fight, apparently "for the new sensation": "They were mostly of the peroxide blonde order, and some of them were not particularly difficult to classify."[20]

The crowd clearly was in Corbett's corner. Perhaps his fans believed that it was inevitable that the popular Irishman from San Francisco was about to defeat the cheeky New Zealander on St. Patrick's Day. At 12:10 the bell sounded for round 1, and the event that some eastern newspapers had for nearly two years labeled the "Fight of the Century" was finally under way. After years of verbal sparring that had enlivened newspaper reports, both men were ready to inflict real damage upon an opponent they detested. In the early rounds, the skilled boxing instructor Corbett put on a "scientific" clinic by smacking Fitzsimmons's face time and again with quick left-handed jabs, while avoiding most of Fitzsimmons's punches. In his own detailed description of the fight sent out to his clients, Siler wrote that in the early rounds, Corbett "boxed well" and "landed and landed at will," but that Fitzsimmons throughout responded with a peculiar wry smile, as if "he liked it. . . . [He] really looked to be worse than he really was."[21]

Corbett opened several cuts on his opponent's freckled face, and late in round 5 he nailed Fitzsimmons with a vicious left-and-right combination that bloodied his nose and split his lip. But Fitzsimmons smiled back through the torrent of blood that ran down his face.

The fight nearly ended in the sixth round when Corbett caught Fitzsimmons squarely on the jaw with a left uppercut and a follow-up right hand to the nose sprayed a stream of blood across the ring. Fitzsimmons seemed powerless to block the barrage of blows. Another shot to the head sent him crumpling to the canvas. The man from Cornwall grasped Corbett's legs, and for a few moments Siler seemed uncertain of how to react. By most accounts he did not start the count immediately. Those at ringside heard Corbett imploring Siler to "count faster!" Corbett's supporters would later claim that Fitzsimmons lay on the canvas for as much as fifteen seconds, but he struggled to his feet as Siler's official count reached nine. He avoided further punishment, bobbing, weaving, and clinching until the bell sounded. He slumped onto his stool as his seconds feverishly worked to revive him, and his wife, Rose, breaking all sorts of gender rules by working in the corner as an unofficial second, shouted encouragement in his ear.[22]

Corbett apparently used up much of his reserve energy attempting the knockout and did not press his advantage in round 7, and in round 8 the two men exchanged punches as Fitzsimmons continued to bleed profusely. Thomas T. Williams, writing from ringside, reported that the scene was "sickening." Most spectators believed Fitzsimmons survived only due to his "gameness," while "the betting men got ready to cash in their Corbett tickets." A confident Corbett smiled as the rounds went on as the two fighters cautiously circled each other, content to maneuver defensively without throwing many punches. Senator Ingalls wrote that the entire spectacle had been transformed into a bizarre theater in which "the object apparently was to avoid rather than inflict injury." Most spectators believed Corbett was winning, but in fact he had little energy left in reserve.[23]

"Hit 'im in the Slats!"

In his autobiography Corbett recalls observing during the fight a very animated woman at ringside near Fitzsimmons's corner. She was, he said, "a big, blonde and very excited woman, her hair loose, hat jammed down over one ear, the blood from Fitz spattering her own face, and she, meanwhile yelling at me things that were not at all flattering either to my skill as a fighter or my conduct as a gentleman." Rose Fitzsimmons's behavior, the *Chicago Tribune* reported, was anything but ladylike: "As the battle went on, she became more and more demonstrative, sometimes breaking out with exclamations which bordered on the profane."[24]

At one point Rose shouted encouragement to her husband: "Punch him! Kill him, Bob! Hit him in the slats [ribs]! Hit him in the slats!" As the fight progressed, a tiring Corbett continued to land punches, but they lacked the force of earlier rounds, and he became more and more a defensive boxer while Fitzsimmons pushed his advantage. In round 14, Fitzsimmons found his opening. Corbett raised his gloves to protect his face after absorbing a blow to the neck, leaving his body momentarily unprotected. With lightning speed, Fitzsimmons uncorked his favorite "solar plexus punch," a short, powerful blow to the body that caught Corbett just under the heart. Corbett's face went white, and his eyes closed as he fell into the ropes. He moaned so loudly that even those in the high cheap seats could hear his cries. A *New York Times* reporter described this telling moment: "The Australian's small eyes twinkled, and with panther-like speed he drew back his left with the forearm rigid and ripped it up into the pit of Corbett's stomach a little under the heart. Corbett was lifted about a foot off the ground, and as he pitched forward Fitzsimmons swung on the jaw and Corbett came heavily down to his knees." Or as Alf Doten wrote in the *Nevada Appeal:* "Fitz landed a terrible left hand to Corbett's wind."[25] Just as he had predicted.

Although Corbett had not been knocked unconscious, he was immobilized by intense pain and unable to breathe normally. He attempted to rise to his feet but could not do so. Corbett recalled in his autobiography that he had dominated the fight and was supremely confident of victory: "I punched him at will. . . . I had bothered him by cutting his face to ribbons, jolted him pretty badly, and he was rather tired. . . . He was missing most of the time, and . . . when he did land, he had to hit so quickly that he lost much of his force and I wasn't hurt." All that changed when Fitzsimmons landed his powerful left hook to "the pit of my stomach and I sank to my knees. . . . I was conscious of everything that went on, the silence of the crowd, the agony on the faces of my seconds, but my body was like that of a man stricken by paralysis."[26]

Siler's count reached ten as the excited crowd, after a long moment of stunned silence, stood and roared its approval. As often occurs just after a dramatic ending to an important fight, excited seconds and fans charged into the ring, creating a mob scene that seemed on the verge of mayhem. Into the melee rushed several Pinkerton detectives, their pistols drawn, shouting for order. For a few moments an apparently disoriented Corbett attempted to get at Fitzsimmons to resume the fight, while Rose fought through the crowd toward Corbett, shouting, "I'll kill him! I'll kill the coward!" Siler jumped out of the ring to avoid the crush of people, but informed the timekeeper that he had counted Corbett out. In the crush of people who climbed into the ring, Corbett's manger, William A. Brady, shouted out an impromptu speech, claiming that Corbett had reached his feet before the count of ten, but he later confessed that he was simply attempting to plant seeds for a rematch, or, as he called it, "a little engineering and scheming" to sway public opinion to the conclusion that " 'lanky Bob' had been actually knocked out in the sixth round and that Corbett had been robbed of the match."[27]

Corbett regained his composure, congratulated Fitz, and asked for a rematch, one that would never come. Several Corbett supporters appeared to threaten the winner, and to his rescue came Wyatt Earp, who grabbed him by the shoulder and assisted him out of the ring with his handlers. Back in his dressing room, Corbett slumped into a chair, rubbing his hand over his torso, and told his gloomy seconds, "How my heart hurts me. I thought I'd die when I went down. . . . The pain was awful. Awful. It may kill me yet." That evening, while riding aboard the "*San Francisco Examiner*'s Lightning Special" back to the Bay Area, Corbett said that he had been caught off guard by a "sneaky little punch," implying that he still was the better man. "I believe in the main I fought as well as I ever fought in my life, but luck was against me. The blow which won the fight for Fitz was in large measure an accidental one."[28]

Fight fans across the country eagerly read detailed reports—many of them describing the details round by round, blow by blow—and it was the subject of considerable discussion everywhere men gathered. Wyatt Earp, writing in the *New York World,* confirmed what many believed: "I consider that I have witnessed today the greatest fight with gloves that was ever held in this or any other country."[29]

Dan Stuart's Belated "Fistiana" Payday

The paltry gate did not diminish Dan Stuart's delight that his fistic carnival had finally taken place. He had delivered on what he had promised, and in so doing had overcome enormous obstacles in the form of angry ministers, stiff-necked politicians, a squadron of Texas Rangers, even a deployment of Mexican regulars. However, his ticket sales had not even approached his expenses. He was out as much as seventy-five thousand dollars. But this clever Texan was not dismayed, and in fact believed that he was about to reap a bountiful return on his investment.

The secret to his eventual financial bonanza rested in the small wooden hut constructed just a few feet from ringside that contained three square openings, through which Enoch Rector's three cameras manufactured by Thomas Edison's company—now called the Veriscope —captured the entire spectacle on 11,000 feet of film, from the pre-fight ceremonies through the confusion that engulfed the ring at the end. Rector's technicians edited the precious film down to 2,880 feet that produced a one-hundred-minute feature-length film. Unlike the drizzling rain of Langtry, the bright skies and penetrating late-winter sun had given Rector a perfect day in which to capture the fight on film. One of the stipulations of the filming contract was that the fight would take place during the middle of the day, when the sunlight was at its brightest. Had the snow continued to fall on St. Patrick's Day, the three Veriscopes would not have been able to produce a film of the quality necessary for distribution and Stuart would have suffered a huge loss.[30]

Two months after the fight, the first showing of the edited film, entitled simply *Corbett vs. Fitzsimmons,* took place in the Academy of Music in New York City. It sold out to an enthusiastic audience of men *and* women. Within a few weeks copies of the film were being shown daily across the United States and in parts of Europe. For many Americans, it was the first motion picture they ever viewed. Showings were originally held in community opera houses and upscale vaudeville theaters, later in rented rooms, county fairs, and even public parks. Admission was initially set at a premium one dollar, but as the months went by and the film was shown in smaller towns with less affluent populations, admission charges were reduced to twenty-five cents. Although Stuart never released any figures, it was reasonably estimated that the film grossed three-quarters of a million dollars, which meant a net profit for him of one hundred thousand dollars, more than enough to cover his losses and return a sizable profit. The two fighters split 30 percent of the film's profits, giving them a significant postfight payday. The unique film contract negotiated by Dan Stuart anticipated by nearly a century the use of television rights by which fight promoters made the bulk of their money.

Film historians have credited *Corbett vs. Fitzsimmons* with being the first genuine feature-length film in history. Many Americans purchased tickets because they were curious about the new technology, but their interest had also been piqued by the vast publicity that had surrounded the fight. Stuart publicized the film with language that appealed to middle- and upper-class customers, consciously seeking to avoid long-standing stereotypes that associated prizefighting with the dregs of society. Advertisements encouraged women to attend special midweek matinee showings. The film was advertised as an educational experience, and in some venues the silent film was accompanied by a live narrative by a professorial type who played down the blood and bruising and emphasized the "scientific" techniques of the manly art. Never mentioned was the implied erotic appeal to women who would have a unique opportunity to see two muscular men, stripped to the waist and wearing revealing shorts, engage in serious battle. As film historian Miriam Hansen concludes, the film "afforded women the forbidden sight of male bodies in seminudity, engaged in intimate and intense physical action." That the handsome "Pompadour Jim" Corbett, who already was an established stage star, was one of the fighters and wore surprising revealing boxing trunks undoubtedly enticed many women to attend a matinee.[31]

How many women actually saw the film during its three-year run in theaters large and small is difficult to ascertain. Certainly, the campaign unleashed by the Women's Christian Temperance Union to ban the film's showing in many states only contributed to women's curiosity. Press interest in the issue undoubtedly overstated the percentage of women who actually attended a showing, but film critic and historian Dan Streible concludes that although many of the estimates were "exaggerations," sufficient numbers attended to the point that women's attendance at future prizefights was no longer an issue. Future fight films never enjoyed the popularity of *Corbett vs. Fitzsimmons*. Stuart had capitalized upon the unique conjoining of curiosity about both the technology of motion pictures and what a prizefight actually looked like. Women would be admitted to future prizefights without much of a fuss, but the sport remained overwhelmingly one that primarily appealed to males.[32]

The impact of the fight upon Nevada's fragile economy proved to be much less than Governor Sadler and his supporters hoped for. The anticipated flood of high rollers ended up being a mere trickle, and the economy of western Nevada received only a mild uptick. Although a few individuals were reported to have inquired about relocating to Nevada as a result of the crush of national publicity, few apparently actually did so. The census of 1900 revealed a 6 percent decline in population from 1890 to a mere 42,335. Eastern newspapers now had Nevada in their sights, often referring to the "Nevada Disgrace" with searing commentary upon the lack of public decency in the frontier western state. It was an attack that would soon intensify with legislation that encouraged easy divorce and, three decades later, legalized casino gambling. A Boston newspaper, for example, editorialized that Nevada "has won the reputation of being the lowest in the rank of intelligence and decency among American states." The fight had helped create the stereotype that would flourish for much of the twentieth century: Nevada as the "Sin State." Nevada editors responded by defending Nevada's sense of frontier openness and liberation, while reprising the standard stereotype of an elitist, effete East. And in response to the harsh criticism emanating from southern pulpits and newspapers, the *Reno Gazette* caustically observed, "The Southern States have the latest styles in lynchings, but not one of them would tolerate a prizefight."[33]

The fight thrust Nevada into the national spotlight of a sport that was inexorably moving out of the shadows into legitimacy, and it would host major prizefights in the next two decades. For the next century, Nevada's popular culture would forever be closely identified with the most primal of all sports. Beyond that, in his dogged determination to promote a fistic carnival, Dan Stuart had set the stage for the legalization of prizefighting in the United States and had created a business model that would conjoin boxing, mass media, and investors into a lucrative, if often shady, enterprise. When famous promoters like Bob Arum and Don King reaped millions of dollars in television and closed-circuit rights to their bouts in Las Vegas and Reno in the 1980s and '90s, they were merely following in the path that Dan Stuart had created a century earlier.

Round 2

Low Blow in the Desert

It's just a little promotion stunt to help sell stocks in the gold mines we have around here. —Tex Rickard, August 1906

As memories of the great fight between Jim Corbett and Bob Fitzsimmons began to recede, the possibility of future fights naturally came up in conversations over drinks and card games. The appeal of a good prizefight always lingered in the Nevada air because the primal masculine sport reflected the harsh life in which mining and ranching were the heart of a small and fragile economy. When the vast deposits on the Comstock began to peter out in the late 1870s, Nevada entered into a severe economic crisis. The state's population fell from 62,266 in 1880 to a scant 42,335 in 1900. In the halls of Congress, informal discussions deliberated over rescinding Nevada's statehood and returning it to territorial status, or perhaps merging it with Utah or California. Nevada's leadership anxiously pondered various schemes to reverse the economic slide. The most promising solution prompted Nevada's lone congressman, Francis Newlands, to push legislation through Congress in 1902 to make "the desert bloom" by constructing, with federal funds, a massive irrigation project that would divert Truckee River water away from Pyramid Lake on the Paiute Reservation to create new farmland in Churchill County. However, the Newlands Project was considered a long-term solution that would take decades before anticipated returns could be realized.

The discovery of gold- and silver-bearing ore in southwestern Nevada near the small mining camp of Tonopah by rancher, attorney, and part-time prospector Jim Butler in 1900, however, rekindled hopes

34

of immediate salvation in the form of another mining boom. When assays revealed high-grade ore, prospectors and miners rushed to Nye County. In 1904, however, attention shifted from Tonopah to a discovery of even higher-quality ore thirty miles due south, on Columbia Mountain. This discovery set off a gold rush reminiscent of the Comstock Lode. By 1906 the boomtown of Goldfield had exceeded the population of Reno, becoming Nevada's largest community virtually overnight.

Not content with the riches being extracted from the sagebrush-strewn hillsides, the leading citizens of Goldfield decided to attract new capital by selling vast quantities of penny stocks in hundreds of undeveloped mining claims. What better way to generate publicity, attract visitors, and sell speculative stocks than by putting on a championship prizefight? The result was one of the most famous fights in the early history of the new gloved era, an event that proved to be successful far beyond the dreams of its promoters, none of whom had any experience whatsoever in promoting a major sporting event.[1] The prizefight also provided a template for future Nevada leaders who aspired to attract tourists and potential investors to the state. Leading the improbable parade was a thirty-four-year-old former cowboy from Texas who ran the busiest saloon in town.

The Magnificent Rube: Tex Rickard

He arrived in Goldfield in late 1904, lured by the smell of gold. Always the optimist, the street-smart George Lewis Rickard was confident that there was money to be made in the Nevada boomtown—big money.[2] He was born in Clay County, Missouri, on January 2, 1871, at a time when memories of the recent border warfare between the pro- and antislavery forces in "Bleeding Kansas" still resonated. Clay County, located just north of Kansas City and hard by the Missouri River, had been settled by migrants from the upper South and was a haven for Confederate sympathizers. According to family legend, Rickard's first cries at birth were not heard because the sheriff and a posse were rushing by the house firing their six-shooters at two fleeing bank robbers, the notorious James brothers. The mother of Frank and Jesse James, a sister to Rickard's mother, lived just down the road from the Rickards. This tale, unsubstantiated but somewhat probable, set the template for a life of adventure and excitement for the voluble salesman and prizefight promoter who came to be called "Tex."

Rickard once told a reporter, "The hard side of life was an old story to me long before I grew up. I never had any boyhood in the sense that the average boy does today. Circumstances forced me into cutting my own way at a time when most boys are out flying kites and playing marbles. I lived the life most boys imagine they want when they read a dime novel."[3] When Rickard was four, Pinkerton detectives surrounded the James house next door, believing the bank-robbing brothers were inside. They tossed a smoking flare through a window to flush them out, but the brothers were nowhere to be found. The flare exploded, ripping off the arm of Tex's aunt. Fearing further violence, his parents decided to relocate to the frontier town of Henrietta, Texas, also located in a county named after Henry Clay. There his father's inability to find work continued, and by the time Tex was eight, he was working at odd jobs and shining shoes for the cowboys to help his family make ends meet.

Tex grew up fast. When his father died in 1882, he quit school and hired on as a hand at a nearby ranch. He witnessed his first employer being shot dead in a barroom saloon following a disagreement over ownership of a few head of cattle. By the time he was fourteen, he was riding the line on the dusty cattle trail that led to the railroad center of Abilene, Kansas. On these long, hard drives, he observed a bunch of resilient cowboys who risked life and limb, confronting angry Indians, dangerous rustlers, and treacherous winter snows and summer thunderstorms. He also watched in amazement when they drank heavily and gambled away their pay after reaching the Kansas railhead. In 1894, after spending his teen years herding cattle, he was elected town marshal of Henrietta and established a reputation for defusing confrontations with lawbreakers by employing his considerable powers of persuasion. He was paid two and a half dollars for each lawbreaker he arrested, which enabled him and his young bride, Leona, to live well. The youthful sheriff won many admirers among the ladies of Henrietta for his charitable deeds and admiration from the menfolk for his facility for winning at faro and poker. In 1895, however, tragedy struck when his wife and infant daughter died at childbirth. It was time to move on. He turned in his badge and headed for a new adventure in frontier Alaska, where he heard that vast quantities of gold were there for the taking.

Rickard lived in the unforgiving Yukon and Klondike Territories for seven years.[4] It did not take long for him to appreciate that he was not cut out for the hard labor that prospecting and digging for gold entailed. He naturally drifted into a line of work that befitted his talents—he tended bar, dealt faro, ran craps tables, and served as the front man for clubs. He also gambled heavily, winning some and losing some. After one particularly good night at the tables, he used his winnings to open his own place in Rampart, but soon thereafter lost ownership in an all-night card game to a couple of sharpers. Moving on to Nome in 1900, he parlayed a profitable evening's winnings at the card tables into half-ownership of a flourishing saloon and casino he called the Northern. It returned him, he later estimated, five hundred thousand dollars over the next four years, much of which he lost gambling or making bad investments in mining claims. Throughout, he enjoyed a reputation for honesty: trusting sourdough prospectors would leave their sacks of gold nuggets in his care without asking for a receipt.[5]

The rip-roaring success of the Northern owed much to his reputation as an honest operator. Journalist Rex Beach recalled his first encounter with Rickard in Alaska: "He was a slim, dark, likable fellow with a warm, flashing smile and a pleasing Southern accent. He could be friendly and animated, or as grim as an Apache. Tex had been raised in the cow country, and showed it."[6]

The Northern—at forty by sixty feet—housed the longest bar in the territories, behind which a team of bartenders relentlessly poured twenty-four hours a day. Whiskey straight from the barrel went for a heady fifty cents a shot, chased by a ten-cent mug of beer. Tex became famous for feeding prospectors down on their luck and buying many a round for the house. He also learned that he could pack the house when he sponsored prizefights featuring young men flailing away with their bare fists while the crowd drank, cheered, and bet on the outcome. Rickard left Alaska in 1902 with sixty-five thousand dollars deposited in a Seattle bank.

He thereupon lost his Alaska stake when he traveled by steamer to South Africa in search of a lost diamond mine, having been bamboozled by a small-time burglar turned con man he encountered in Seattle. He remained unperturbed by his setback. "What the hell?" he said later. "It was a wonderful trip and well worth what it cost." Back in San Francisco in the autumn of 1904, he was on the lookout for a new adventure when he encountered H. S. "Kid" Highley, who had been an associate in the Northern saloon. Highley excitedly told him that major gold deposits had been discovered in south-central Nevada. Figuring that he had plenty of experience making money amid a gold-seeking frenzy, and positive that the weather would be more hospitable than he had endured in Alaska, he and second wife Ellie Mae and their young daughter soon established residence in a newly constructed Victorian house, complete with indoor plumbing and the only grass yard in town. It was the first brick structure built in the primitive mining camp.

Two years earlier the town of Goldfield did not exist. According to legend, just two men were the sole occupants of the land. By the time the Rickards arrived in November 1904, an estimated ten thousand fortune seekers had already taken up residence in an unplanned sprawl of makeshift shacks and tents. An estimated two million dollars of gold ore had already been milled, and the best was yet to come. All across the United States, interest in Goldfield spread like a prairie fire. Inflated reports of one mine alone producing five million dollars of gold-bearing ore in just three months lured the adventurous to try their luck prospecting and many more to invest in speculative mining stock. Much more than Nevada's first mining boom on the Comstock that had begun on the eve of the Civil War, this boom was characterized by an orgy of stock speculation, much of it operated by a pack of scofflaws and con artists. A gold frenzy seemed to grip otherwise relatively staid citizens all across the United States, who bought vast quantities of speculative stocks in a mining town they had never visited. George Graham Rice, one of the leading con artists who contributed mightily to the town's speculative ambience, later wrote in his autobiography that penny stocks in yet-to-be-developed gold mines held a special appeal to aggressive, naive investors: "Tens of thousands of people . . . whose incomes were not sufficient to permit them to indulge in stock-market speculation in rails and industrials, found in cheap mining stocks the thing they were looking for—an opportunity . . . to give full play to their gambling, or speculative instinct."[7] The name of the new boomtown—Goldfield—seemed appropriate, as did the town's informal motto: "The greatest mining camp ever known."

Tex Rickard and Kid Highley opened their saloon and gambling parlor in the heart of the action on the corner of Crook and Main Streets, giving it the sentimental name of the Northern. Although they faced competition from approximately fifty other watering holes and gambling houses, the Northern quickly became the popular hub of the town's male-dominated social life. Rice relates that the Northern was "the popular rendezvous," where men "gathered nightly . . . talked mines and mining, and sold properties." It was not unusual, he wrote, for brokers "to trade 30,000 or 40,000 shares of stock" on a typical evening in the Northern. Three shifts of six bartenders worked around the clock behind the sixty-foot bar, and fourteen gaming tables—faro, poker, craps, roulette, blackjack—saw steady action around the clock. Highley worked as a pit boss, sharing time for a while with Wyatt Earp, whose reputation earned in Dodge City and at the O. K. Corral in Tombstone helped keep the peace. Business was especially good because Rickard enjoyed a reputation for running honest games. His accountant, Billy Murray, later recalled routinely counting more than ten thousand dollars daily in receipts, which roughly totaled seven million dollars during the four years Highley and Rickard operated the Northern. Murray also safeguarded sacks of gold dust and nuggets that trusting prospectors left in Rickard's care. Highley, a man who did not smoke, drink, or chase women, left Goldfield a very rich man; decades later he recalled that he never ceased to be amazed that the street-smart Rickard could still lose large sums in a card game or be suckered into a bad investment in a mine, but never seemed to mind. He recalled that Rickard's gift of gab came naturally: "He could always draw a crowd. His very name and reputation attracted the customers."[8]

In 1955 the eighty-six-year-old Highley, now living in a luxurious hotel suite in San Francisco, told a journalist that he could never understand how Rickard, who had been around gold mining for a decade, could still get snookered by a con man who once sold him stock in a salted mine, one of the oldest tricks in the business. But then Highley smiled, his eyes twinkling, and recalled that Rickard had also pulled off the most improbable of promotions: a championship prizefight in Goldfield that put the town on the map. "There has never been anything like it since," the Kid said with a laugh. Indeed there wasn't.[9]

Boosters, Scam Artists, and Promoters

It did not take Rickard long to establish himself in the fluid social milieu of the boomtown. His saloon and gambling emporium was the talk of the town, and he was soon sharing the company of Goldfield's business elite that included such prominent mine owners as George

Wingfield and George Nixon, along with such shameless scam artists as Larry "Shanghai" Sullivan and George Graham Rice. Rickard looked and dressed the part of a successful businessman. Affable and approachable, he was a popular man about town. When he ventured out, his normal attire included a stylish suit set off by a jaunty fedora and a gold-headed walking stick. Journalist Bob Edgren, in town for the prizefight, commented that unlike many hucksters he had encountered in the fight game, Rickard was "neither short nor fat. He is tall, lean and sinewy as a cowboy, dark-tanned from exposure to desert sun and wind, and has a sharp eyed, thin lipped, straight-nosed countenance, and is as alert as an eagle." But it was his reputation as a straight talker that truly set him apart: "He bites his words off in a decisive manner when he talks. He is a typical frontiersman . . . a gambler by profession—just the kind of gambler Bret Harte pictured so delightfully in his stories of California life in the Fifties."[10]

Goldfield was brimming with optimism when Rickard and Highley arrived in town, and in the ensuing months the town's prospects grew ever brighter. Whereas most western gold mines produced ore valued between $5 and $20 a ton, Goldfield ore was bringing between $100 and $150 a ton. By the time Rickard arrived, an estimated ten thousand newcomers had turned the area into a haphazard settlement of tents and wooden shacks; soon evidence of permanence began to appear in the form of imposing brick and stone commercial buildings. Goldfield was, in fact, already the largest city in Nevada, with its bustling dirt streets reflecting a rich tapestry of a desert frontier camp melding into a modern community. The scene was aptly described in a 1907 edition of the *Mining and Scientific Press* as a mélange of "nondescript promoters, irresponsible mining engineers, highgraders, and agitators, [who] rubbed elbows with brokers and businessmen from New York, Philadelphia, Chicago and other large cities. Its changing tempo was best exemplified by seeing on the same street, the prospector with his burro, and the mining engineer with his automobile."[11]

The lure of easy money attracted a small army of unscrupulous promoters and speculators, who exploited the national psychology that had been deeply affected by a serious economic downturn and subsequent banking panic. These scammers inundated eastern newspapers with incredulous tales of immense riches being made in the Nevada desert.

By 1905 more than a hundred mining companies had been formed, most of which owned only unproven claims, and many more came and went with the passing of the years. Some legitimate operators sought investment capital to develop their properties. Others, however, had little interest in actually developing claims that they knew, or at least presumed, were worthless, and instead sought to capitalize upon the get-rich-quick mania that gold fever encouraged by peddling worthless stock. They shrewdly exploited the gold craze that swept across the country in the wake of hard economic times. They took out advertisements in midwestern and eastern newspapers, contingent upon the newspapers also publishing as fact their "news releases" that told of incredible bonanzas. At a time when there were no effective regulations governing the content of stock prospectuses and advertising claims, these con artists fleeced gullible investors who accepted at face value the most outlandish promotional claims without even a cursory examination. As historian Russell Elliott concludes, they callously "promoted mining claims against all of the rules of mining, mining custom, and accepted promotional methods. . . . They made false claims of ore values, used false advertising, and resorted to all the tricks of mine salting which were known to their particular breed of men."[12]

Or as historian Richard Lillard states, tongue in cheek: "Promoters with rascally motives flourished in Goldfield as they never had in Virginia City, ingenious though its citizens were in fraud and chicanery. Suave crooks were so thick in Goldfield that they needed badges for identification so that they wouldn't try to sell wildcat to each other."[13]

Two of the most successful of these rogues were George Graham Rice and L. M. "Shanghai" Sullivan. Rice, whose real name was Jacob S. Herzig, was born in New York City in 1870 and landed in Nevada after having done three years of hard time in Sing Sing for forgery. He was drawn to Goldfield as a fly is to sugar, and he established an advertising company that he shortly thereafter merged with the L. M. Sullivan Trust Company, which was little more than a vehicle to promote the sale of mining stocks to easy marks. They published many a misleading story in their house organ, the *Nevada Mining News,* which they circulated across the nation. Sullivan had come from Seattle, where he had operated a flophouse whose drunken residents sometimes awakened from a stupor to find themselves newly anointed stevedores aboard a steamer heading for the Orient—hence the nickname of "Shanghai." Rice used the slow-witted and semiliterate Sullivan as the front man in the elaborate scam operation.[14]

Throughout his lifetime, Rickard exhibited a curious combination of shrewd promoter and naive country rube. Hence, he easily developed a cordial relationship with the two scam artists. At some point, probably over a drink or two, Rice and Rickard hit upon the idea of a championship prizefight to publicize the town's good name and in the process unload vast quantities of stock. When they proposed such a scheme to a few leading citizens, they were immediately inundated by pledges of financial support from local businessmen, stockbrokers, and mine operators. Within a few days, the Goldfield Athletic Club (GAC) was formed, its sole mission to put on a big fight on Labor Day, the participants yet unknown.

Rickard had witnessed firsthand the appeal that boxing matches between rank amateurs enjoyed in the male-dominated mining culture of remote Alaska, but he apparently become interested in professional prizefighting in San Francisco, where the sport flourished. He was especially impressed by the excitement generated by recollections of the ring exploits of local hero James J. Corbett. Rickard had also followed the news of what was purported to be a championship heavyweight fight held the previous July in Reno. The prizefight between Marvin Hart and Jack Root had been the brainchild of two local sportsmen, state senator Al Livingston of Carson City, who had played a role in landing the Fitzsimmons-Corbett fight in 1897, and businessman Joe "Kid" Egan of Reno. They formed the Reno Athletic Club with their own funds to promote the fight and announced that because Jim Jeffries had vacated the title in 1904, the bout would be for the world championship. They announced a five-thousand-dollar purse, with the winner taking 65 percent. Their enthusiasm, however, did not resonate with boxing experts elsewhere, who exhibited, at best, lukewarm interest. Both fighters had respectable records, but their talents paled in comparison to those of Jeffries, who now was attending to his Southern California alfalfa farm. Although Livingston and Egan aggressively promoted the fight, it attracted little attention outside of northern Nevada. Despite an appearance by the vaunted Jeffries as referee (which cost Livingston and Egan a thousand dollars), only an estimated four thousand fans, most of them locals, watched the match in the sixty-five-hundred-seat wooden arena they erected on the east edge of Reno. The fight itself was exciting enough, with Root dominating for much of the match. He knocked Hart down in the seventh round and seemed well on his way to victory when Hart connected with a powerful blow to the stomach in the twelfth round that sent Root to the canvas, where he lay writhing in pain as Jeffries counted to ten.[15]

Much to Livingston's and Egan's chagrin, Jeffries refused to declare that Hart was the new heavyweight champion. That issue was soon resolved when Hart lost a lopsided decision to Canadian Tommy Burns in Colma, California, the following February, the beginning of a chain of events that would help catapult Rickard into national prominence as the leading promoter of championship prizefights.

At the organizational meeting of the GAC on July 30, Sullivan was elected president, while others claimed honorific roles (such as ring announcer, time keeper, and bell ringer). But no one stepped forward to do the heavy lifting, at which point all eyes turned toward Rickard. "All the tony jobs had been passed out," he later recalled, but then those present realized the obvious: "Somebody would have to do a lot of work, like negotiating with the managers and seeing about an arena and all the rest of it. In other words, running everything from start to finish." Kid Highley sealed the deal when he wryly said to the very busy saloon owner, "You got the time for it, Tex. The rest of us haven't."[16]

The GAC members knew their man. With the event planned for Labor Day—just thirty-three days away—Rickard moved quickly and decisively, armed with sufficient cash raised from several other businessmen and mine operators. Tex put up ten thousand dollars of his own money, although he was usually a firm practitioner of the principle that it is always best to wheel and deal with other people's money. The *Goldfield Sun* reported that within twenty-four hours after Rickard assumed command of the adventure, the GAC had received sufficient contributions to offer a theretofore unheard-of purse of thirty thousand dollars, one that guaranteed the fight would attract attention: "Business men, saloon keepers, bankers, mine owners, gamblers and miners, all rushed into the office of Tex Rickard and planked their contributions down in good hard cash, not promises or conversation money; with the total amount subscribed reaching a grand total of $52,000." Twenty-four hours later, Rickard had reportedly booked another forty thousand dollars . . . of other people's money. The *Goldfield Review* glowingly proclaimed that this outpouring of hard cash was evidence to the world that the town was awash with money and predicted that the upcoming extravaganza would succeed in promoting the rapidly growing boomtown as a place in which to invest in mining stock.[17]

Although his only experience with boxing had been organizing amateurish bare-knuckle slugfests in Alaska, Rickard proved adept in handling the many complex facets of promoting a championship prizefight. Possessed of astute insights into the foibles of human nature and experienced in making large bets, he fearlessly plunged ahead. When it was over, Rickard had put on a classic championship fight, lured five thousand persons to town (some extravagant claims placed the number as high as fifteen thousand), and in so doing facilitated the sale of vast amounts of (mostly worthless) mining stock. The publicity that he generated indeed placed Goldfield on the map. In the process, Rickard became a national figure and launched himself upon an improbable career as America's first great boxing promoter.

The Old Master and the Durable Dane

The American people became incredibly curious when Rickard announced that the freshly minted Goldfield Athletic Club was offering an unprecedented purse of thirty thousand dollars to attract two leading lightweights, Joe Gans and Battling Nelson, for a championship "finish fight" in Goldfield. (The purse was worth approximately three-quarters of a million dollars in 2012 currency.) Americans everywhere wanted to know more about the audacious man who had made the stunning offer. Overnight, Rickard became famous. As events leading up to Labor Day unfolded, he increasingly became the center of attention, more so than the two fighters.

Rickard often remarked that he was a man blessed with good luck. That certainly was in evidence when he made his first move as a fledgling promoter. In May he had visited New York City, and while there he attended a prizefight between two prominent lightweights, Jimmy Britt and Terry McGovern. The excitement generated by the event intrigued him, and he managed to have a brief conversation ringside with McGovern's manager, Joe Humphreys. Shortly after assuming command of the Goldfield Athletic Club, he fired off a telegram to Humphreys, who had apparently forgotten his brief encounter with the cowboy from Nevada: CAN MAKE YOU AN OFFER OF FIFTEEN

THOUSAND DOLLARS FOR A FIGHT TO A FINISH BETWEEN TERRY MCGOVERN AND JIMMY BRITT TO TAKE PLACE AT GOLDFIELD, NEVADA. WIRE ANSWER IMMEDIATELY. TEX RICKARD. Humphreys was irked that the telegram had been sent collect, a fact that led him to dismiss its contents as a practical joke. The large amount proposed was obviously a hoax, or so he told himself. Irritated that he had forked over five dollars to accept the telegram, Humphreys fired off an immediate one-word rejoinder: NO! And he sent it collect.[18]

Humphreys did not bother to mention the telegram to his fighter, but a few days later he was stunned when McGovern shoved a newspaper in his face, demanding to know why he was not the fighter to get an offer to share a thirty-thousand-dollar prize! "Joe Gans is half dead," he fumed, "but his manager gets him a thirty-thousand dollar fight!" The newspaper reported that an unknown promoter in distant Nevada had lured the champion Gans and leading challenger Battling Nelson to Goldfield for a Labor Day dustup by dangling before them an offer that was the largest known to mankind. Three years later, Rickard and Humphreys happened to meet, and McGovern's curious manager had to ask why that telegram had been sent collect. "Hell, I didn't send it collect," Tex replied. "I wrote out that telegram and gave my porter a ten-dollar gold piece to send it. I guess the young feller just put the whole ten dollars in his pocket, forgetful-like."[19]

Humphrey's mistake was a stroke of immense good luck for the novice fight promoter. Another McGovern-Britt fight would have been old news and not have stirred nearly the level of public attention as did the first-time pairing of two prominent lightweights that fight fans wanted to see. Having received Humphrey's blunt rejection, Rickard did not hesitate. He knew that Battling Nelson was in Salt Lake City, and he sent an initial offer of twenty thousand dollars to his manager, Billy Nolan, who studiously ignored the offer. Meanwhile, Rickard had tracked down Joe Gans in San Francisco, where the champion, having been abandoned by his longtime manager, was down on his luck and out of money. He readily agreed to whatever terms Rickard considered fair and borrowed enough money for train fare to get to Goldfield. With Gans signed, Rickard wired Nolan and raised the offer to thirty thousand and left for Reno, where he contracted to purchase enough cheap green lumber (214,667 board feet to be precise) to build an arena capable of seating eight thousand spectators. Nolan's acceptance awaited Tex upon his return to Goldfield. Back in New York City, Joe Humphreys studiously avoided telling Terrible Terry McGovern how he had missed out on a historic payday. Only later did Rickard learn that the well-established San Francisco fight promoter Sunny Jim Coffroth had been trying for months to arrange the same fight to be held in the Bay Area; Coffroth was reportedly steamed that he had been outfinagled—and seriously outbid—by a rank amateur from Nevada.[20]

Despite the fact that he was a black fighter at a time when virulent racism raged across America, the soft-spoken, gentlemanly Gans enjoyed widespread popularity. At age thirty-one, he had won all but 5 of 144 fights, and 3 of those losses were attributed to his naive willingness to satisfy the betting schemes of his unprincipled manager, Al Herford, by dumping fights. Fans appreciated that while he was the consummate "scientific" boxer, he was also capable of unleashing a powerful knockout punch with either hand. Boxing journalist and historian Bert Sugar has written that Gans "was one of the classiest boxers of all time—the greatest boxer pound-for-pound and punch-for-punch of all time."[21] Hence, the nickname "Old Master" seemed appropriate.

Born into poverty in Baltimore in 1874, Gans had worked as a youngster at the arduous job of shucking oysters down by the waterfront. Life on the streets was tough, and he became well known for his ability to defend himself. His fistic skills brought him to the attention of Herford, a local saloon owner, gambler, and all-around hustler, who became his manager. At age seventeen, Gans began his professional career fighting in local clubs and then moved on to bigger venues, appearing in theaters and private clubs across the country, sometimes even joining traveling carnivals. Unlike talented black heavyweights Sam Langford, Joe Jennette, Sam McVey, and Jack Johnson, who were systematically denied matches by leading white heavyweights, Gans was able to challenge leading white lightweights because the symbolism of masculine supremacy was not in play as with heavyweights. Nonetheless, he had learned to deal with racial slurs and slights of all kinds, including accepting lesser slices of the prize money than white fighters. At the time, there were only two recognized weight classifications: heavyweight and, for fighters under 133 pounds, lightweight. His natural fighting weight was 140 pounds, and to make the weight limit he often had to undergo extreme methods of losing weight to avoid paying a forfeiture fee.

Gans won the lightweight championship in 1902 when he knocked out Frank Erne in the first round before a crowd of five thousand near Niagara Falls in Fort Erie, Ontario. In assessing the many fights that were required for Gans to reach the pinnacle of his profession, boxing historian Nat Fleischer concludes, "No fighter has ever faced a tougher field in the journey to the title."[22] His many fights against the best opponents, however, had made Gans a wily craftsman. He was famous as a counterpuncher, well known for exceptional endurance, whose footwork enabled him to avoid danger while wearing down his opponents with his lightning-fast jabs, before unleashing knockout punches with either hand. His punches were reportedly so powerful that he would destroy a leather punching bag in a furious assault; one journalist compared the sound of his punches hitting the bag to that of a Gatling gun.

By 1905 Gans had defeated all worthy challengers. Unable to find willing opponents, deserted by Herford, and having lost his bankroll gambling, Gans was destitute when the call from Rickard arrived. His reputation was also in serious question. In Chicago in 1900, Terry McGovern knocked him down five times in the second round in a bout in which Gans seemed totally inept. Even blows that apparently did not land sent him reeling to the canvas. Angry spectators doubted that McGovern had delivered any blow that would have led to a knockdown; referee George Siler wrote in the *Chicago Tribune* that "the few blows [McGovern] delivered were the weakest ever seen from a man of his known hitting ability." It was widely believed that Herford had ordered Gans to take a dive as part of a convoluted conspiracy that would, ironically, provide him an opportunity to fight champion Frank Erne for the lightweight title. Herford naturally had covertly bet big money on McGovern. Public reaction to this unsavory spectacle with McGovern led directly to prizefighting being banned in Illinois for twenty years. Again in 1904, Gans was accused of attempting to dump a fight when he fought with suspicious ineptness for five rounds in San Francisco against Jimmy Britt before being declared the winner on a low blow. Free from Herford's influence, Gans publicly proclaimed that he would never again agree to throw a fight, but these two highly publicized episodes became an underlying issue when bets were made in Goldfield.[23]

In the days leading up to the fight, concerns about Gans's ethics were soon overshadowed by the overwhelming negative reaction to the arrogant and offensive behavior of Nelson's manager, the pugnacious Billy Nolan. Upon his arrival in town on August 9, Nolan began making outrageous demands that taught Rickard an essential lesson: everything is negotiable in the fight business. "From the day Nolan came into town, he put us in a high fever," he recalled. "He made trouble almost every day with his endless naggin'. If I hadn't been able to protect poor Joe Gans to some extent, Nolan would have skinned him out of everything down to the gold in his teeth."[24]

Nolan succeeded in alienating most everyone in Goldfield by threatening to pull out of the fight unless his preposterous demands were met. For starters, he told Rickard that he assumed the $30,000 was for Nelson's share. After a heated give-and-take, Tex raised the total purse to $33,500, with Nelson being guaranteed $22,500 to Gans's $11,000. Desperate for a payday, Gans readily agreed to the arrangement even though *he* was the defending champion. Then Nolan insisted that Gans, well known for having difficulty making the 133-pound limit, be subjected to three separate weigh-ins the day of the fight *and* that he be weighed wearing his shoes. Nolan apparently intended that Gans would have to forego adequate sustenance the day of the fight and that he not drink sufficient water, thereby forcing him to enter the sun-drenched outdoor ring dehydrated. Nolan even demanded and was granted that the standard-size ring of twenty-foot square be reduced to eighteen square feet, theorizing that his fighter, whose primary tactic was to bulldoze his opponents, would gain a tactical advantage in a smaller ring.

Nolan's outrageous behavior culminated in a long and contentious session with Rickard, who ultimately threatened to cancel the fight and leave Nolan and Nelson stranded in Goldfield without their hefty payday and to face the wrath of thousands of locals, many of whom were reputed to be quick to employ violent solutions. Nolan backed off, but continued his daily sniping. In sharp contrast, Gans won many supporters among white residents with his respectful demeanor, accessibility, and good humor.

Battling Nelson's image was not much better than his manager's.

Although seven years Gans's junior at age twenty-four, Nelson had already brawled his way to fifty victories. His well-deserved reputation for illegal head butts and low blows, coupled with his manager's demands, made him the villain in the days leading up to the fight. Nelson's image was compounded by conventional wisdom that held he was deficient in the mental-acuity category. All of this contributed to Gans being made an early ten-to-seven favorite among the betting class.

As the fight drew near, the best thinking among those planning to place a wager centered upon the perception that Nelson's major strength was his ability to wear down opponents. His unconventional style was to absorb multiple punches, round after round, inviting his opponents to give him their best shots. After several rounds of banging blows off his skull, his arm-weary opponents proved unable to ward off the relentless Bat. He also fought out of a deep crouch that enabled him to launch his powerful head butts. One writer aptly summarized his basic ring strategy: "Nelson has a curious way of fighting. First he plunges in again and again, inviting the other fellow to hit him on the jaw. When his rival was so tired of hitting Bat's lower maxillary that he couldn't raise his arm above a whisper, Bat took his turn and delivered the final punch. Usually, by that time the other fellow was too tired and discouraged to care to get up, even if he wasn't knocked out."[25] Little wonder that Nelson carried the nickname of the "Durable Dane."

Oscar Mattheus Nielson was born in Denmark in 1874, and his name was Americanized to Oscar Matthew Nelson when his parents migrated to Chicago when he was two. He was raised in the nondescript industrial Chicago suburb of Hegewisch and began fighting for money at the age of fourteen. His lack of verbal acuity was irresistible to journalists, who gleefully made his reputed low intelligence part of their narratives. One New York journalist was so curious about Nelson's mental sluggishness that he talked him into undergoing a series of medical tests that supposedly revealed a slow heartbeat and a skull that was reported to be about 60 percent thicker than the norm. The conclusion of the medical examiner was telling: "It would be difficult to hurt Nelson with a gloved fist. It would be impossible to kill him with the hardest blow of any human being since the Neanderthal man."[26]

Just how thick the Durable Dane's skull actually measured remains unknown, but his reputation as a brawler who could take the most powerful of blows, round after round, and wear down his opponents in the process was beyond question. Experts estimated that he took three blows for every one he delivered. His battered face and artfully mangled nose testified to the many punches his face had absorbed. His inability to articulate even the most basic of concepts tended to reinforce the popular image that he was a dullard who had one essential pugilistic skill: he could take one helluva punch. In response to these curious evaluations, Nelson liked to say, "I ain't human," and after the fight Gans would admit that, in comparison to his other foes, "Nelson is simply impervious to punishment."

Stacks of Double Eagles

The self-assured Tex Rickard had pulled off the seemingly impossible. Within less than two weeks after being selected to head the Goldfield Athletic Club, and without any experience in the arcane business of prizefight promotion whatsoever, he had put together a championship fight that attracted enormous national interest. In the process, he had become the center of much of the prefight publicity. When reporters descended upon Goldfield in the days before Labor Day, their first objective was to interview Rickard rather than the two fighters.

A major point of curiosity when reporters arrived in town was the front window of the town's biggest bank, the John S. Cook & Company, where Rickard had stacked thirty thousand dollars in the form of fifteen hundred glistening twenty-dollar double-eagle gold pieces. He did so to erase any doubt that he had the money to guarantee the fighters' purses. The neat stacks of coins became a convenient lead story in newspaper reports, providing substance to the underlying intent of promoting Goldfield as a major gold-mining center where large fortunes were being made. Because he had often handled such amounts of money, Rickard saw nothing unusual about his ploy and apparently did not anticipate the media frenzy that the stacks of coins created. Upon more than a few occasions, he had reputedly won or lost that amount in an evening at the gaming tables. Shrewd promotional instincts were undoubtedly part of his DNA, but he seemed genuinely surprised by the response his gimmick had generated.

When out-of-town reporters approached him, they discovered a courteous and outgoing man who was more than willing to provide them with as much information as he possessed. The seasoned reporters who descended upon Goldfield had previously encountered many a conniving fight promoter. Not surprisingly, they were smitten with Rickard. His candid responses to questions, his affable "aw shucks" demeanor, and his easy accessibility overcame initial suspicions that he was out of his league. San Francisco reporter (and soon-to-be-popular cartoonist) Rube Goldberg was one of the many such journalists: "Rickard seemed a shy, self-effacing man who dressed quietly and appeared to consider himself too unimportant—at first—to be interviewed or photographed. His hair was already thinning. He has small, piecing eyes, but he was frank and honest with you, regardless of what you asked him. He always seemed interested in you. If you walked into his office, he would get up and greet you by name. No matter how busy he was he would take a minute or two out to chat with you. And he was like that with everyone."[27]

Goldberg also took note of one of Rickard's signature expressions of confidence and friendship: "Every once in a while, Tex would call one of us to one side and hand him a twenty-dollar gold piece. Somehow, crude, uneducated guy that he was, he managed to do this graciously. You had the impression that it was you who was doing him the favor by accepting the money. It was always a token of friendship, never a bribe." Goldberg appreciated that Rickard was doling out the gold pieces to journalists like himself who were on small expense accounts and working for low salaries.[28]

By matching the smooth black boxer with the white brawler, Rickard had stumbled onto a formula for success that he would replicate many times in the future: creating a sharp contrast by pitting a popular fighter against someone whose race, ethnicity, or personal traits sparked disdain (and a desire to see the match) on the part of potential ticket purchasers. In this instance, however, he had the atypical mixture of a popular African American versus an unpopular white fighter in a town not known for its racial tolerance.

By the weekend of the fight, a fleet of two hundred Pullman sleeping cars had been assembled on the new sidings the Tonopah and Goldfield Railroad had hastily constructed just days before the fight. With the few local hotels and boardinghouses booked solid, the Pullman cars provided sleeping quarters for the influx of fight fans. With incoming passenger cars filled to capacity, the overflow of passengers was accommodated on wooden benches placed on flatcars. Business in the town's saloons was nonstop. Meanwhile, business was booming at

George Rice's place of business. One of his best-selling stocks was that of the "Stray Dog Mining Company." The editor of the *Bullfrog Miner* in nearby Beatty wrote that the fight had proved to be "a great drawing card for Goldfield," because "hundreds will come from all over the east that [*sic*] that have scarcely heard of Goldfield, and many of them will invest in mines and stocks while there."[29]

To commemorate the big event, the Goldfield Athletic Club published an ornate fifty-page program that included brief biographies of the club's officers with a few pages devoted to the fighters and the "history-making glove contest," but the bulk of this self-congratulatory publication was devoted to extolling Goldfield and "the wonders of southern Nevada" that focused upon the many investment opportunities that existed in its mines. Advertisements proclaimed the vast potentials of various stock issues, and pictures of allegedly producing mines were prominent. Massive mailings of the program were sent out across the land, predicting a bountiful future for Goldfield. Twenty-five thousand postcards with a scenic picture of the gold-laden hills were distributed. The *San Francisco Journal of Commerce* lauded the upstart community, noting that the "producers of the mining camp have shown again their indomitable spirit of getting what they go after."[30]

Lost in all the ballyhoo was the adamant opposition to prizefighting by Nevada governor John Sparks, who, pointing to the potential for the death of one of the pugilists, called the upcoming bout "a disgrace to our state." The governor's refusal to attend the fight and his public statement, however, did not dampen enthusiasm. Ethical and moral concerns voiced by pastors were brushed aside. In this mining town, where injuries and even deaths occurred with numbing frequency, the dangers of a "glove contest" seemed relatively minuscule. Writing about the mining town of Butte, Montana, historian Mary Murphy concludes that the dangers of mining naturally led to boxing becoming a major focus of leisurely activity in a town where "excessive violence was not unusual" and "an ethic of working-class manliness" prevailed. Working daily in dangerous conditions, Butte's miners demanded a similar intensity in their leisure activity. Boxing was a sport that displayed an individual's manliness and courage, and as such was an apt metaphor for the difficult and dangerous lives led by miners. In her perceptive study of life and labor in Goldfield, historian Dee Kille believes that prizefighting provided an apt metaphor for a harsh and uncertain existence in an environment where "a culture of manliness" prevailed.[31]

Matters of Gender and Race

In the days leading up to Labor Day, the issues of gender and race became a prominent part of the public dialogue. Although women had been permitted to attend the Fitzsimmons-Corbett fight in Carson City in 1897, albeit restricted to an enclosed area, the question of whether women should watch the upcoming prizefight was raised once more. Presbyterian minister James Byers took the offensive by threatening to "expel any woman who attends the prize fight from my flock," but his threat had little impact upon public opinion. Women were permitted to watch both fighters in their training sessions, and Rickard announced that he welcomed ladies who wished to purchase tickets. Women were prominently seen at both training camps, but Billy Nolan articulated concerns for the sensibilities of ladies by announcing "ladies days" on Wednesdays, at which time Nelson and his sparring partners would "appear in long tights such as are worn in theatrical exhibitions" rather than conventional boxing trunks.[32]

Rickard was not hesitant to take a stand on behalf of equal opportunity: "We are going to make it possible for women—good women—to see the fight."[33] Accordingly, he issued orders that any man who displayed unrefined behavior in the presence of the ladies, such as swearing or drunkenness, would be ejected. Picking up on the issue, one San Francisco newspaper sent writer Pauline Jacobson to report on the fight "from a woman's point of view." The number of women who actually attended the fight itself appears to have been relatively small. The *National Police Gazette* estimated the number of women "of seeming refinement" in the crowd at about two hundred. Rickard apparently learned an important lesson regarding gender issues; in the 1920s he openly encouraged female attendance at his megapromotions and helped make prizefighting an acceptable form of public entertainment for both genders.

The issue of Gans's race, however, was not so easily dismissed. This was a time, after all, when African Americans were being lynched and harsh segregation policies were enforced across the country. Even at the highest levels of government, blacks were either ignored or, worse, subjected to blatant discriminatory policies and practices, undergirded by racist assumptions that were palpable. By a vote of seven to one in 1896, the US Supreme Court had made racial segregation constitutional by creating the facade of "separate but equal" in the infamous decision of *Plessy v. Ferguson.* Southern Democrats in Congress were resolutely determined to maintain the racial status quo in their states, and even the White House was at best indifferent if not downright hostile to the treatment of African Americans. Even reports of brutal lynchings did not merit a response. Theodore Roosevelt may have made headlines when he invited the gradualist black spokesman Booker T. Washington to the White House for dinner, but he studiously avoided using his "bully pulpit" to advance even marginally the nation's African Americans toward equal rights.

The few blacks who had moved to Goldfield worked at menial jobs and were subjected to the conventional racial rules of the day, in-cluding living in the same section of town. These attitudes readily surfaced when Gans arrived in town. Local newspaper accounts casually referred to him as the "Baltimore brunette," the "colored whirlwind," and the "black demon." On the streets as well as in newspaper accounts, he was frequently called "boy." With Gans emerging as the betting favorite, the *Goldfield News* took due notice of the "unique position" in which many conflicted white citizens found themselves, "wishing to see a Negro defeat a white man." Gans's affable personality that was on display in Goldfield created an uneasy ambivalence among the whites who got to know him, especially when compared to the negative image that Nelson and his manager projected. According to imprecise accounts, a few blacks attended the fight.

The public comments by the infelicitous Nelson provided a jarring contrast to Gans, but he was merely regurgitating widely held racist assumptions. He bluntly placed the upcoming battle into a crude racial context: "I am going to put Gans out just as sure as I sit in this auto. White men and Mexicans, colored gentlemen and Indians, all look alike to me and I don't think there lives one of either race that can wallop me in my class." He later became even more explicit: "While I can even crawl, I will not let it be said that a nigger put me out. I am going to go after him while I've got a breath left in my body. I will let Gans wear himself out, and then I'll come through and get him. Watch me. There will be crepe in Coontown on Labor Day while the Danish descendants are celebrating."[34]

Long Afternoon in the Sun

The sun was bright and the sky clear on the long-anticipated day. By 3:00 p.m. the temperature neared the hundred-degree mark. Heavy betting over the weekend had produced more Gans money, pushing street odds down to as low as ten to six at the stock emporium and temporary betting poolroom run by George Rice and Shanghai Sullivan. Some of the largest bets were placed by owners of mines, who wagered copious amounts of stock shares: Jim Riley, owner of a popular Tonopah saloon, put up twenty-five thousand shares in a Tonopah mining company valued at $25,000 against four hundred shares in a Goldfield mine; control of the two mines reportedly rested on the outcome of the fight. Rickard himself was believed to have placed a substantial wager on Nelson.

On the weekend of the fight, a festive holiday mood surged through the crowded town. Spectators cheered youngsters running footraces and bet on hard-rock drilling contests that attracted energetic entrants who performed before large crowds. Prospectors drifted into town from out of the hills, leading their heavily laden burros. For the first time since the town was founded, the mines and mills shut down. Untold thousands of visitors—estimates varied from five to fifteen thousand—had inundated the town, drinking heavily, placing their bets, visiting the busy brothels, and squeezing into the packed Northern casino to test their luck. Many also purchased stocks. Rickard announced that all eight thousand tickets had been sold, producing revenues of $69,715. When he presented a final accounting to the directors of the GAC, he reported that in addition to paying the fighters, he had spent $23,000 in expenses ($13,000 for construction of the arena) and declared a profit of $13,215, after returning the up-front money advanced by investors.

While the visitors were enjoying themselves in the days leading up to the fight, Gans was waging a gallant fight to shed four pounds, reportedly spending considerable time in a "Turkish bath" and consuming only smidgens of nourishment and water. He apparently managed to take in good humor Billy Nolan's unrelenting effort to distract and annoy him both physically and psychologically. Much to everyone's relief (Nolan and Nelson excepted), when Gans stepped on the scales three times during the day, he came in under the 133 limit. At 1:30 on Monday afternoon, two California lightweights, Bobbie Lundie and Jack Clifford, were introduced for what was a noteworthy prelim, because they were squaring off for an unprecedentedly large purse of $1,000 for an undercard bout. Clifford was counted out in the second round, and the capacity crowd squirmed uncomfortably on the green bleachers that were oozing sap in the hot sun as they awaited the championship bout scheduled for 3:00 p.m.

Notable guests took their seats at ringside, although the president's son Theodore Roosevelt Jr., whose anticipated presence was widely rumored in newspapers, was nowhere to be seen. Employing his typical mangled verbiage, Shanghai Sullivan introduced the two fighters, with the crowd greeting Nelson with hisses and boos and showering Gans with cheers. Sullivan also informed the crowd that three hundred deputy sheriffs were in attendance, many wearing their holstered .45s in plain sight, and pointedly announced that guns would not be permitted in the ring. Across the entire United States, fans gathered for blow-by-blow descriptions of the action that were to be tapped out at ringside by a Western Union telegrapher.

Referee George Siler, who had arrived from Chicago to officiate as well as write accounts for the *Chicago Tribune,* gave the two men their instructions that included a pointed comment about head butting, obviously for the benefit of Battling Nelson. It would be a fight to the finish, he said, or in the extraordinary circumstance that the fight went forty-five rounds of three minutes each, he would declare a winner. As he prepared to return to his corner, Gans told Siler in a loud voice that he had instructed his seconds that they were not to throw in a sponge; he wanted no suspicion about a fixed fight, something that, given his history, had been widely rumored among the betting crowd.[35]

If the length of the fight was any indication, spectators got their money's worth. It was a long and brutal fight under a relentless Nevada sun. Rickard had initially considered hanging a large canvas high above the ring to protect the fighters from the sun, but because the fight was to be filmed for commercial release by the Miles Brothers Company from San Francisco, he vetoed the idea in order to provide adequate light to ensure a quality film print. Gans put his peerless boxing skills on display in the early rounds, easily avoiding Nelson's bull rushes while peppering his face with picturesque jabs and counterpunches. The Old Master put on a pugilistic demonstration that was worthy of his nickname, but one hour into the fight he began to tire.

The steam went out of his punches, and he moved more slowly. With neither man able to land a knockout punch, they settled in for a long afternoon, producing many a lackluster round highlighted by plenty of clinches and arm wrestling. Despite downing copious amounts of water between rounds, dehydration problems for both men further slowed the pace of the fight. Nelson lived up to his reputation for illegal head butts, as he repeatedly used his reputed hard head as a battering ram. The crowd rose in anger several times after he seemed to land blows well below the waistline, but Siler did nothing but issue warnings. The seasoned referee later told the press that he knew many spectators had traveled long distances to witness the bout and that he did not want to disappoint them with an early disqualification.

In 1959 Brittie Caynor recalled that as a seven-year-old, she had accompanied her father down to the arena after the fight had begun. They were permitted to enter the arena at a discount one dollar. She recalled the loud cheering of the crowd, but most of all the sight of blood: "It was dreadful. I couldn't stand to see much of it. Nelson was a dirty fighter. Everyone was screaming at him."[36]

By the twentieth round, both men were showing signs of exhaustion, as they gasped for air and grappled each other in long clinches. But the fight marched inexorably onward, and a restive mood began to spread throughout the crowd. Not only were spectators feeling the effects of the hundred-degree temperature, but many had become bored with the lack of action. Perhaps they were merely anxious to hit the saloons. In the thirty-third round, Gans broke a bone in his right hand when he hit the Dane on that famous skull; he retreated in pain but feigned that he had twisted an ankle to conceal the wound. He slogged on, determined to defend his title, fighting with one hand. The fight, ringside reports indicated, had deteriorated into "a bloody, back-alley brawl." Instinct took over, as both men sought to survive under the hot sun.[37]

By the fortieth round, long shadows began to creep across the ring, as the sun dropped behind Malpais Mountain. Their bodies sunburned, bruised, and stained with blood, Nelson and Gans bravely went on. In the forty-second round, however, after Gans nailed Nelson with a ferocious left hook that seemed to have no visible impact (maybe his skull was indeed thicker than normal), the Durable Dane unleashed a powerful blow directly to the groin that sent Gans to the canvas, writhing in agony. The crowd rose in angry protest, and after a few moments of indecision, referee George Siler declared Gans the winner by disqualification. It had been a close fight, and it was unclear how he would have awarded the "fight to the finish" had it gone the maximum forty-five rounds. The postfight analysis was that Gans's left hook had convinced Nelson that he could not win, and so he opted to end the fight by deliberately uncorking a low blow.[38]

Supporters carried the wounded Gans from the ring, while Nelson departed upright to a loud chorus of catcalls. The two battlers had waged the longest championship fight in the history of glove contests and had displayed incredible courage while putting on an enduring display of the manly art under a hot sun. The sunburned fans, their clothing blotted with pine tar, headed for nearby saloons to settle their bets and quench their thirst. George Graham Rice was pleased that he had made a bundle betting on Gans and gave expression to the undercurrent of racial sentiment: "Even the partisans of Nelson agreed after the fight that the battle put up by the negro was a white man's fight and he was entitled to the win."[39]

The Bubble Bursts

By all measures the fight was a great success. Goldfield had become, at least for a brief moment, the center of the nation's attention. Rice was pleased that the fight "was sufficient to keep the Goldfield news pot boiling." No tally of the mining stock sold was announced, but newspaper reports indicated that a major infusion of capital had resulted. Restaurants and saloons had a banner weekend, and Rickard's Northern, the premier gambling house in town, reportedly set records. The Goldfield Athletic Club directors were delighted with the success of the endeavor, and the two fighters walked off with unprecedented paydays. Local sportsmen were already discussing the possibilities of putting on another championship fight. Reports on the box-office receipts from films of the fight, however, were disappointing. The fact that the fight had lasted for more than three hours meant that the film had to be severely edited; after a few months of lukewarm response by moviegoers, the Miles Brothers Company recognized that the only moment moviegoers wanted to see was the bout-ending low blow; a shortened version was thereupon produced that enjoyed a long run in burlesque houses, where it was shown between live artistic performances. No accounting of the film's gross was made public, but it appears that the GAC and the two fighters divvied up fifty thousand dollars in revenues.[40]

As the visitors departed, the future of Nevada's largest city seemed bright. Some fifteen million dollars was on deposit in three local banks, real estate prices had skyrocketed, and the mines and the mills were working around the clock. But the euphoria did not last for long. For a time, simmering tensions arising out of the militant demands of the Western Federation of Miners—reputed to be closely associated with the notorious Industrial Workers of the World—were kept in check. Within days after the fight, the bottom fell out of the Sullivan Trust Company, as nervous investors dumped their stocks. The company's indebtedness was estimated at nearly three hundred thousand dollars, and George Rice was forced to flee to the safety of Reno, from which he would hatch his next scam. Shanghai Sullivan also felt compelled to leave town for his own safety, taking up residence in nearby Tonopah, where he went on an extended drinking binge.

The demise of Sullivan Trust had no perceptible impact upon the town's economy, and mining receipts continued to grow in 1907. Then came the national banking panic that emanated from the major banking houses in New York City in late October. The ensuing crisis hit Goldfield like a sledgehammer because the San Francisco banks—only recently reopened after the great earthquake of April 18, 1906—were forced to shut their doors. Two of the three banks in Goldfield closed, and the largest, the John S. Cook & Company, faced the same fate until bailed out by a large infusion of funds by George Wingfield and George Nixon. In December Wingfield attempted to stop the massive theft by workers of high-grade ore (the pilfering employees were known as "high-graders"). This prompted a strike by the Western Federation of Miners.

Wingfield moved forcefully to destroy the union. Although there were no overt acts of violence, Governor Sparks, who was closely allied with the mine operators, persuaded President Theodore Roosevelt to dispatch federal troops to maintain order. By April 1908 the Goldfield Consolidated Mines Company had resumed full operations by importing scab workers, and the union was broken. The mines reached their highest level of production in 1911, but both the quantity and the quality of ore had begun to decline. Goldfield actually began losing population shortly after the prizefight, and the town's economy entered into an inexorable decline that had no end. At the height of the boom in 1906–7, the population of Goldfield was reasonably estimated to be as high as 22,000, although some overly exuberant local boosters claimed 30,000. When the Bureau of the Census took an official tally in 1910, however, a population of only 4,838 remained. By 1920, with the Gold-field Consolidated Mines Company in the process of shutting down operations, the population had dwindled to just 1,558.[41]

The great prizefight that had briefly captured the nation's attention proved to be a mere blip in the spectacular rise and fall of one of Nevada's great mining booms. It had served its purpose of exploiting the emotions generated by an engaging prizefight to secure much-needed capital, but it proved to be a onetime event for an overgrown mining camp that some feared might eventually become yet another Nevada ghost town.[42] It managed to avoid that ignominious fate; its population, however, dwindled to just a few hundred: the census of 2010 recorded 285 residents.

George Wingfield had already moved his banking and investment operations to Reno, where he would wield enormous political and economic power as the undisputed "owner and operator" of the state of Nevada until the Great Depression brought him down. Individual investors lost an estimated $150 million in their misbegotten plunge on legitimate Goldfield mining stock, but historian Sally Zanjani estimates that an equal amount had also been lost by those foolish enough to trust their money with such rogues as George Graham Rice, Shanghai Sullivan, and other purveyors of "wildcat" stock. Well before stock values plunged with incredible rapidity, a newspaper editor in nearby Death Valley had already noted that most of the losses were borne by naive small investors who had believed the outlandish promises that had induced them to buy what proved to be worthless penny stocks:

> Wildcat promotions depend upon the small investor. They always sell stock cheaply, because they can tempt the easy dollars in their direction by appealing to the cheap investor. They have cheap bait and they expect to catch a cheap public, but they have a well-schemed plan, and they succeed. The money which they receive and with which they are to promote the mine goes into the pockets of the wildcatter, and the mine remains just what it was in the beginning—a worthless piece of land near some good mining camp.[43]

Rex Beach watched the unfolding spectacle as a guest of Tex Rickard, and four months later he wrote that the fight had accomplished its goal of publicizing the town and its mines. He was also impressed with the raw attraction that prizefighting enjoyed:

> I grew amazed at the hold this sport has on the American people. For these were typical Americans, gathered from every quarter of our land. Not merely prospectors but men from universities and farms and the cities of the East. . . . In the journals countless columns are given to it. It is discussed in every club East and West, fortunes are wagered on its outcome, it shares importance in the press with wars and Presidential messages and stock-yard scandals. Moving pictures are taken and thousands pay to see them for months after.[44]

Recognizing that the sun was setting on Goldfield, in 1908 Tex Rickard moved on to another Nevada mining-camp adventure. As he drove out of Goldfield, he stopped briefly at an abandoned church and hung a sign on the front door: THIS CHURCH CLOSED. GOD HAS GONE TO RAWHIDE!

Round 3

Reno, "Center of the Universe"

Tex Rickard was a good friend of mine. Money was never his main interest—it was just stuff to move around. He loved publicity and wanted to be known as the greatest promoter of all time. That was all. In this he was and will remain safe. He was the greatest. —Grantland Rice, *The Tumult and the Shouting: My Life in Sport* (1954)

America's preeminent boxing historian Randy Roberts aptly described the famous prizefight for the heavyweight championship held in Reno on July 4, 1910, as a "racial Armageddon." It was an epic spectacle that captivated the attention of the American people because it was defined by journalists, ministers, and politicians, as well as gamblers, hucksters, and bartenders, as a supreme contest that was "for all the racial marbles."[1] Sportsmen everywhere made their bets and eagerly followed the prefight "dope" in the newspapers. Cornelius Vanderbilt had a special telegraph machine installed in his Newport, Rhode Island, mansion to receive round-by-round reports for the benefit of invited guests, and in cities large and small across the country crowds gathered outside Western Union shops to hear reports. Even from distant Africa where he was on his famous safari, former president Theodore Roosevelt wrote expressing concern whether "Jeffries can get back into form."[2]

Although black boxer Jack Johnson had won a lopsided contest over Tommy Burns to claim the title at Rushcutter's Bay in Australia the day after Christmas in 1908, many white Americans were reluctant to recognize him as the legitimate champion. Writing from ringside after witnessing Johnson administer a humiliating and painful beating to the undersize champion, Jack London telegraphed a story for the *New York Herald* that described how Johnson had verbally taunted the hopelessly outclassed Burns throughout the fight, smiling broadly to reveal his gold-capped teeth as he punched away with impunity. London concluded his report with the oft-quoted message to the retired former champion, the undefeated Jim Jeffries: "But one thing now remains. Jim Jeffries must now emerge from his alfalfa farm and remove that golden smile from Jack Johnson's face. Jeff, it's up to you. The White Man must be rescued."[3]

Throughout much of 1909, the boxing world was consumed by a search for the Great White Hope, a white pugilist who could dethrone the black champion. When he arrived back in North America in March 1909, Johnson was accompanied by Hattie McClay, a white woman who had been his companion for two years after leaving the life of an upscale New York City prostitute. She accompanied him down the gangplank in Vancouver, British Columbia, arm in arm, adorned in a stylish plumed hat and a full-length fur coat. Although McClay had remained out of public view until after Johnson had dethroned Burns, she was now put on full public display. "Dressed in silk and furs," Roberts writes, "she seemed as prized a possession of Johnson's as his gold-capped teeth."[4] She was but one of many white women with whom Johnson was seen (and photographed) in public, and his open defiance of a fundamental component of America's unwritten racial code contributed to the urgency of the search for a white savior.

The Search for the Great White Hope

Devoted to a life of extravagance and excess, Johnson spent his money as fast as he earned it. He once claimed to have burned sixty thousand dollars on luxuries in one week. He was especially taken with fast, expensive automobiles. After returning from Australia, he overturned a snazzy Thomas Flyer while driving hell-bent between Chicago and South Bend. It was the first of many automobile crashes in his life. (In 1946 he would die on a country road in North Carolina when he smacked his Lincoln Zephyr into a tree). To support his expensive lifestyle, he fought five times in 1909 against inferior opponents, all of them white. In October 1909 in Colma, California, near San Francisco, he met the formidable middleweight champion popularly known as "the Assassin." Stan Ketchel had a well-deserved reputation for savagery both in and out of the ring. "He would pound and rip his opponent's eyes, nose and mouth in a clinch," one reporter wrote. "He couldn't get enough blood."[5]

Although Stan Ketchel was reputed to be a formidable challenger, Johnson knew that his size and strength would enable him to win easily. As he had done in the past and as was not uncommon at the time in the shady ethical world of prizefighting, Johnson acceded to promoter "Sunny Jim" Coffroth's request that he not knock out his smaller (by some forty pounds) opponent so that the film of the fight would have commercial value. For eleven rounds, Johnson remained true to his pledge, content to jab away at his overmatched opponent, but refraining from using his most powerful punch, an uppercut that had produced several knockouts for him. In the twelfth round, however, Ketchel hit Johnson on the side of the face with a roundhouse that sent him to the floor; all commitments to let the fight go the full twenty rounds were forgotten as Johnson rose from the canvas with a grin on his face and unleashed a volley of powerful blows that sent Ketchel to the canvas, where he lay "lifeless as a log." The telling blow was straight to the mouth, and as Johnson followed the count to ten, he calmly picked two of Ketchel's teeth from his bloodied glove.[6]

Journalists covering the fight did not appreciate that Johnson had toyed with his undersized opponent and quickly jumped to the conclusion that an opponent of Johnson's size and strength could easily return the heavyweight crown to white America. That man, beyond question, was Jim Jeffries. "If Johnson shows no more class than he showed today, Jeffries with one-half his old-time form, can clean up the Negro in jig time," one writer smugly concluded.[7]

After spending nearly a decade in his pursuit of the heavyweight crown, a quest that was repeatedly rebuffed by refusals of leading white boxers to meet him in the ring, Johnson felt liberated from the racial codes that had held him back. He no longer felt the need to accommodate himself to the opinion of whites. Johnson's flaunting of Hattie McClay as well as his new companion, Etta Duryea, the former wife (with a reputation as a "sporting woman") of a prominent New York City man-about-town well known for his ownership of racehorses, reflected that conviction. Etta was tall and slender with long blonde hair, and she was soon being introduced as his "wife," although they did not marry until 1911. As Roberts concludes, "Now more than ever Johnson was expected to conform. And now more than ever Johnson felt he did not have to. The collision course was set."[8]

Unfortunately for those seeking to dethrone the new champion, there were no viable options among active white heavyweights. This led to attention being focused on the retired former champion Jeffries, who operated a Los Angeles saloon and tended an alfalfa farm. Born and raised on a farm outside Carroll, Ohio, Jeffries had worked for a time as a boilermaker but was drawn to California and the flourishing boxing scene in the Bay Area. He first was noticed when he knocked Jim Corbett down while serving as a sparring partner in Carson City before the fight with Bob Fitzsimmons. He signed on with Corbett's manger, Bill Brady, who provided guidance and instructors to teach him the finer points of the fight game. He developed a low crouch from which he threw powerful right hooks. At six-foot-two and 220 rock-solid pounds, "Jeff" displayed pure athleticism unusual for a man of his size: he had run the hundred-yard dash in eleven seconds and high-jumped five feet, ten inches, both superb achievements at the time.

By 1899 Jeffries had defeated the leading heavyweight challengers and entered the ring on June 9 at the Coney Island Athletic Club in New York against Fitzsimmons. The aging champion could not penetrate Jeffries's defenses and after two trips to the canvas in the ninth round was knocked unconscious by a powerful left hook to the jaw. The new champion defended his title seven times against all white contenders, including ending the comeback hopes of both Fitzsimmons and Corbett by knocking them out. He retired undefeated in 1904 after dispatching the Canadian Jack Munroe in San Francisco in the second round. In his prime Jeffries was a picture of power and resilience. He could readily absorb the best punches thrown his way—conventional wisdom was that he had a "granite jaw"—and he had never been knocked down in a professional fight.

For a time Jeffries resisted all pleas that he make a comeback, even drawing attention to the fact that, like white champions before him, he had not accepted a challenge from a black fighter: "Tommy Burns' mistake was in giving Johnson the chance to fight for the championship," he said. His resistance crumbled before an onslaught of appeals that insisted even after six years of retirement and at the age of thirty-five, he still could handle the arrogant champion. He had stopped training and ballooned to three hundred pounds. By October, how- ever, he decided to accept the challenge and began a workout sched- ule designed to shed seventy-five pounds and regain his fighting trim. The prospect of recapturing the title was enticing, but so was the allur- ing fact that he could earn an unprecedented payday by agreeing to a prizefight that all of America wanted to see. After a series of negotia- tions, he and Johnson agreed that they would sign with the promoter who submitted the best offer in a closed bidding process.

Their handlers announced that they would accept sealed bids on December 1 in New York City. This announcement set off a flurry of speculation about the match, and it would continue to grow, produc- ing one of the most anticipated championship fights in history. With the potential for a large payday looming, a reported thirty-five would- be promoters from several countries expressed interest. Ultimately, four experienced men entered the bidding, although a fifth bidder also decided to give it a whirl. Everyone with any knowledge of the fight game viewed that person as a naive neophyte, clearly someone who was out of his class. Such a situation was ready-made for Tex Rickard.

Showdown in Hoboken

The opportunity to promote the fight that Americans were eager to see attracted the biggest names in the fight game: "Tuxedo Eddie" Graney and Sunny Jim Coffroth, both of whom wanted to hold the fight in San Francisco; "Uncle Tom" McCarey of Los Angeles; and Hugh McIntosh, an Australian who had put on the Burns-Johnson fight. Little did they know that in the gentleman from Nevada, they had met their match. As historian Richard G. Lillard observes, Rickard was "a master manipu- lator of publicity, a gambler who could lose all and win again, withal a businessman." As such, Tex Rickard was a "representative figure of an era in Nevada history."[9]

Rickard's luck had turned sour after he left Goldfield. He opened his third Northern saloon in Rawhide in the spring of 1908 and joined forces with George Graham Rice to promote mining stocks. In Sep- tember much of the town, including Rickard's saloon, was leveled by a fire. A flash flood the following August swept away tents, buildings, and mining equipment. By that time, however, the town's population was already in a steep decline, as the reality had set in that the hills contained insufficient amounts of gold. Rawhide, for a time promoted as the next Goldfield, was on its way to becoming a ghost town. Rickard prudently relocated to eastern Nevada, where a copper mine was drawing residents to the town of Ely. He was attracted by the prospects of opening yet another Northern saloon and dabbling in mining stocks as a bank official. It was there that he learned Johnson and Jeffries were soliciting bids.[10]

Rickard went east, armed with a secret infusion of cash from a wealthy Minnesota investor, Thomas E. Cole, whom Tex had advised regarding mining stocks. Cole owned stocks in gold and silver mines in Alaska and several western states. Rickard was informed that Sunny Jim Coffroth had already signed Jeffries to a deal and assumed that Johnson would have no choice but to accept whatever terms were offered. Rickard, however, believed that the winning bidder would be the individual who had lined up the champion, not the challenger. So he stopped off in Pittsburgh, where he knew Johnson was appearing in a vaudeville show. He apparently reasoned—correctly, it turned out—that the publicly disparaged Etta Duryea would appreciate being treated civilly by a white man, and she informed him that Johnson had not yet signed with another bidder. When Rickard offered her the bounty of a fur coat to put in a good word for him with her "husband," she arranged for him to meet with the champion backstage at the theater. Strapped for cash as usual, Johnson suggested that he would be favorably inclined to sign with Rickard if he could advance him $2,500. Tex promptly whipped out two $1,000 bills and one $500 and laid them on the dressing-room table. The wide-eyed Johnson told Rickard that the top bid would be $100,000 to be split between the two fighters and suggested that a bid for $101,000 would do the trick. In return, Rickard assured Johnson that he would treat him fairly, something that Johnson had learned over his career not to expect from a white fight promoter. The first thing Rickard did when he arrived in New York was to purchase a fur coat for Etta. Johnson trusted Rickard.[11]

The much-anticipated bid opening was announced for December 1 in Hoboken. Threats that local authorities would arrest those present for violating New York's antiboxing laws led to moving the bid opening across the Hudson River to the Meyer's Hotel in Hoboken. Anticipating that he would hold the fight in San Francisco, Rickard quietly cut a deal for an equal partnership with one of that city's major promoters and a longtime associate of Coffroth, Jack Gleason, who he believed would be able to help him traverse the shark-infested political waters in the City by the Bay. Gleason would remain behind the scenes throughout the adventure, permitting Rickard to be the front man. At the Hoboken bid opening, a large crowd of reporters and other hangers-on had congregated to witness the opening. Coffroth's bid was for $125,000 but did not mention motion picture rights; Graney's bid was more complicated, a minimum guarantee of $70,000, but with the fighters to share 100 percent of the film rights and 90 percent of the gate; the Australian McIntosh offered $100,000 plus 25 percent of the film rights. Rickard's bid was opened next, and when the envelope was ripped open the assembled crowd let out a gasp. Out tumbled a certified check for $5,000 and fifteen $1,000 bills, along with a written bid of $101,000 and two-thirds of the movie rights. In addition, Rickard promised both fighters an up-front $10,000 signing bonus. The bid by Tom McCreary, who wanted to hold the fight in Los Angeles, was the final envelope to be opened, and it topped Rickard's bid by $24,000, with 50 percent of the movie rights. The next day it was no surprise that Rickard was proclaimed the winner. He later said that he knew he had sealed the deal when he saw "Johnson's eyes bulge out" when the large bills fell onto the table. "I knew we had him. . . . All you fellows were talking in big figures," he told his vanquished adversaries at the hotel bar, "but a bunch of thousand-dollar bills is the biggest argument in the world." Rickard announced that the fight would occur on July 4, 1910 . . . in San Francisco.[12]

Crisis in Black and White

As soon as news reports out of Hoboken informed the nation that the black champion would defend his title against Jeffries in San Francisco, a frenzied protest erupted across the nation, demanding that the governor of California stop the fight. Much of the campaign was generated by Protestant ministers, but others joined in the crusade as well with various motivations. At a time when the average annual income for a factory worker was somewhere around $500, the huge payday that both men would receive seemed outrageous. Critics noted that the income from film rights would more than triple the payout received from the $101,000 purse that the winner and loser would divide on a 75 percent to 25 percent basis. One critic, writing in the *New York Evening Sun*, complained, "A new era is at hand. . . . These honey-fisted survivors of the Stone Age are . . . the real moneymakers. Primitive Nature seems to reward her followers handsomely, despite civilization's boasted triumphs."[13]

A second angle soon developed that drew heavily upon the dubious reputation that had long engulfed prizefighting. Within days after the contract had been signed, rumors began to circulate wildly and widely that the fix was in. No one knew which fighter had agreed to take a dive and for what payoff, but the consensus was that Johnson had agreed to throw the fight because, well, that is the way blacks operated. This was, of course, a time when many fights were fixed; even Joe Gans, the masterful ring craftsman and longtime lightweight champion, had engaged in such skullduggery at least twice, so the possibility of a fix did not seem beyond the realm of possibility. The heavy amount of early betting on the fight, much of it on Jeffries, fueled further the rumors of a fix; the lopsided odds against Johnson that professional gamblers had posted suggested that they somehow were in on the deception. In fact, the betting trend that made Jeffries a prohibitive favorite was derived from the underlying assumption that the white challenger possessed the racial traits—both physical and mental—necessary to win back the title for white civilization.

In the months before the fight, Johnson's nonchalant attitude toward training added to the speculation that he was on the take. Jeffries, however, also seemed averse to entering into a rigorous training regimen, suggesting to the suspicious that he knew that the outcome was already decided. So, it seemed reasonable that he could understandably spend his days fishing rather than doing roadwork. The inability of the two camps to agree upon an acceptable referee further stimulated wild rumors that fueled belief that some dark conspiracy was afoot. Ultimately, Rickard decided that his large investment would turn sour if the rumors continued, and so with the concurrence of both camps, it was agreed that he would referee the fight because his presence as the third man in the ring would calm the furiously churning rumor mill.

These side issues, however, paled before the standard narrative that this was much more than a classic contest between two worthy athletes. It had all of the makings of a Shakespearean tragedy. It was viewed as an epic struggle for racial supremacy. By 1910, despite occasional efforts at the enforcement of nineteenth-century laws prohibiting prizefighting, the "manly sport" had come to be generally tolerated. Public officials were increasingly willing to permit what were posited as "gloved contests," "scientific exhibitions," or "sparring matches" as means around the laws. These exhibitions, however, usually pitted two white men against each other—or two black men. Now the heavyweight champion was, incredibly, a black man, and the challenger was white. For many Americans, that fact denoted race supremacy at a time when scientists and social scientists agreed that there were demonstrable racial characteristics—physical, psychological, and cultural—that were widely believed to be measurable.

Tex Rickard shamelessly took advantage of the inflamed racial attitudes of the era, advertising the fight as "the ultimate test of racial superiority." Commentaries on the upcoming fight were couched in the conventional wisdom shaped by such popular writers as Jack London ("The Great White Hope") and Rudyard Kipling ("The White Man's Burden"). Cultural achievement was also seen through a racial prism. One newspaper account predicted a Jeffries victory because he had "Runnymede and Agincourt behind him" and Johnson had "nothing but the jungle."[14] Scientists reported on different sizes of brains as a racial characteristic, and a climatologist even suggested that blacks and whites had differing levels of energy due to the amount of sunlight to which their ancestors had been exposed. But much of the rhetoric inspired by the upcoming fight was reflective of simple ignorance and racial hatred. One of those outspoken "experts" was former champion James J. Corbett, who had become a member of Jeffries's inner circle and would be in his corner the day of the fight: "Take it from me," he snarled to a cluster of reporters, "the black boy has a yellow streak and Jeff will bring it out when he gets him into that ring."[15]

How much of the anti-Johnson sentiment stemmed from his open flouting of the unwritten racial code of the day is difficult to determine, but it was substantial. His reputation as having a preference for white women—he often traveled simultaneously with two or three white females in his entourage—and his attraction to expensive automobiles, expensive champagne, gambling, and stylish clothes, even his gold-capped teeth, were targets for attack. The list of critics and scolds even extended to the presumed spokesman for black America, Booker T. Washington. This famous educator, the first black man ever to be invited for dinner at the White House, and who in 1895 at the Atlanta

Exposition thrilled an all-white audience when he tacitly accepted as sound public policy the separation of the races, joined in the criticism in a speech before the Detroit Young Men's Christian Association (YMCA): "Jack Johnson has harmed rather than helped the race. I wish to say emphatically that his actions do not meet my approval, and I'm sure they do not meet the approval of the colored race." Other more perceptive black leaders, however, saw much to fear in the upcoming bout. If Johnson were to win, they said, the likelihood that African Americans would be targeted by angry mobs of whites was a very real possibility.[16] And many a white newspaper in the South ominously predicted a "race war" if Johnson won.

California Flip-Flop

To the more perceptive observers, the simple fact that a white man was about to enter the ring to challenge a black champion meant that an important symbolic barrier had been breached. In a real sense, the black man had won an important psychological victory by that very fact. Randy Roberts has correctly written, "Just to allow the fight to take place was to admit a sort of equality," signifying that "blacks had an equal chance to excel in at least one aspect of American life."[17] Within this inflamed context, Rickard set about tending to the myriad details required to put on what was being widely proclaimed as the "Fight of the Century." His winning bid had stated that the fight would be held somewhere in California, Utah, or Nevada, but his intent was clearly San Francisco, where prizefights were routinely held and a large core of fans existed. The Bay Area was rightfully considered the boxing capital of America, a place where the sport openly flourished despite legal obstacles. Assured by political insiders that there would be no serious opposition to the fight—state law explicitly permitted "boxing exhibitions"—Rickard rented office space in downtown San Francisco and signed a thirty-five-thousand-dollar contract for the construction of a thirty-thousand-seat arena at the corner of Sixth and Market Streets.

As soon as San Francisco was announced as the location, the insurgent progressive coalition that was in the process of making the Golden State a model of political reform mobilized to stop the fight. They were joined by progressive activists from across the country. Progressives were a diverse group, representative of both major parties and focused upon many diverse causes: trust busting, public utilities regulation (or even public ownership), overturning the power of political bosses, railroad-rate regulation, pure food and drug laws, public education, Prohibition, amending state constitutions to provide for primary elections, the recall of elected officials, and the right of citizens to initiate legislation. However varied their interests might have been, the progressives were also white, middle- and upper-middle class, and overwhelmingly Protestant. Few supported civil rights for blacks, and their crusades to improve America often included ugly anti-immigrant and antiminority sentiments based upon racist assumptions. Boxing's image of corruption and violence, coupled with its appeal to working-class males, made it a natural target for a wide swath of the multilayered and complex agendas posited by various elements of the progressive movement.

The public images of Jack Johnson and prizefighting neatly encapsulated many fears and phobias that sparked a national outpouring of protest. Johnson was a "Negro" who stood astride the sporting world, his championship belt symbolizing to many racial supremacy. Johnson, of course, was a prime example of all that the progressives found repugnant. His reputation as a drinker, profligate spender, and frequent customer of (white) prostitutes was well established. He earned his living in a blood sport that presented a degrading spectacle that debased the public morality. He was also black and as heavyweight champion stood as a powerful symbolic threat to the superiority of the Anglo-Saxon, a perception that many progressives embraced.

Thus did progressives unleash an angry campaign to force Governor James N. Gillett to stop the fight. The first-term governor was a probusiness Republican who had initially signaled to San Francisco businessmen eager to host the fight that he supported their plans. He was fully aware that California law permitted gloved "exhibitions" conducted under the Queensberry rules. He also knew that professional fight cards were routinely held in Los Angeles and San Francisco without stirring a public protest. But this fight, which carried with it emotional racial baggage, was something out of the ordinary. His desk, he later ruminated, was suddenly overflowing with letters, postcards, and telegrams demanding he intervene. One group of opponents in Cincinnati mailed penny postcards across the country, proclaiming: "STOP THE FIGHT. THIS IS THE 20TH CENTURY." A large gaggle of Protestant ministers held a prayer vigil on the steps of the state capitol building.[18]

In April Johnson began training at Seal Beach, while Jeffries set up camp high in the Santa Cruz Mountains at rustic Rowardennan. For several weeks Gillett was unmoved as plans moved forward and San Francisco hotel and restaurant managers eagerly anticipated an influx of affluent visitors to fill the thirty-thousand-seat arena nearing completion. But on June 16, less than three weeks before the scheduled prizefight, Gillett suddenly reversed positions. He seems to have been motivated by a communication from New York congressman William S. Bennett, a member of the House of Representatives Committee on Foreign Affairs, informing him that should the "prospective fight" be held, funding for the location of the much-anticipated Panama-Pacific Exposition in San Francisco in 1913 would be imperiled. Gillett thereupon determined that Jeffries and Johnson were in training not for a "sparring exhibition" but for a "prizefight," which was not permissible under state statutes.

Rickard was stunned. He had already invested considerable money, and the governor's reversal threatened him with financial ruin. He had already banked $133,000 in ticket sales that would have to be returned at great clerical expense, paid the two fighters their $10,000 signing bonuses, and invested $35,000 in constructing the arena. He floated the possibility of suing the governor and the State of California, but backed off when Gillett angrily responded: "If Tex Rickard is looking for a fight with me he will get a bigger one than he has advertised for the Fourth of July. We've had enough of prize fights and prize fight promoters. They've been breaking the law long enough and we'll have no more of it."[19]

Rickard desperately sought to move the fight to a location where it would be welcomed. And he had to move fast . . . very fast.

All Roads Lead to Reno

Rickard reportedly received communications expressing interest from thirty-five cities, but the only ones he considered were from Salt Lake City, Ely, Reno, and Goldfield. He decided against Utah because the state legislature would have to pass a special permit requiring the governor's signature. Located in eastern Nevada, the small town of Ely was too isolated to attract a large crowd. Goldfield, scene of his triumphant first venture into the prizefight game, however, seemed viable. For several days he openly expressed interest in the offer he had received pledging to build a six-thousand-seat arena along with a guarantee of $120,000 in ticket sales. Although Rickard favored Reno because of its location on the main line of the Union Pacific just two hundred miles from San Francisco, he publicly hinted that the Goldfield offer might be too good to pass up. Reno's business leaders, eager to host the fight, took the bait and countered with an offer to construct an arena to hold twenty thousand and pay the state license fee of $1,000.

Assured in writing by Governor Denver Dickerson that there would be no legal hurdles should any Nevada site be selected, Rickard set up shop in the Hotel Golden in Reno, meeting with representatives from the three Nevada towns on June 20 and 21. Mayor Arthur Britt, a former saloon owner and beer distributor, urged Rickard to select Reno. Rumors abounded, including a legitimate one that the gold barons of Goldfield had upped their ante to $200,000. Rickard nonetheless announced that Reno's superior railroad service was the deciding factor and that the fight would occur on the afternoon of Monday, July 4. His rationale was one even his disappointed friends from Goldfield could not dispute. Jeffries and Johnson thereupon broke camp in California and boarded the train for Reno to reestablish their training camps. Thus did the eyes of the nation turn to the small city of Reno, population seventeen thousand, nestled along the Truckee River and protected by mountains on all sides.[20]

Immediately following Rickard's announcement, the national network of opponents immediately turned its attention to Carson City, bombarding Governor Denver Dickerson with telegrams, letters, postcards, and petitions. The thirty-eight-year-old governor had a well-deserved reputation for decisiveness, and that trait was quickly manifest as the bundles of mail poured into his office. He said that the messages were being deposited in a wastebasket as they arrived and issued a statement that the State of Nevada was prepared to host what was now being called the "Battle of the Century": "Prize fights are licensed under the laws of this state. My duties are to enforce laws, not make them. There will be no interference from the Governor's office if requirements of law are complied with." And in words intended to reassure Rickard, he emphasized with finality, "This decision is irrevocable."

Nonetheless, rumors continued to circulate almost up until the day of the fight that Dickerson would capitulate to the crusade that had been joined by the Nevada branch of the Women's Christian Temperance Union, led by the Reverend L. M. Burwell of the Reno Methodist Church. Burwell delivered a fiery sermon entitled "Reno's Disgrace" to an overflow congregation of four hundred at the First Street church and published a statement in Reno newspapers in which he linked his opposition to Reno's growing national reputation as a "Sin City": "Reno and Nevada sees [sic] the saloon and the gambling hall as the greatest asset, placing them above even the divorce industry. . . . We have a reputation for that but if we have this prize fight and show that we are delighted over getting it, there will be nothing too bad for the rest of the world to think about Reno and Nevada."[21]

Burwell's condemnation did not deter Reno's leadership one little bit. In fact, the *Reno Evening Gazette* used his message to create a different spin: "[The reformers] point out the fact that under the existing law, Nevada has the reputation that goes along with allowing prizefighting. And as long as the state has that reputation, it should reap some of the benefit." With the fight only two weeks off, its reputation as a "Sin City" not a concern, the town's business and political establishment mobilized for action. They optimistically anticipated upwards of twenty thousand visitors would descend upon the city and prepared for the anticipated bonanza on the long Fourth of July weekend. Plans were made to place cots in the hallways of hotels, and a registry was established so that local home owners could rent out rooms. The Union Pacific routed two hundred Pullman sleeping and several dining cars to Nevada to be placed on sidings to accommodate the overflow unable to find space in local hotels. The railroad announced special trains would arrive from the Bay Area, Los Angeles, Portland, Seattle, and even as far away as New York City, Chicago, and Denver. Automobile caravans were reportedly organized in Denver, Salt Lake City, and several West Coast cities.[22]

Just beyond the city limits along East Fourth Street, the same site as the 1905 Hart-Root fight, 175 construction workers were busily erecting the wooden arena under the direction of local contractor Jim

McLaughlin. They pounded away furiously at four hundred thousand board feet of uncured yellow pine lumber and five tons of nails to erect, in just thirteen frenetic days, an arena that would seat nearly seventeen thousand spectators and accommodate several thousand standees. The final nails were driven into place on the eve of the fight.

Anticipating an influx of pickpockets, prostitutes, muggers, and scam artists, Governor Dickerson ordered all fifty of the state police (popularly known as the Nevada Rangers) into Reno, where they were joined by forty Southern Pacific detectives. Washoe County sheriff Charles Ferrell announced that he and his deputies appreciated the assistance and issued reassuring statements that public safety would be preserved. Although Sheriff Ferrell did not say so publicly, he and others worried that a riot could engulf the town should the black fighter emerge victorious. Rickard announced that detectives would be at all entrances to the arena to search for concealed weapons. These concerns were well grounded. Jack London's plea written at ringside the day that a battered Tommy Burns lost the title in Rushcutter's Bay had set the tone, and many a dire prediction or racist threat punctuated news reports across the country. Rickard himself exploited the racial theme with a pronouncement that this would be a fight between the "hope of the white race" and the "Negroes' deliverer."

The racial overtones produced sharply contrasting perceptions. Coverage in newspapers that targeted white readership was devoted to the return of the heavyweight title to white America. African Americans, however, saw the fight as an important symbolic historical event: two men, one black, one white, would enter the ring with an equal opportunity for victory. The significance of this reality was not lost on perceptive whites, especially since it came hard on the heels of the creation of the National Association for the Advancement of Colored People the previous summer. That the NAACP was established by a biracial group of distinguished journalists, educators, professors, clergy, lawyers, and social workers that included such luminaries as John Dewey, Jane Addams, Oswald Garrison Villard, William Dean Howells, and W. E. B. DuBois was compelling. DuBois had assumed the editorship of the NAACP's journal, the *Crisis,* and was outspoken in advocating equal rights for African Americans. The issue of race focused the nation's attention upon Reno, and because the fight would occur during the long Independence Day weekend, emotions were intensified.

Commentators failed to recognize the enormous symbolic significance of a championship prizefight to be held celebrating the Declaration of Independence that proclaimed in the second paragraph: "We hold these truths to be self evident, that all men are created equal . . ."

The NAACP had sparked a great deal of attention when its leaders announced that its goals were nothing less than effecting a fundamental change in public policy across the entire United States, demanding the integration of public education, creation of greater employment opportunities, guarantee of the right to vote for all citizens, passage of federal legislation to prosecute lynch mobs, and equal protection under the laws. Racial segregation had long existed in the boxing game. During his prime John L. Sullivan had announced that he would take on "all comers." "In this challenge I include all fighters—first come first served—who are white. I will not fight a negro. I never have and never shall." As champion Jeffries had continued that discriminatory tradition. When he retired undefeated in 1904, he said the reason was that there were no qualified challengers he had not already defeated, casually overlooking such formidable foes as Sam Langford, Joe Jeanette, Sam McVey—and, of course, Jack Johnson. It was superbly ironic that one of the most prominent celebrities who announced they would attend the fight was the pompous John L. Sullivan.

The arrival of the two fighters in Reno provided a sharp contrast. When Jeffries arrived on the afternoon of June 27, a loud and enthusiastic crowd estimated at five thousand met his train at the passenger terminal on Commercial Row in downtown Reno. Jeffries, typically, was not in a cordial mood and slipped out the back of the train into a waiting car, sending former champion Jim Corbett to greet the welcoming horde of supporters. Jeffries went directly to the town's most prestigious spa, the luxurious Moana Springs resort, with its therapeutic geothermal waters located three miles south of town. Jeffries had initially balked at coming to Nevada because he had left town in 1905 after refereeing the Hart-Root fight without settling a five-thousand-dollar gambling debt, a delicate matter that Rickard apparently resolved. As the day of the fight moved closer, the more sullen and reclusive Jeffries became. Perhaps he had actually believed that Johnson would take a dive in San Francisco, but that possibility was now gone, put to rest by Governor Dickerson, who issued a special statement that "this would be an honest contest. I have received that assurance, and I am satisfied." Nonetheless, journalists as far away as the East Coast repeatedly speculated that the fight was fixed, prompting Rickard to issue yet another statement denouncing rumors of "a frame-up." "We have tried our best to avoid any move in the staging of this contest that would lend the least semblance of truth to the vicious rumors and opinions that have gone the rounds," he said.[23]

Jeffries seemed indifferent to his training, a fact that prompted Rickard to speak privately with him and Corbett about his concerns. Several public sightings confirmed that "Jeff" was spending several hours each day casting for trout along the banks of the Truckee River. Despite the fact that the fight was scheduled to go forty-five rounds (the last prizefight ever scheduled for such a duration), he definitely was not engaged in a training regimen commensurate with that possibility. He did little sparring and seldom worked the punching or heavy bags, spending his days doing roadwork in the early morning, fishing in the afternoon, and playing cards after dinner before retiring early. A steady stream of supporters and journalists came to Moana by trolley, but they were repeatedly disappointed when he failed to appear for an announced workout.

Journalist Arthur Ruhl reported in *Collier's* magazine, "There was nothing winsome about Jeffries. He was as surly and ugly as a caged bear." Reporting on a time when a crowd surrounded his open touring car as he returned from a fishing excursion, Ruhl noted, "He would sit there without moving for five or ten minutes, still glowering straight ahead, chewing gum and seeing only, as it seemed, the vision of his black rival coming to meet him from across the ring."[24] Obviously distracted, Jeffries did not eat well and complained about not being able to sleep. He apparently was overwhelmed by the enormous publicity that the fight had generated and felt uncomfortable in his anointed role of the Great White Hope, a fact he later made explicit in his autobiography.

One episode stands out: Shortly after he arrived in town for the big event, the rotund John L. Sullivan went out to Moana Springs to pay his respects, one former champion to another. Much to his embarrassment, the great John L. was detained at the gate by Jim Corbett. Sullivan had been falsely quoted in the *Boston Globe* that a "frame-up" was in the works. That story was picked up and given extensive play across the country. Corbett and Sullivan still carried residual mutual hostility from their epic fight in 1892, when Corbett knocked Sullivan out and took away his title. Words were exchanged, and for a time onlookers thought that they were about to reprise their epic fight. Sullivan snarled, "If you're running the camp I don't want to see him anyway," and abruptly departed. Popular vaudeville performer Walter Kelly, who had joined Jeffries's entourage, recalled, "I had a lump in my throat as I watched John L. drive away. He was leaving the camp of a heavyweight champion without even the tribute of a handshake or a goodbye. For some reason that just didn't seem right."[25]

Unlike the plush garden setting at Moana Springs, with its geothermal baths, swimming pool, graceful gardens, and a beer garden complete with piano player, Rick's Resort was new and relatively primitive. Johnson arrived there on June 28, after being greeted by a much smaller crowd at the train station, perhaps due to his train being three hours late. Johnson was accompanied by his new companion, Etta Duryea, who many erroneously believed was his wife. The resort consisted of a recently constructed three-story building that contained a restaurant and a small gaming area. Johnson's entourage took over the entire second and third floors. Out back a ring had been erected on a wooden platform, and one punching bag hung nearby. Unlike the surly Jeffries, Johnson was relaxed and put on a fistic demonstration each afternoon with sparring partner George Cotton. Afterward he mingled with the crowd, exchanging banter and enjoying a good laugh. He even occasionally broke out his cello and played for the crowd or performed parts of his standard vaudeville performance. Ruhl found the contrast to Jeffries striking: "Light-hearted, humorous, witty . . . he was quiet, well-mannered, generous in what he said of his opponent, and, indeed not without an almost winsome charm." What the easygoing atmosphere tended to conceal, however, was that each day he engaged in serious training, doing upwards of ten miles of roadwork in the morning before engaging in a severe workout regimen that would be capped by his riveting attack upon the punching bag, followed by several rounds of sparring in which he concentrated upon fine-tuning his defensive tactics. If the fight went the full forty-five rounds, he would be ready.

Despite the glaring differences evident at the two camps, the betting was heavily skewed toward Jeffries, indicating that gamblers were following their hearts in hopes that the "white grizzly" would triumph. The reality was, however, that Jeffries had not been in a ring for nearly six years, and at age thirty-five he was facing a quick and superbly conditioned boxer who was in his prime. Although the general public was overwhelmingly putting their money down on Jeffries at the betting parlors in Reno and San Francisco, those who understood the nuances of the game tended to favor Johnson because of his athleticism and conditioning. Sullivan conceded that after considering "all of the dope," he believed Johnson would win, as did Stan Ketchel, who had every reason to respect Johnson's prowess. Especially significant were the comments of the ring-savvy sparring partner George Cotton: "Johnson is the greatest boxer who ever pulled on a glove. It is next to impossible to hit him. I know that he can hit. I know that he has the heart and the confidence. He will surprise some wise bettors. I know Jack will win decisively, but it will be a hard fight."[26]

As the day of the fight approached, the town became overrun with visitors. The dusty streets were crowded with milling fight fans. Expensive touring cars prowled the town, having made the arduous trip over crude dirt roads across the Sierra. Much of the action was confined to a compact five square blocks that contained fifty saloons and several small gambling emporiums that operated around the clock. Restaurants were overwhelmed, and customers lined up to eat in shifts, the last meals of the day being served shortly before midnight. When the dishes were cleared, cots were set up in the dining rooms and connecting hallways. Newspaper accounts indicated that the beefed-up security force maintained public safety, with the most pressing problem stemming from pickpockets. Public drunkenness kept officers busy, but there were no major crimes reported. Meanwhile, Reno's working prostitutes were reportedly doing a land-office business in the cluster of brothels located near the Truckee River, their hospitality efforts supplemented by a large contingent of newcomers brought in to help meet the demand. By the day of the fight, some five hundred newspaper reporters were filing stories to their home offices, producing 150,000 words a day being sent out by Western Union. Many of their stories merely repeated and rehashed rumors already published by one of their peers. Out-of-state reporters also devoted considerable space to their fascination with crowded casinos operating openly without interference by law enforcement. The stories often featured the daring revelation that some of the gamblers at the tables were women.[27]

Showdown in Reno, July 4, 1910

Monday, July 4, 1910, dawned clear, cool, and bright, a glorious Independence Day in the high desert. The dry air was clear with a crystal-blue sky and lingering pockets of snow high in the Sierra Nevada providing an inspiring backdrop. The cool morning air would not linger, however, as the relentless sun pushed the temperature to ninety degrees by the opening bell. The heat and blistering sunlight did not bode well for Jeffries, whose dedication to returning his thirty-five-year-old body to fighting trim had been tepid at best. The enclosed design of the arena tended to keep out cooling breezes, creating an uncomfortable setting for fans unprotected from the sun's unrelenting rays. The last nails had been driven into the arena the previous afternoon, and just hours before the gates opened workers placed numbers on the reserved seats so that ushers could assist ticket holders.

Although the gates did not open until noon, by eleven a large throng had gathered outside the arena. The lucky ones had hitched a ride on the trolley cars operated by the Reno Street Railway, but most walked the one mile from downtown. By one thirty the seats were filled. Rickard reported that approximately sixteen thousand tickets had been sold and that morning three thousand additional standing-room-only tickets were sold for five dollars each. In the crowded confusion after the gates had opened, an unknown but substantial number of "scalawags" scaled the fence or slipped by officers at the gates. Among the estimated twenty thousand spectators were two hundred women, including Etta Duryea. Mrs. Jeffries remained in seclusion at Moana Springs. It did not take long for the men to take off their jackets and loosen their ties as the bright sun beat down upon the arena. Many squirmed uncomfortably as the wooden planks oozed sap under the penetrating sunlight. Those who wanted to quench their thirst had only one option: lemonade. Fearing violence in the charged racial atmosphere, Rickard had prudently decided that alcohol would not be permitted within the arena, and he had issued a stern order that no handguns could be carried onto the premises. Fourteen physicians were on duty around the arena to tend to those suffering from the heat. No preliminary bouts had been scheduled, but the Reno Military Band entertained the restless crowd with a medley of patriotic tunes, including the white southern battle song "Dixie." According to some newspaper accounts, the crowd cheered raucously when the band broke into a popular song of the day, "All Coons Look Alike to Me," although that fact remains in dispute.[28]

At two o'clock, rotund announcer Billy Jordan climbed into the ring and began a long series of introductions of the many dignitaries who had made the trek to Reno. Among those who acknowledged cheers from the sweltering crowd were Governor Dickerson, Sullivan, Corbett, Bob Fitzsimmons, Ketchel, Tommy Burns, the prominent black heavyweight Sam Langford, and the current featherweight champion, Abe "the Little Hebrew" Attell (who would later become a key figure in an unrelated historical sports scandal).[29] At two thirty promoter-turned-referee Tex Rickard entered the ring, wearing a straw hat to protect his thinning pate from the blistering sun. Johnson appeared first, wearing a gray robe that he tossed aside, revealing blue trunks with an American flag wrapped around his waist. Johnson was greeted by a telling silence until a smattering of applause rippled gently across the arena, punctuated by catcalls and hisses. Ignoring the tepid reception, Johnson flashed his golden smile and waved to the crowd. He could not help but notice that he was in hostile territory, surrounded by a sea of twenty thousand white faces.

Then an eruption of cheers and applause engulfed the arena as Jeffries and his large entourage made their way toward the ring. Leading the parade was Jim Corbett, a fierce scowl frozen upon his handsome face. He not only was emotionally dedicated to Jeffries; the previous day he had plunked down five thousand dollars on his man. The crowd rose to its feet as if it were one to welcome their favorite. Wearing purple trunks, Jeffries's hulking hair-covered body exuded an aura of strength and power. As he glared across the ring at his smiling opponent, Jeffries's formidable appearance reinforced the popular descriptions offered up by journalists: a "grizzly bear," a "bull," or, as Jack London colorfully described him, "an abysmal brute." Johnson's appearance prompted a *Los Angeles Times* reporter to reveal his personal sentiments on the upcoming fight when he described how he interpreted Johnson's reaction to the arrival of his imposing adversary: "I never saw any human soul so shaken with fear. When the fight began Johnson was so frightened that his face was deathly, ashen gray. His lips were dry and his eyes staring with a sort of horrified terror."[30]

That was not the most perceptive of journalistic observations, according to others witnessing the same scene; they described a smiling, relaxed, confident Johnson who playfully engaged those seated at ringside in casual banter. The language would quickly turn sour once Rickard had finished his instructions and sent the fighters to their corners. Even before the bell for round 1 sounded, Johnson and Corbett began a nasty exchange of words that would continue throughout the afternoon. The rhythm of the fight was set early, as Jeffries plodded toward his quicker and faster opponent, flailing away with both hands, most of which missed their mark. Johnson's defensive skills were evident from the beginning, as he easily dodged or blocked most punches. Jeffries used the same strategy he had used during his championship reign: able to take a solid punch, he waded in, willing to absorb punishment in order to deliver his own blows. Johnson clearly was the better boxer, scoring time and again with counterpunches, as Jeffries futilely attempted to tie him up in clinches. According to the detailed descriptions published by newspapers, as well as from watching a film of the fight, the match shaped up as one between a slugger and a boxer. By the end of the third round, Jeffries had become engulfed in perspiration. He already seemed to be tiring from a combination of the oppressive heat and the energy he was expending trying to catch up with his elusive opponent.

In the fourth round, Johnson took control of the fight, blistering Jeffries with sharp jabs and uppercuts. He also intensified his running commentary with both Jeffries and the enraged Corbett, repeatedly asking in a voice loud enough to be heard by those in the front rows what happened to the powerful punches for which Jeffries had once been famous. By round 6 the enthusiasm of the crowd had greatly diminished, as emotions began switching from exuberant optimism to a somber realization that Jeffries was hopelessly outclassed. It was apparent that his once-vaunted skills had seriously eroded, his punches no longer carrying the same impact. It seemed that Johnson was content to enjoy the afternoon, punishing his lumbering opponent at will. By the sixth round, Jeffries's right eye, red and swelling, had nearly closed, and blood trickled steadily from his nose. Before the bell for round 8, Corbett fired another verbal barrage across the ring at Johnson, who simply smiled and replied, "It's too late now to do anything, Jim. Your man is all in."[31]

And indeed he was. In the next several rounds, Johnson seemed to toy with the tiring former champion, often shouting out to Corbett so that those near ringside could hear his barbed comments. By the twelfth round Jeffries's body was drenched in his own blood. Johnson had suffered only one minor cut when Jeffries opened an old wound received during training. Corbett ended his angry exchanges with Johnson, spending his time instead encouraging his fighter and warning him about impending blows that arrived from all angles with telling effect. The crowd grew increasingly quiet and periodically roused itself to cheer when Jeffries uncorked a lunging punch that missed its mark.

Round 15 brought a swift end to the lopsided affair. As he had done at the sound of the bell for each round, Jeffries rushed across the ring toward his opponent, but this time he was once again met with a flurry of punches, as Johnson took to the offense. For several rounds Johnson had been content to coast, apparently prolonging the fight to inflict pain and humiliation upon his opponent. The fight having lasted for nearly an hour, Johnson apparently decided that the time had come to end it. He unleashed a furious combination of punches that the exhausted Jeffries could not escape. The *New York World* reported that Jeffries "shambled after the elusive Negro," but "Johnson simply waited for the big man to come in and chopped his face to pieces." A powerful left uppercut landed squarely on the jaw, sending Jeffries reeling into the ropes. Stunned, his famous defensive crouch abandoned, Jeffries dropped his guard, and Johnson sent him to the canvas with a volley of rapid-fire punches.[32] For the first time in his entire career, Jeffries had been knocked down. It was a dramatic moment that signaled the end was near.

Jeffries rose tentatively when timekeeper George Hartung reached the count of nine, only to be knocked partway out of the ring by the onrushing Johnson. He made it back into the ring with the assistance of his seconds and a couple of friendly reporters as shouts from the crowd now implored Rickard to stop the fight. He ignored them, but it was only a matter of a few seconds before the end came when Johnson once more sent Jeffries sprawling into the ropes with another shot to the head. Jeffries appeared unable to rise, and Corbett and other members of Jeffries's corner came rushing into the ring before the count could reach ten. Rickard declared the fight over. Technically, Jeffries had not been counted out, although it was evident that Hartung would have reached the count of ten long before Jeffries could have risen. The fight went into the record books as a technical knockout (TKO).

An eerie silence fell across the arena as the partisan crowd sullenly watched as their man was carried from the ring. He was lugged to an open automobile and driven back to Moana Springs, where he arrived still groggy. He would later say that he could not recall the last round or the trip back to his training camp. His handlers had planned a large banquet at the Hotel Golden to celebrate an anticipated victory, but that event was summarily canceled and a small dinner was held at Moana Springs. Less than half of his invited friends and supporters showed up. They had apparently lost heavily betting on their man, and their absence prompted Jeffries later to make the acerbic comment: "It did not take long to find out who my friends were after my downfall. The real ones were there, trying to cheer me up and show me they were loyal."[33]

The subdued crowd left the arena quickly and quietly, many heading for downtown Reno to alleviate their distress in the awaiting saloons. The disappointed Jeffries fans, however, were engaged in the process of coming to grips with a new reality, which historian Thomas Hietala aptly summarizes: "Johnson stood proudly at the summit, and symbolically, millions of African Americans stood beside him. For Johnson and his people, the championship seemed a partial but promising fulfillment of their collective hopes and dreams, a portent of a future brighter than their troubled past."[34]

Aftermath

Johnson had no plans for a victory dinner. Midway through the fight, sensing victory and apparently concerned about the safety of himself and his entourage, he instructed one of his associates to go to the train station and purchase one-way tickets to Chicago to depart that evening. By nightfall Johnson and companion Etta Duryea were safely out of town, heading toward an uncertain future that would soon spin out of control.[35] In 1905 Jeffries had infamously left town with a five-thousand-dollar gambling debt, and this time he likewise skipped, leaving a caterer stuck with a one-thousand-dollar bill for the victory banquet he had ordered but canceled after the meal had been prepared.

The *Reno Evening Gazette* dutifully informed its readers, "James J. Jeffries put the crowning touch on his monumental unpopularity in this city when he welched on a big wine supper he had ordered at the Thomas Café."[36]

Any fears of violence in Reno were soon forgotten, as a subdued calm spread across downtown Reno. Conversations were muted as the realization grew that the black champion had decisively demonstrated he was the better fighter. The general consensus was that Jeffries's six-year layoff had taken its toll, but there was no denying the fact that a black man reigned supreme in the world of prizefighting.

Johnson had refused to respond to the many crude racial comments that were directed his way in the months leading up to the fight. He had maintained his good humor, winning him many friends. In the afterglow of his victory, he felt vindicated. He would later recall that before he left the ring that afternoon, he "felt the auspiciousness of the occasion. . . . I realized that my victory in this event meant more than on any previous occasion. It wasn't just the championship that was at stake—it was my own honor, and to a degree the honor of my race."[37]

Those who had believed in the inevitability of a Jeffries victory eagerly grasped the rumor that began circulating within hours after the fight that Jeffries had somehow been drugged. Jeffries himself discounted the fable, issuing a statement that said, in part, "I simply couldn't fight. I am the only one to be blamed for losing that fight." And he stated, in a telling observation about his own thinking in the days before the fight, "When thousands of people came to me and told me I could redeem the white race, I was foolish enough to believe them. I honestly believed I could do it, but I was wrong." With the passing of the years, however, Jeffries came around to embracing the conspiracy thesis, ultimately concluding that evil gamblers had somehow slipped an unknown potion "known to athletics" into iced-tea drinks that he sipped after doing roadwork. In his 1929 autobiography, Jeffries recalled that he felt listless the morning of the fight and that two decades later, he still had private detectives working the case: "I will never cease trying to get to the bottom of the affair." Jeffries had finally decided that nefarious gamblers, not his long absence from the ring and his desultory approach to training, explained his loss.[38]

Within a few minutes after the participants had departed the ring, several hundred fans descended upon the ring, seeking souvenirs. With knives in hand, they began slashing away at the ropes and canvas. The demolition of the ring, however, was the only significant violence that occurred in Reno that evening. Downtown, bets were paid off, drinks studiously downed, the fight reconstructed and deconstructed by sunburned spectators. Visitors began departing on special trains, and within twenty-four hours most visitors had left town. In the days that followed, the streets were cleaned, the cots removed from hotel hallways, merchants added up their receipts, and Sheriff Ferrell sent the railroad detectives and Nevada Rangers on their way. Life in Reno soon returned to its normal languid pace. The Fight of the Century was in the hands of historians.

Fallout

Outside of Reno, however, reaction was not so pleasant. The American people had been electronically connected to the arena by telegraph wires, and so the news spread rapidly across the United States. On this national holiday, large crowds had gathered in public places to hear the round-by-round descriptions read from the Western Union wire. Within minutes after Tex Rickard declared Johnson the winner, nasty events began to occur thousands of miles away. Riots erupted in several cities, most notably in New York City, where police had to break up several attempts by white gangs to lynch innocent black passersby. Randy Roberts wrote in 1979, "Never before had a single event caused such widespread rioting. Not until the assassination of Martin Luther King would another event elicit a similar reaction."[39] Roving bands of young white males, their numbers estimated in the several hundreds, randomly attacked unsuspecting persons.

New York newspapers reported that a "reign of terror" spread across the city that lasted well into the early hours of July 5. Six black men were killed in the city and several dozen treated for serious wounds. Similar outbursts of racially charged violence—beatings, knifings, shootings—occurred in several southern states, most notably South Carolina, Georgia, Virginia, Louisiana, Texas, and Tennessee. Attacks were also reported in other cities, including Boston, Philadelphia, Cincinnati, and St. Louis. The gruesome totals varied from one report to another, but hundreds were injured, while at least eighteen deaths were confirmed.

When all the bills were paid, Rickard and his silent partner, Jack

Gleason, split a net profit of $120,000. A total of 15,760 reserved-seat tickets had been sold that amounted to $277,775, the largest box-office take on a sporting event up to that time; as a point of comparison, receipts for the 1910 World Series totaled only $174,000. They were able to pay off all of the expenses incurred in San Francisco, but their anticipation of a large residual payoff from film rights proved negligible.

Rickard had every reason to expect large royalty checks when the film was released to theaters in August, but anticipation was negated by a wave of protests that led to the film being suppressed in many states and communities. In part, the protest was merely an extension of the long-extant antiprizefighting impulse, but it was prompted primarily by heightened anxieties and racial hatred that Johnson's victory produced among some whites. Even Theodore Roosevelt, who had earlier expressed interest in the bout while on African safari and had engaged in sparring from his teenage years into his presidency, joined in the rising tide of voices when he issued a statement couched in the middle-class rhetoric of progressivism: "I sincerely trust that public sentiment will be so aroused, and will make itself felt so effectively, as to guarantee that this is the last prize fight to take place in the United States."[40] The unanswered question, of course, was whether TR and his fellow moralists would have been so eager to reignite the antiprizefighting fires had the white man won.

White politicians joined forces with antiprizefight reformers and rabid segregationists to demand that the film showing the systematic bludgeoning of the Great White Hope by a black man be repressed. Fears that the commercial film would encourage black viewers to become "uppity" were widespread. Many southern newspaper writers had set the stage for this reaction with editorials before the fight, warning that a Johnson victory would produce an undesirable attitude among African Americans. While some proponents of censorship feared that the film would inspire black aggression, others worried that it would debase the morals of white children and innocent women. "Decency and good order require that the public exhibition of these pictures should be prohibited," *Independent* magazine editorialized. All across the South, governors issued orders to prevent the showing of the film. Several governors in northern and western states followed suit, but for the most part they were successfully opposed in court by advocates of free speech and operators of motion-picture houses. The mayor of the capital city of Pennsylvania summarized the rationale behind the censorship movement: Harrisburg, he said, had "many colored people and . . . could not take any chances on disturbances." In Chicago the issue stoked great controversy, but after considerable vacillation on his part, the chief of police, Leroy Steward, ordered the film banned.[41]

Eventually, the film was widely shown outside of the South, sometimes clandestinely in private clubs. But the public did not flock to the theaters in anticipated large numbers; the novelty of prizefight films had apparently worn off. The General Film Company reportedly lost approximately two hundred thousand dollars on its investment, so Rickard, Gleason, and the two fighters did not receive their anticipated royalties. Both fighters, however, had already pocketed their signing bonuses from American Vitagraph, the company that actually filmed the fight (sixty-six thousand dollars to Jeffries, fifty thousand to Johnson).

Black spokesmen responded furiously to the effort to ban the film, charging reformers with gross hypocrisy for their selective censorship. A writer in the Chicago black newspaper the *Defender* noted with appropriate sarcasm that white Chicago authorities had permitted the presentation of hateful stage presentations of such plays as *The Nigger,* but somehow found a film of an actual sporting event to be harmful. "Why not let the Johnson-Jeffries pictures be shown? These show equality in every particular."[42] Randy Roberts observes that before the fight, when white Americans overwhelmingly believed Jeffries would win, there was no effort to censor the avalanche of newspaper reports that emanated from Reno: "Why, indeed, was there no talk of censorship of printed material about the fight before the result was known? As long as many whites believed that Jeffries would win, the fight was seen as an acceptable contest between the races. Now, with Jeffries bruised and defeated, the same white writers were saying that it was wrong to see any racial significance in the result. Why, too, would the Johnson-Jeffries fight film be banned when other prizefight films had not been outlawed?"[43]

Thus did the Fight of the Century take on a new sense of urgency after the ring and the arena had been dismantled and the crowds had dispersed from Reno. Johnson was euphoric as he and his "wife,"

Etta, rode their own "Victory Special" toward Chicago, but he had no inkling of what the Department of Justice had in mind for him. He and Etta married in 1911, but their relationship was tempestuous, punctuated by his serial infidelities and his physical attacks upon his wife. Depressed, criticized by both whites and blacks for the interracial marriage, she committed suicide with one of Johnson's pistols in 1912. Johnson was shortly thereafter indicted on charges of transporting an unmarried woman across state lines for immoral purposes under the nebulous stipulations of the Mann Act, which was passed in 1910 by Congress as a means of thwarting interstate prostitution rings. Convicted by a federal court in Chicago in 1913, and while out on bail awaiting sentencing, Johnson fled to Canada to avoid incarceration and later lived in France, where he earned money staging exhibitions and appearing in stage revues. In 1915, in Havana, he lost his title when he was knocked out in the twenty-sixth round by Jess Willard and in 1920 returned to the United States to be arrested. He spent a year in the federal prison in Leavenworth. At a time when African Americans were expected to know their proper place, the proud and undaunted Jack Johnson paid the price for his notable assertions of independence.

It could be argued that Jack Johnson's persona that was on display in Reno anticipated the dawning of a new age in America that would round into full view during the 1920s. Black Americans, especially those in urban areas, would embrace the doctrines of equality and black pride as flamboyantly articulated by Marcus Garvey through his Universal Negro Improvement Association. However, the hatred and resistance that Johnson engendered would come full flower during the 1920s, when the Ku Klux Klan enjoyed a major growth in membership; Congress took careful aim at ethnic, religious, and racial groups through discriminatory immigration policies; and various organizations sought to repress modernist impulses by demanding censorship of sexual themes in motion pictures and imposing their social values through passage of state laws attacking Darwinian biology, attempting to enforce the disastrous Prohibition amendment to the Constitution, and waging concerted attacks upon new forms of expression revealed in popular music and dancing.

Unlike Jack Johnson, however, Tex Rickard had emerged as a popular national figure, his reputation as a skillful, if colorful, entrepreneur firmly established. After a curious interlude spent in Paraguay running fifty thousand head of cattle on a 325,000-acre spread, he returned to the United States in 1915 to renew his career as the nation's premier promoter of prizefights. He had presided over the promotion of two major fights and left behind a legacy that Nevada would accept, indeed embrace. By the time of the Jeffries-Johnson fight, Reno had already been singled out for criticism for its active exploitation of the law that required only a six-month residency by one of the marriage partners before the granting of a divorce. The state's largest city, albeit with a population of fewer than twenty thousand, was well on its way to embracing a maverick label that was marked by an aggressive moral relativism that produced an outcry of condemnation across the country. That became reality in the 1920s under the colorful leadership of Mayor E. E. Roberts, who openly embraced a strident form of social liberalism that included toleration of prostitution, illegal booze, and backroom gambling. Himself an attorney who specialized in divorce law, Roberts publicly stated that Reno's tolerance of social practices under his administration that were illegal elsewhere was merely "tearing off the mask of hypocrisy and doing in the open what we know is going on all over the nation today behind closed doors." Others, however, took a different view, denouncing the city in a steady stream of newspaper and magazine articles, all of which portrayed the "Biggest Little City" as a general repository of immorality and decadence. "Reno and what it is doing presents a distinct menace to the ideals and concepts for what this country has always stood," one Methodist minister typically wrote in a national journal.[44]

It was acceptance of prizefighting that had begun the tradition that would lead to the negative image of Nevada as a maverick state where unconventional behavior was not only tolerated, but in fact encouraged.

Round 4

Nevada Loses Its Boxing Mojo

They came to see the fight, but any fight almost would have done as well. They wanted to see Reno and there is only one Reno.
—Nevada State Journal, July 5, 1931

The three championship fights held by 1910 gave Nevada a national reputation as a safe haven for those seeking to promote major championship prizefights. They also contributed significantly to the growing image of Nevada as the "Sin State." They were promoted on the critical assumption that at least half of the spectators would come from out of state for a sporting holiday. Nevada's slender population was not capable of sustaining a financially viable prizefighting culture, and following the First World War the center of American prizefighting culture shifted eastward as state after state legalized the sport. This transfer was clearly revealed when Tex Rickard snubbed his many friends in Nevada and became the driving force for the relocation of big-time boxing eastward.

Tex Rickard Snubs Nevada

The flamboyant Rickard, of course, always had his sights firmly fixed on the spotlight and the money, and he abandoned Nevada without a second thought. A new era in American popular culture emerged during the 1920s, and prominent in this development was an upsurge in the popularity of high-profile spectator sports, including prizefighting. The economic realities of the new trend became disappointingly apparent to Nevada's economic stewards in 1919. After his soaring success in promoting the Johnson-Jeffries fight in 1910, Rickard spent a few years in the eastern Nevada copper-mining town of Ely, where he operated his fourth version of a Northern saloon and dealt in mining stocks. He remained attuned to the semiclandestine world of prizefighting. Seeking a new adventure, in 1913, he invested the $400,000 he had amassed in Nevada in a 325,000-acre ranch in Paraguay that he stocked with fifty thousand head of cattle, and to which he lured several cowboys from Texas to do the wrangling. He lived the life of a landed aristocrat, overseeing his new enterprise, but he also dabbled in other ventures: touring with a small circus he purchased, promoting prizefights and wrestling matches, and even holding a friendly meeting with Theodore Roosevelt as he was making his grand tour of South America. The South American venture turned sour in 1915, and Rickard cashed out at a huge loss. He and his wife returned to New York City to start anew, and upon debarking their ship he learned that five days earlier the unheralded Jess Willard had knocked out Jack Johnson in Havana in the twenty-sixth round to capture the heavyweight title. Within a few months, Rickard had signed Willard to defend his crown in Madison Square Garden in March 1916 against journeyman Sailor Frank Moran.

Although the enormous six-foot-six, 252-pound Willard easily dispatched the gutsy but overmatched Moran, Rickard had to contend with a flurry of antiprizefighting attacks in William Randolph Hearst's *New York Journal*. Nonetheless, he attracted the largest indoor crowd up to that point in New York's sports history to witness the one-sided affair. An estimated fourteen thousand spectators gave Rickard a record-setting $152,000 gate, but he was especially pleased with the fact that many of the city's prominent and powerful were in attendance, decked out in formal eveningwear and accompanied by ladies in evening gowns. Their presence gave the fight a touch of class that he had long hoped would become part of the sport's appeal. A couple of days before the March 25, 1916, fight, he told an associate, "Wait till you see all of the nice people I'm going to have at the fight. A lot of millionaires and governors and society ladies are going to be there. I can hardly believe what is happening to this business."[1]

The composition of the audience convinced Rickard that public opinion regarding boxing was changing, despite the fact that in 1917 the Republican majority in the state legislature managed to narrowly repeal the Frawley Act of 1911 that had legalized prizefighting in the

Empire State. Once again prizefighting was illegal in New York. In late 1918 Rickard secured the signature of Jess Willard to a contract to defend his title against the best contender that he could find, but he needed to find a venue where he would not risk arrest. After considering several candidates, he concluded that Jack Dempsey was the logical choice. Dempsey had learned his trade as a teenager fighting for small purses in western mining towns, including some in Nevada. He served a difficult apprenticeship, losing several fights early in his career, some by knockouts. When he turned twenty-one, however, Dempsey began to put weight on his scrawny frame and was transformed into a box-office sensation, thanks to the tutelage of his new manager, the ethically challenged but equally talented Jack "Doc" Kearns. Dempsey had managed to finagle a deferment from the military draft on the dubious premise that he had to provide for his indigent mother, and he fought about once a month throughout 1917 and 1918, winning twenty-seven bouts by knockout, and in the process emerged as an up-and-coming fighter. Under Kearns's guidance, he was transformed into a ruthless ring assassin. He became a crowd-pleasing dynamo, described by one journalist as a "cyclone in action, a bobbing, weaving, slugging marvel" who had "the cruelty necessary for a ring killer, and [who] belted away as only a man can who has often been desperate and hungry and frightened."[2]

By the spring of 1919, Dempsey had emerged from among a dozen or so contenders to face Willard, the so-called Pottawatomie Giant, who had not fought since winning the title in 1916. News that Rickard was looking for a place where he could hold the fight without interference from politicians and law enforcement stirred great interest among the political and business leaders of northern Nevada. For several months Rickard shamelessly promoted interest in the fight by leaking tips to journalists to stimulate speculation on which challenger he would sign to meet Willard and his selection of a location. On February 11 Rickard solved one-half of the puzzle when he and Kearns announced that Dempsey had agreed to a fifty-thousand-dollar payday to challenge Willard. But the matter of the location remained clouded in mystery, and he encouraged speculation to hype interest in the fight.

Newspaper stories mentioned several cities as possible hosts; even the possibility of a few European cities was thrown into the mix. It was only natural that Rickard would casually mention Reno as one of the possibilities. In fact, he had already determined that it would be Toledo, Ohio, but he continued the speculative charade. Business and political leaders in northern Nevada were optimistic that Rickard would bring the fight to Reno, where he had many friends and had established himself as a can-do person with the Johnson-Jeffries fight. Nevada boxing fans remembered Dempsey from his formative years fighting in Tonopah, Goldfield, and Reno, and others recalled that in 1913 Willard had fought at Moana Springs, the bucolic resort located on the south edge of town.

The obvious location for Willard-Dempsey had to be Reno, or so it seemed, and that conclusion prompted one of the nation's leading sports authorities, *Sporting News* editor Alfred Spink, to authoritatively state just that in a lengthy article on March 10 that was reprinted in newspapers across the country. "There is every reason in the world why Rickard should take the fight to Reno even outside the fact that the financial returns there are sure to be greater than those that could possibly be obtained elsewhere." Among the intangibles he cited were the "cool climate" that would provide comfort for spectators on a July afternoon and the typical "clear skies" that provided an ideal "place where moving pictures of a fight can be taken." Reno's location on the main east-west line of the Union Pacific, Spink said, further made a compelling case for Reno.

For those reasons, as well as the fact that Rickard had many friends in high places in Nevada, Spink concluded, "Rickard is making arrangements to build a big arena in Reno, one that will make the Johnson-Jeffries arena look like thirty cents." Spink went on to say, "The people out there have some sense. They know it will benefit their town financially and that their merchants and hotelkeepers will benefit greatly by bringing the fight out there."

Central to Spink's confidence was the accommodation provided by the Nevada state legislature to help bring the fight to Reno. In this instance, legislators inserted themselves into an ongoing cultural war that had consumed Nevada politics ever since the late nineteenth century. For more than a decade, Nevada elections and legislative sessions had revolved around an embittered fight between the state's economic-political establishment controlled by mining, banking, and railroad interests and an energized group of progressive reformers, many of them women, who demanded far-reaching social and moral reforms.

The progressive movement crested in the elections of 1910 and did not ebb until the United States entered the Great War in April 1917. During the hotly contested 1910 election, maverick Republican Tasker L. Oddie upset incumbent governor Denver Dickerson in the governor's race. A lawyer and mine owner who had made and lost a fortune in the Tonopah-Goldfield boom, Oddie campaigned vigorously against the "entrenched power" of the railroad and banking interests, promising to abolish "boss control" of the state. During the ensuing four years, Oddie and his supporters succeeded in amending the state constitution to provide for the initiative and referendum and established regulatory commissions to oversee railroad and mining interests. The crowning achievement of Nevada progressives occurred in 1914, when women won the right to vote.

Oddie and his supporters also took direct aim at the moral decay they saw in Nevada life. In 1909 the legislature had passed a bill making all forms of gambling illegal, but in the next biennial legislative session made some forms of card playing legal. In 1913 the reformers counterattacked and passed comprehensive antigambling legislation. In that same session, the legislature also took aim at the perceived social ills associated with prizefighting by amending the original prizefighting bill of 1897 that had made possible the Fitzsimmons-Corbett fight. The law stipulated that "any contest or exhibition in a public place with gloves between man and man" could not last for more than ten rounds. It was that law that stood firmly in the way of attracting what Rickard was promoting as the "Fight of the Decade" because the standard length of a championship bout was twenty-five rounds.

Permitting "Glove Contests Between White Men"

If Reno had any hope of securing Rickard's selection of Reno, the 1913 law restricting a prizefight to ten rounds had to be amended. That effort set off a furious struggle in the legislature in February 1919. By this time the influence of the progressives had seriously eroded, just as it had waned across the entire nation. By 1919 the conservative push back against all things progressive was in full swing. US attorney general A. Mitchell Palmer launched his Red Scare, taking dead aim at radical unionists, anarchists, socialists, and communists. The once-persuasive progressive appeals to man's better instincts now seemed to ring hollow. Thus, on February 2, Republican assemblyman

Elbert Stewart of Washoe County confidently introduced a bill permitting "boxing matches for purses, not to exceed twenty-five rounds." The *Carson City Appeal* reported that the intent of the bill was specifically to secure for Reno "the proposed match for the heavyweight championship between Jess Willard, the title holder, and Jack Dempsey, who recently attracted the attention of devotees of the boxing game as the local contender for the stellar honors of the fistic arena."[3]

In the state senate on February 19, an amendment offered by William P. Harrington, a Democrat from Ormsby County, passed without debate. It stipulated that any person "over the age of twenty-one" could obtain a license to promote "any contest or exhibition with gloves between *white men*" (emphasis added). The *Carson City Appeal* devoted just one sentence to this substantive amendment by duly informing readers that the bill "makes it unlawful for contests between whites and blacks." The historical record does not indicate that this amendment sparked any disagreement or concern among members of the all-white male legislature, and no editorial or public comment or criticism seems to have been forthcoming.

Resentment still lingered among many Nevadans because Jack Johnson had whipped the Great White Hope a decade earlier. In reports about the frequent prizefights held in the state at this time, Nevada newspapers routinely identified those participants who were "colored" or "Negro." Racial identification and discrimination were deeply imbedded in the culture of a state where there were relatively few black residents and many whites whose roots were in former Confederate states. Consequently, the Harrington amendment passed without serious reflection or debate.

A few legislators did voice their opposition to Stewart's bill as a "disgrace," but their concern was not the Harrington amendment but rather the morality of permitting prizefighting itself. Because both Willard and Dempsey were white, supporters of the bill had no qualms about the racial implications of their action, as both houses of the legislature passed the amended bill by substantial majorities.

The racial issue was not the reason that Governor Emmett D. Boyle vetoed the bill. In a sharply worded veto message on February 26, he denounced the bill in words that reflected the long-standing moral outrage against boxing itself that opponents had been expressing for decades, and he disingenuously sought to skirt the obvious underlying reason for the bill's enactment: "Whether this bill is designed to invite prizefighting in general or whether it be designed to invite a particular prize-fight, I am not prepared to say." He went on to state that "public opinion has registered its opposition, not to boxing or glove contests, but to the existing debased and wholly discredited sportsmanship represented in the commercialized aspect of the professional pugilism which this measure invites to Nevada. From one of the finest and most beneficial of all sports, boxing under professional auspices, has degenerated into as mean, as unsportsmanlike, and as dubious an enterprise as could be found parading under the cloak of true sportsmanship in any of the four corners of the wide world." The governor concluded his message with an appeal to the "civic pride of the better side of the citizenry," suggesting that "Nevadans, in the vast majority, prefer to prosper under a type of laws which do not invite, even for short periods, the troops of undesirables who constitute the professional and habitual following of the prize ring."

Undaunted, Assemblyman Stewart quickly mobilized his forces, and the veto message was placed on the legislative agenda for reconsideration. He apparently took no chances on mustering the necessary two-thirds majority required for a veto override. The *Carson City Appeal* reported that at one point, he postponed consideration because of illness among some supporters. He wanted to wait "until all hands are on deck," and when that time arrived the governor's veto was overwhelmingly overridden.

But the damage had been done. Despite the fact that the bill had been passed over the governor's veto by healthy majorities, Rickard was unwilling to risk the possibility of mischievous guerrilla warfare by progressive opponents, a group that now clearly included the governor. Boyle's stern veto message, which mentioned "debased and wholly discredited" promoters, could have offended Rickard and even hurt the governor politically with Rickard's old friends. The governor's strong words provided a strong indication that he might not have the cooperation from the governor as he had received in 1910 from Governor Denver Dickerson. Even Rickard's overly optimistic prediction that this fight would attract eighty thousand spectators to Reno for a long Fourth of July holiday weekend was insufficient for the governor to back off of his antiprizefight stance.

Those Nevadans who had worked hard to pave the way for Rickard to hold the Willard-Dempsey fight in Reno had every reason to be disappointed when Rickard announced that the July 4 extravaganza would be held in Toledo, which had mainline railroad service linking the city with New York, Cleveland, Detroit, and Chicago. Perhaps the most acutely disappointed Nevadans took some satisfaction that on fight day, fewer than twenty thousand spectators watched a one-sided Dempsey victory in a cavernous eighty-thousand-seat arena Rickard had built at a cost of $160,000. Although the gate receipts totaled $452,000, that amount fell far below the goal Rickard had predicted: the first $1 million gate. Nonetheless, Rickard and his associates cleared $100,000 for their efforts, and he now was in a position to dominate the fight game during the 1920s, during which he would promote five $1 million fights featuring the charismatic Dempsey.

Jack Dempsey's Fistic Carnival in Reno

Although Nevada fight fans were provided period fight cards in local clubs in Carson City, Tonopah, Ely, Winnemucca, and Reno that matched hopeful locals with itinerant fighters from nearby states, they could only follow through the newspapers the big fights that captured major headlines throughout the 1920s. The Frawley Act lost its appeal in New York as a new era in American life emerged in the wake of the decline of progressivism. Symbolic of impending cultural changes, boxing once more was legalized. In 1920 the New York Legislature passed a bill introduced by Senator Jimmy Walker legalizing prizefighting and establishing the New York Boxing Commission to oversee the enterprise. The popular Walker Law also set a limit of fifteen rounds, required a physician to be present at ringside, and stipulated other safety measures, including the abolition of head butting. Nevada no longer commanded prizefighting's center stage.

In May 1931, however, prizefight fever once more rippled across northern Nevada when rumors began to spread that Jack Dempsey was in Reno to promote a prizefight. The legalization of gambling two months earlier also opened up the excitement to be generated by public betting on the fight. The possibility of hosting a major boxing match excited the residents of Reno who saw it as a potentially large payday at a time when the Great Depression was beginning to take a serious toll upon the economic vitality of the city of fewer than twenty thousand. The Depression had been rough for Dempsey, too. By his own admission, Dempsey had lost more than $3 million in the stock market collapse that had sent the Dow Jones market index down 85 percent from its midsummer highs in 1929. Dempsey was eager to find a profitable new line of work, and he had done some promotional work with Rickard before his friend had died of peritonitis in January 1929, with a tearful Dempsey cradling him in his arms in a Miami hospital.[4]

The year 1931 was a pivotal time in the history of Nevada. On March 19 of that year, the state legislature had enacted far-reaching legislation legalizing wide-open gambling. The operators of the recently opened (or at least now licensed) casinos along Commercial Row and Center Street in downtown Reno were anxious to lure visitors to their new emporiums, and a major prizefight promoted by the immensely popular Dempsey seemed just the right ticket.[5]

Dempsey was invited to Reno by two businessmen who were also well-known gamblers believed to have close connections with bootlegging and other criminal enterprises. Dempsey had apparently become acquainted with Reno's reputed underworld bosses James "Jimmy the Cinch" McKay and William "Curly Bill" Graham as an impoverished itinerant novice boxer in Tonopah in 1915. McKay and Graham were now firmly established in Reno, where they operated several enterprises, some legal and some not. The thirty-six-year-old Dempsey was rumored to be considering a comeback to regain the heavyweight title that he had lost to Gene Tunney in 1926. McKay and Graham were quite likely angling to become his financial backers should he make the attempt, which did not seem all that improbable given the rather unimpressive group of challengers to Max Schmeling.

A major prizefight would figure to benefit McKay's and Graham's Reno enterprises. They owned and operated the largest casino in town, the Bank Club, and had interests in several other casinos. Before gambling was legalized, they had operated several clandestine gambling establishments in Reno without serious interference from local law enforcement. As soon as the governor signed the bill, they merely opened wide the doors of the Bank Club, hung out a sign, and ran an advertisement in local papers that admitted as much: "Grand opening today of the Bank Club. The club has been greatly enlarged, however the management remains the same." They also owned the Willows, a popular supper club and speakeasy on the west edge of town, and the popular Cal-Neva Lodge and Casino at North Lake Tahoe. The Willows featured big-name entertainment and served gourmet food and the best liquors available to carefully screened guests during these final years of Prohibition. It actually had a peephole in the front door that the greeter-bouncer used to screen would-be customers.

These two enterprising men also operated the city's largest brothel, located on the east edge of the business district, near the Truckee River. At this time prostitution was legal within the city. The Stockade featured fifty cribs that employed working ladies in round-the-clock eight-hour shifts. McKay and Graham were also widely believed to control the lucrative bootlegging industry across northern Nevada. Among their alleged acquaintances was the notorious gangster George "Baby Face" Nelson, who spent considerable time in Reno with their protection. In 1934 McKay and Graham faced felony charges for mail fraud resulting from an investigation by the Federal Bureau of Investigation (FBI), but the government's prime witness, a bank clerk named Roy Frisch, disappeared on the eve of the trial and was never seen again. Widespread rumors were that he had been "rubbed out" by Baby Face Nelson and his body dumped down one of many abandoned mine shafts in the area, apparently a favor to McKay and Graham for providing him a sanctuary from the long arm of the law. The widely assumed murder of Frisch remains the great unsolved murder mystery in Reno history and vivid testimony to a period of general lawlessness in the town. Both men ended up serving six years during the 1940s in the federal prison at Leavenworth on new charges of conspiracy and mail fraud.[6]

Graham and McKay had close ties with the powerful banker, businessman, and political operative George Wingfield. One of Wingfield's favorite avocations was operating a stable of thoroughbred racehorses, and he planned to inaugurate a twenty-nine-day thoroughbred racing meet at the state fairgrounds in Reno in the summer of 1931. That the prizefight would take place in a newly constructed wooden arena located in the racetrack's infield was no coincidence. Born in 1876 in Arkansas, he moved to Oregon when a child. Wingfield came to Winnemucca in 1896 and initially worked as a ranch hand, but before long he was earning his living playing poker. Skill at the card tables led to ownership of a saloon and card parlor. He moved on to Tonopah in 1901 to open a saloon and gambling emporium, where the enormous gold and silver mining boom was under way.

In 1903 Wingfield became a business partner with banker George Nixon, and together they began making large investments in mining leases. Wingfield became a multimillionaire (with an estimated worth of twenty-five to thirty million dollars) by the age of thirty through what his biographer explains was "an incredible combination of ability, luck, and gambling prowess." He and Nixon acquired several profitable mining operations under a holding company named the Goldfield Consolidated Mines Company that was initially capitalized at fifty million dollars in 1906. When Goldfield went into sharp decline, Wingfield moved his operations to Reno, concentrating his attention upon banking while also diversifying his holdings with investments in ranch land and other businesses, including construction of the largest hotel in Nevada, the luxurious Riverside along the Truckee River that replaced an earlier Riverside Hotel that had burned down.

By 1912, when US senator Nixon died, Wingfield controlled four of the largest banks in the state. Nominally a Republican, Wingfield naturally gravitated to state politics as a means of enhancing his economic power, and from his office in the Reno National Bank, the largest in the state, he wielded unquestioned power as the political and economic boss of the small state. He was both respected and feared as he conflated his own economic interests with those of the state. Ultimately, his financial empire expanded to twelve banks before it collapsed in 1932, a victim of the banking crisis that swept the nation. Until his financial collapse, Wingfield was accurately known as the "owner and operator of Nevada." By mixing his financial ambitions with his control of state politics, Wingfield worked assiduously to promote projects that would help the thinly populated state grow.[7]

Thus, it was natural that Wingfield became a major, if silent, financial backer of Dempsey's foray into the arcane world of prizefight promotions. Wingfield was, after all, a member of the Nevada Agricultural Commission, which owned the fairgrounds racetrack, and for good measure he was also a founding and longtime member of the Nevada State Racing Commission. By becoming the front man for McKay, Graham, and Wingfield, Dempsey had all the financial backing and political clout necessary to stage a major prizefight. By his own admission, Dempsey was in severe financial distress due to his investment setbacks in the stock market crash and had no money himself to invest in the promotion.

Dempsey was well known in Reno, having won his first professional fight in 1915 at the Jockey Athletic Club and soon thereafter fought several times in Goldfield and Tonopah before he became one of the most famous Americans of the 1920s. His return to Reno in April 1931 sparked rumors on several levels. Because he had rented a house, it was widely rumored that he wanted to establish residency in Nevada in order to divorce his second wife, Estelle. Because he had lobbied legislators to legalize gambling as part of Wingfield's covert campaign to do so, rumors circulated that he was scouting about for investment opportunities in a casino. He did not deny concurrent speculations that he was contemplating a ring comeback and told reporters on April 11 that he wanted to referee some prizefights for the money but hinted that he was considering a boxing comeback.[8]

To many Renoites, however, those rumors paled in comparison to the speculations that he was in serious discussions with such heavy hitters as McKay, Graham, and Wingfield to bring a major fight to Reno for the Fourth of July weekend. At a press conference on May 1, along with his business manager, Leonard Sacks, he confirmed that he was hard at work putting together a big-name fight and that prominent local architect Frederic DeLongchamps had been commissioned to design an arena to accommodate an anticipated crowd of twenty thousand. Not coincidentally, Wingfield was in the process of updating the racetrack after several years of neglect. An upscale clubhouse, also designed by DeLongchamps, was already under construction in anticipation of the opening of the racing season on Wednesday, July 1.

The Reno business community strongly supported the promotion and undoubtedly pushed Dempsey, Winfield, and Graham to require the fighters to do their training the month before the fight in Reno. The daily workouts would attract substantial crowds, and the hope, and intent, was that these training sessions would lure boxing fans to town well before the weekend of the fight. State political leaders, strongly conservative and antitax in their outlook, also recognized that increased tourism would generate additional tax revenues so that they would not have to emulate other western states and raise taxes to match the trickle of public works projects being introduced by the Hoover administration (which would become a gusher when Franklin Roosevelt took office in 1933).

Putting Reno on the Map

This announcement met with widespread approval in Reno. It rekindled memories of 1910 when Tex Rickard had truly "put Reno on the map" on another Fourth of July. Two weeks later Dempsey announced that he had signed two leading heavyweights who were considered prime candidates to challenge reigning champion Max Schmeling. Max Baer was a handsome, charming twenty-two-year-old from California who as a teenager had delivered meat for a California grocer, and so was dubbed the "Livermore Butcher."[9] His opponent, Paulino Uzcudun, was a native of the Basque country of northern Spain and the reigning European champion, and in a day when every fighter had to have a catchy nickname, he was dubbed the "Basque Woodchopper," or the "Bouncing Basque." The genial Uzcudun had come to America to seek bigger paydays and a chance to get a crack at the world heavyweight title.

In matching these two fighters, Dempsey demonstrated a keen understanding of what sells tickets: the *Reno Evening Gazette* estimated that ten thousand Basques lived in Nevada and contiguous western states and that Uzcudun would attract many of them to Reno to support a kindred soul. A report in the *Humboldt Star* confirmed that perception: "Basques in Winnemucca were joyous over the prospects of their countryman staging a battle in Reno and indications are that should the fight details be completed, an almost 100 per cent exodus of his countrymen here to the fight in Reno will result."[10] The handsome Baer was a popular up-and-coming fighter from the Bay Area whose flamboyant lifestyle had created the reputation of a serious playboy. Dempsey believed that thousands of Bay Area fans would make the trek over the Sierra Nevada to support their man.

Dempsey essentially sought to reprise the magic that Tex Rickard had created in an earlier period of Nevada's history. The Baer-Uzcudun match, however, did not generate the national media attention as did the three great earlier championship fights, but it did attract large numbers of visitors who were probably more intrigued by the several new casinos than they were by the fight itself. Thousands of fans came from Northern California by rail and automobile to cheer for the flamboyant Baer, but an even larger number of visitors arrived from as far away as Southern California, Colorado, Arizona, and Idaho to cheer for the first Basque athlete to rise to national prominence in the United States.

At the insistence of his financial backers, Dempsey required that the two fighters do their final four weeks of training in Reno. Their presence became daily fodder for local newspapers and attracted serious fight fans who came to Reno to watch them smack punching bags and go a few rounds with sparring partners. It was determined that Baer would train at Lawton's Hot Springs, west of town along the Verdi road, and Uzcudun would encamp south of town at Steamboat Springs. On May 19 Dempsey opened his ticket office in downtown Reno on Virginia Street and announced that tickets would also be sold in San Francisco, Oakland, and Salt Lake City. Reno's flamboyant mayor, E. E. Roberts, purchased the first ticket, a twenty-dollar ringside seat. Basking in a wave of local adulation, Dempsey was soon thinking in an expansive way, telling local reporters that he was anxious to prove that Reno had not lost its ability to host a major prizefight and that if his first venture proved successful in luring a capacity crowd, he would go after even "bigger" matches in the near future.[11]

Baer arrived first in Reno on May 28, a pleasant surprise for Dempsey, because Baer had neglected his training before previous fights while pursuing an aggressive social life. Aware of that reputation and Dempsey's concern for his dedication to the task at hand, Baer had pledged that he would stick to business and avoid the newly opened casinos. Evidence that Baer was in town to win a fight was revealed when his entourage included ten sparring partners and a trainer. Upon his arrival, Baer told a gaggle of reporters and onlookers: "I'm serious. No more playing around for me from now until this fight is over. I'm going out and get that big spiggoty [sic] quick! This is my big chance to get somewhere. If I muff it, I might as well hang up the gloves. So I'm getting down to business. A four or five round kayo of Paulino ought to get me a chance at the championship. That's what I want." He reiterated his seriousness of purpose by saying he had brought only three of forty-one fashionable suits from his Livermore home. Nonetheless, Dempsey had reason to be concerned, because Baer arrived in a sixteen-cylinder sports car driven by his chauffeur decked out in proper livery and accompanied by a full-time social secretary. Upon Baer's arrival in town, the chatter among soon-to-be divorcées at area dude ranches reportedly became quite animated.[12]

Uzcudun did not make it to Reno as planned on June 1, remaining in New York City until his favorite sparring partner, Juanito Olaquibal, arrived from Spain. According to his manager, Lou Brix, the Woodchopper planned a stop in Ogden, Utah, where a large celebration in his honor was planned by "several thousand Basques of that vicinity." After spending time with his well-wishers in Ogden, he proceeded westward, where he was formally welcomed to Nevada at the Elko train station by Reno businessman Martin Goni, who owned and operated Toscano's hotel and restaurant in Reno. Uzcudun was greeted at every whistle-stop across northern Nevada by cheering Basques, including an enthusiastic crowd numbering in the several hundreds in Winnemucca. His train arrived in Reno at eleven on the night of June 4, but despite the late hour, an enthusiastic crowd of several thousand welcomed him. A brass band decked out in traditional Basque garb added to the festivities at the train station. After greeting the crowd, Uzcudun was driven by Dempsey to the Riverside Hotel.

The next day he moved into his quarters at Steamboat Springs, which became a destination site for thousands of Basque fans, who were thrilled to watch their man go through his training routine. Before most workouts the outgoing Uzcudun visited with his supporters and signed autographs. Future Pulitzer Prize nominee Robert Laxalt was then eight years old, and he later recalled that he and his father spent nearly every day in June at the training site. His father, Dominique, was an avid boxing fan whose wife ran their Basque hotel and restaurant in Carson City while he spent most of his days tending to his flock of sheep high in the Sierra Nevada. "We practically lived at Steamboat Springs," Nevada's most famous native author would later recall.[13]

On June 14 the Reno Moose Lodge sponsored a barbecue picnic at the resort, with Paulino slicing huge roasts for a hungry crowd estimated at twelve hundred. The *Nevada State Journal* reported that the turnout was "so heavy" that a "whole steer and 12 sheep were roasted over open pits."[14] Uzcudun thereupon thrilled his guests with a lively sparring session. Eleven days before the fight, Dempsey and Nevada governor Fred Balzar traveled to Winnemucca to address a banquet audience at the American Legion post in which Dempsey curiously predicted that Baer would win the fight but urged the many Basques in the audience to come to Reno to support their man.[15]

The crowds at Lawton's Springs were equally large and enthusiastic, but the composition of Baer's audience was decidedly different, featuring a large contingent of what one newspaper called "the pretty, blonde members of the divorce colony." Baer initially attempted to adhere to his promise of focusing upon the upcoming fight, but soon Dempsey began receiving reports that were not reassuring. Baer had been spotted horseback riding in the Sierra foothills with a covey of divorcées and had apparently activated his three fashionable suits for nocturnal visits to Reno nightspots. Dempsey sent a terse letter ordering trainer Dolph Thomas to ride herd on the handsome boxer, with specific orders that he could not use or even ride in his own automobile, could not go horseback riding, and could not be seen in Reno after dark. Baer responded with an angry blast, telling reporters that Dempsey's warning was "hardly justified" because the reports he had received were "outright lies." Nonetheless, he promised to train with a greater seriousness of purpose, adding for good measure that he planned to "plaster 'Upsidedown' all over that ring."[16]

The prefight news reports filed by a growing number of reporters from major West Coast newspapers were filled with inconsequential training-camp news and the usual rumors about secret punches except for the afternoon when Baer's manager, Ancil Hoffman, showed up at Steamboat Springs and attempted to blend into the crowd. He obviously was there "to get a line on the Basque" but was discovered and confronted by Uzcudun's manager, Lou Brix, and told to depart the premises. Words were exchanged, and soon the two managers were clumsily rolling in the grass, attempting to throw a punch or two. Hoffman was summarily tossed out of camp.[17]

Dempsey Dominates the Headlines

Although the upcoming fight matched two prominent heavyweights, the major figure in the news was first and foremost the promoter. Jack Dempsey had lost none of the star power that he had enjoyed during his seven-year reign as champion. News reports, which he attempted to ignore, repeated speculation that he was seeing a divorce attorney and informed readers when he was seen at restaurants in the company of attractive women. During some of his visits to the training camps, Dempsey donned ring togs and went a few brisk rounds with sparring partners, much to the delight of the assembled. That he looked in fighting trim sparked a resurgence of rumors that he might make a serious attempt at a comeback. On June 21 more than three thousand fans paid twenty-five cents to see him mix it up with Uzcudun's sparring partner, Al Gomez. On June 30 he knocked out Ole Johnson at Lawton Springs with a left hook that awed the crowd.

When the eighty-four-page "official program" was released for sale at twenty-five cents a copy, the cover picture was of Dempsey, not the two fighters. The program was designed to appeal not to spectators but toward a larger audience of potential investors in the Reno-Tahoe area; it featured several photographs of the area's scenic attractions and contained scores of advertisements by local businesses that were aimed toward an out-of-town audience. The publication also indicated that Dempsey intended to move aggressively into the fight-promotions business, because it included a moving testimonial to the recently departed Tex Rickard signed by Dempsey.[18] The former champion made more headlines when he announced that he had decided that he would serve as referee, just as Rickard had done for the Jeffries-Johnson match in 1910. He did so after both fighters had objected to the names of several potential referees, but the unstated fact was that his presence in the ring would undoubtedly attract additional fans to the event. Ticket sales had been sluggish, but immediately after the announcement "a rush for tickets" occurred.[19]

By the last days of June, with ticket sales brisk and record crowds predicted, Reno residents advertised rooms in their homes for rent, and some even erected tents in their yards to make a few bucks. Several hastily constructed temporary campgrounds were also pronounced ready for business, having complied with Department of Health regulations. On June 25 Dempsey announced that the elegant arena designed by architect Frederic DeLongchamps had been completed, and a few days later he released a list of thirty special rules he would enforce as referee, among them that should the fight go the twenty-round distance, he alone would decide the winner. Dempsey and Governor Balzar also appeared at a joint press conference, the major purpose of which was to scotch persistent rumors that the fight was "fixed," although those persistent rumors did not specify which fighter would be taking a dive. As an indication of the arrival of a new era in transportation, Gilpin Airlines announced the inauguration of direct service to Los Angeles, while management at Reno's new Boeing Field reported that a ground crew had been hired and a new control tower would be in operation for the arrival of the first scheduled flight on July 1.[20]

Reno public safety officials were also making preparations. The fire department announced it had installed special water lines and hydrants at the fairgrounds, and a temporary building was erected at which a pumper and a chemical truck were stationed. Police chief John Kirkley announced that fifty plainclothes officers were being brought in from the Bay Area to circulate among the crowd to deter pickpockets and that he had purchased a Thompson submachine gun and two high-powered Browning rifles, "just in case." For good measure, Governor Balzar announced that uniformed members of the National Guard would patrol the grounds as well, on the lookout for violators of the prohibitions imposed by the Eighteenth Amendment.[21]

The embrace by Nevadans of this boxing match, and in this instance the role played by the famous Jack Dempsey, reflected the adulation that sports figures received from the American public during the 1920s. Despite the excitement generated by the rapidly expanding economy that brought forth motion pictures, network radio broadcasts, labor-saving electric appliances, and the family automobile, the 1920s also were a troubling time for many Americans because the accelerated pace of social and economic change shook their confidence and diminished their sense of control over their individual lives. The frontier era of American history had definitely ended, and an unknown future loomed. Many social commentators lamented the steady decline of the farm population and the simultaneous demise of the power and influence upon national life of Main Street America. Others were repelled by the suggestive sexuality seen on motion picture screens and heard in the new forms of popular music that provoked unrestrained dance steps. Nineteenth-century America—the increasingly nostalgic America as invoked by the recently departed Populist spokesman William Jennings Bryan—had given way to a nation controlled by large cities, which were home to large and powerful corporations as well as pockets of radicals that, as in the writings of such leading intellectuals as Sherwood Anderson and Sinclair Lewis, openly mocked the traditional ways of small-town and rural America.

As historian Roderick Nash explains, the American people sought reassurance in a troubling and uncertain time. This quest led to the emergence of mass spectator sports, especially professional baseball and college football, with such "star" performers as Babe Ruth and Red Grange becoming acclaimed celebrities whose popularity equaled or even exceeded that of elected presidents. As Nash suggests, with the frontier era receding from memory, the American public substituted sports stars for iconic nineteenth-century heroic figures Daniel Boone and Buffalo Bill. Those "heroic" athletes who dominated individual sports were enthusiastically embraced: Johnny Weissmuller, Bobby Jones, Walter Hagen, Gertrude Ederle, Babe Didrikson, and Bill Tilden. In this so-called golden age of American sports, the one figure who stood out above all of the rest was the boxer possessed of the ultimate form of athletic conquest, the powerful knockout punch: Jack Dempsey. That this man who so aptly symbolized the new order was in Reno to put on a prizefight was self-evident validation for locals that Nevada was the place for a big fight. Or so it seemed.

Betting at local sports gaming parlors—another innovation to the local economy made possible by the legalization of gambling—picked up in the days before the fight, with Uzcudun being made a narrow ten-to-nine favorite. Newspaper accounts reported that heavy betting from Basques skewed the odds slightly in his favor. On Wednesday, July 1, the summer horse-racing meet commenced before large and enthusiastic crowds; special victory cups were awarded in honor of Uzcudun, Dempsey, and Baer. Patrons in the new grandstand downed soft drinks and lemonade under the large sign that urged everyone to "please observe the Prohibition law." Gilpin Airlines began depositing in Reno many Hollywood luminaries that by the day of the fight included Edward G. Robinson, the Marx brothers, Tom Mix, Buster Keaton, W. C. Fields, Jack Warner, and Darryl Zanuck. Dempsey's business manager reported that sixty out-of-town reporters had secured credentials and fourteen Western Union lines had been established at ringside so that up-to-the-minute reports would flow out of the arena to the awaiting world. On the negative side, reports surfaced that downtown hotels had jacked up their prices to as much as an outrageous forty dollars a room, although some rooms in lesser establishments were reportedly available for as little as thirty-five cents. Home owners were even renting out their porches for sleeping because all motor hotels, campgrounds, and hotels were booked, as were the two hundred Pullman cars that had been located on the main sidings just east of town.[22]

Twenty Blistering Rounds

The forecast for Saturday, July 4, was ninety-five degrees. The fight was scheduled to begin at noon so that the fans could then migrate over to the grandstand for the afternoon's races. When the gates opened at 8:00 a.m., several thousand fans rushed into the general admission sections to secure the best of the three- and five-dollar seats located in the back rows of the arena. Some aggressive fans attempted to poach a seat in the more expensive reserved sections, but members of the National Guard escorted them to the cheap seats. The *Nevada State Journal* reported that a "notable feature" of the crowd was the "number of women present," which its reporter estimated to be nearly half the audience. This was in sharp contrast to the earlier Nevada prizefights in which the issue of whether women would be permitted to enter the arena was a topic of considerable concern to promoters Dan Stuart and Tex Rickard—and a sign that the Roaring Twenties had indeed changed women's role in society to some extent. Pictures of the crowd suggest, however, that the reporter's estimate of the percentage of women in attendance was substantially inflated.[23]

At 10:00 a.m. the Reno Municipal Band, dressed in their summer white uniforms, began to entertain, and at 10:30 the public address announcer began introducing the celebrities present, beginning with Governor Fred Balzar, Mayor E. E. Roberts, and the three men who financed the event: Wingfield, McKay, and Graham. The biggest applause was for Dempsey, who appeared in a natty outfit composed of a bright-green shirt and white flannel pants and waved at the crowd before disappearing back to his dressing room to prepare for his task of refereeing.

Spectators were thrilled by a noisy flyover by ten US Army biplanes that had originated out of Mather Field in Sacramento. The pilots did a few rollovers and dives before swooping down low over the arena in preparation for landing on the dirt runway at Boeing Field. At 11:00 a.m. the first of four preliminary bouts began. The sun was beating down hard, and restive fans began to squirm as resin began to seep out of the green wood that had been purchased at a deep discount to construct the bleachers. Sale of "near beer" was brisk, as the four-round prelims proceeded to the cheers of the fans. At noon Dempsey reappeared in the ring and was followed by the two fighters, who were received with loud cheers. The photogenic Baer looked stunning in his bright-blue robe that had a large seal of the state of California embroidered on the back, while Uzcudun wore a dark-blue robe with no inscription.[24]

The near-capacity crowd settled in for the main event. Both fighters, understanding that their progression toward a possible title fight hinged upon this bout, began to throw serious leather from the sound of the first bell.[25] Uzcudun took several sharp blows to the face, but he countered with swift punches of his own. In the second round Uzcudun seemed to want to end the fight, as he tore across the ring at the bell and began throwing a flurry of punches. Baer deftly avoided the assault while scoring with sharp counterpunches. In round 3 Uzcudun landed a sharp blow to Baer's nose, and the first blood of the fight began to trickle down his face. Shortly thereafter, his lip began to bleed from another shot. As the early rounds went by, Uzcudun seemed to be controlling the fight, as Baer was forced on the defensive, struggling to tie up his opponent in clinches. Dempsey repeatedly warned both men for head butts. By round 8 the wise men assembled at the ringside press table had decided that Uzcudun was winning, but in the following rounds the Livermore Butcher Boy began to take the initiative, as the heat and bright sun seemed to slow down the 202-pound European. As round 9 ended, Baer landed a solid blow to the head that sent Uzcudun back to his corner, apparently dazed.[26]

Subsequent rounds passed by with both fighters having their moments, but they had visibly tired under the relentless sun. In the later rounds the number of head butts increased. The force of their blows seemed to have diminished, as arm wrestling and clinching increased, prompting some in the crowd to shout out, demanding more action. The Associated Press reported that both exhausted men "butted like goats" during the final rounds.[27] The irritated fans apparently had scant idea about the amount of energy that the two men had expended, as both now seemed determined to follow a strategy of simply attempting to stay on their feet until the twentieth round was completed.

As the two men were splashed with water and seconds waved towels in their faces to cool them off before the last round, Dempsey leaned over to the press row and said to no one in particular that the winner would be the fighter who won the last round. Both men seemed to sense that reality, and they tore furiously into each other, landing punches that brought the crowd out of its lethargy. In the final minute, Uzcudun scored with several punches to the body, as Baer seemed too exhausted to do anything but try to avoid the incoming blows. The crowd came to its feet cheering, and within a few seconds after the final bell, Dempsey raised Uzcudun's hand in triumph.[28] The crowd's cheers affirmed its approval of his decision.

The "Bounding Basque" had seemingly ended Baer's quest for a title shot, or so the newspapers reported. In a press conference after the fight, Dempsey was confronted by comments from reporters that they thought the fight had been "a little slow," if not boring, but he smiled and suggested that those who held such an opinion should try to go twenty rounds against a formidable opponent under a hot midday Nevada sun. Uzcudun readily confirmed that observation, telling reporters that while he was frustrated by Baer's repeated head butts, his biggest opponent had been the heat: "It was very hot out there in the ring and whenever I drew a deep breath it was like sucking in hot flames. My feet felt like balls of fire. Twenty rounds under a hot sun is like forty rounds under a roof at night."[29]

The pace of the fight had prompted several catcalls from the crowd, and the next day the *Reno Evening Gazette* joined in the complaining, concluding that "the fight was nothing more than a wrestling and head butting contest . . . and only two or three solid blows were delivered during the entire 20 rounds." Because of the "ham and egg" show that Uzcudun and Baer put on, the discontented editorial writer concluded with a sarcastic sneer, "Jack Dempsey, who was referee and promoter of the Reno affair, was the only attraction in the ring. Baer will have to return to his butcher delivery boy job in Livermore," and "Uzcudun really should go back to chopping wood or else get a job herding sheep."[30]

This one note of discord, however, was lost in the euphoria produced by the bonanza downtown of fully booked hotels, overcrowded restaurants, and jammed casino floors. An unknown reporter writing in the Sunday-morning edition of the *Nevada State Journal* tended to confirm the correctness of the decision earlier in the year to permit wide-open casino operations. "It was not the usual fight crowd," the writer noted, emphasizing that "they came to see the fight, but any fight almost would have done as well. They wanted to see Reno and there is only one Reno." He noted that the large crowds in town on Saturday night constituted "a tidal wave of merrymakers" that contributed to "the most colorful, crowded and generally noisy night in Reno's history last night as its thousands of visitors sought pleasure. . . . [T]hat it was the biggest night in the city's history went undisputed. There was never another crowd like it here."[31]

Aftermath

Most of the out-of-town visitors remained in Reno for a boisterous Saturday night on the town, and Reno police chief Kirkley was pleased that for the most part, they remained peaceful. Several arrests were made for public drunkenness, and one pickpocket ended up in the city jail. The fire department had a much busier time, responding to sixteen calls, all of which resulted from careless use of fireworks. The *Reno Evening Gazette* editorialized that the weekend was a great success because the fight had "placed Reno on the Fourth of July map of the United States in large red letters." But in an effort to balance out the editorial with a nod to those few who had protested the holding of a prizefight, the writer carefully added, "As a method of observing the holiday, it may not have pleased everyone, but for those who like that kind of entertainment, it was unquestionably a success."[32]

Once the final accounting had been done, however, Dempsey and his backers were less than ecstatic. They probably were gratified that the early-morning rush for the general admissions tickets had pushed them out of the red and to a modest profit level. Because of primitive bookkeeping, they could not provide a precise accounting of the number of tickets sold, and Dempsey glumly lowered his initial estimate: he now pegged attendance at between 12,000 and 14,000. Local newspapers reported sharply differing reports on attendance and total revenues. When the accountants finished their work, a total gate of $79,666 was reported, but after the two fighters were paid (Uzcudun $18,000, Baer $12,000), the eight prelim fighters received their modest stipends, federal entertainment taxes paid, and all other expenses met (primarily the cost of constructing the arena), Dempsey and his backers reportedly cleared less than $1,000. The two local newspapers, citing different sources, reported that substantial discrepancies had come to light. Because an unknown number of individuals who held tickets to the horse races had been granted free admission to the fight, the total number of tickets sold was further reduced to an estimated 9,260, far below the optimistic early predictions of 18,000.

Dempsey had earlier said he hoped to promote another major fight in the same arena on Labor Day weekend, but such was not to be. The final accounting apparently sobered Dempsey and his backers regarding future promotions. They announced that Dempsey himself would enter the ring against the so-called Aberdeen Assassin, Leo Lomski, in a four-round exhibition instead of the promised fight between Uzcudun and Jack Sharkey. The day after the exhibition, Dempsey departed for Portland, where he began a barnstorming tour of exhibition matches, often taking on four challengers in one evening. On August 19 Dempsey met Jack Beasley at the fairgrounds and, after sustaining a bloody lip in the first round, knocked Beasley to the canvas three times in round 2. Beasley bravely agreed to fight a third round for an additional stipend, but declined to go for an even greater payday by opting out of a round 4. Lomski the Assassin pulled out of the bout two weeks before Labor Day, and in desperation, with hundreds of tickets sold, McKay and Graham announced that Dempsey would take on five little-known challengers. An estimated 10,000 fans were in attendance to watch Dempsey knock out two of the men while going two playful rounds each with the others. He thereupon departed town for another series of exhibitions. Between then and February 1932, Dempsey fought fifty exhibitions, and he enjoyed such easy triumphs that he convinced himself that he could make a real comeback. But in Chicago on February 8, he suffered a humiliating defeat to Kingfish Levinsky and, after completing a scheduled seventeen additional exhibitions, decided to hang up the gloves forever.

Dempsey discovered that he did not have the same promotional magic as Tex Rickard. He moved on to other enterprises, primarily operating his famous New York City watering hole and steak house. He promoted his last fight in Reno on July 4, 1932, when he matched Baer and Levinsky, attracting a modest crowd. Reno's sizzle as a major prizefight location was gone. Shortly thereafter, the exquisitely designed DeLongchamps arena was demolished. Contrary to a wave of negative reports after his loss to Uzcudun, Baer's career had not ended. He won the heavyweight title from Primo Carnera in June 1934, but lost his first defense to James Braddock a year later. He thereupon repaired to Hollywood for an acting career that spanned twenty motion pictures and numerous radio broadcasts. Uzcudun's career leveled out, but he was given a shot at the crown in Rome in 1933, losing a unanimous decision to Carnera. He made one last attempt at glory in early-December 1935, but was knocked out in the fourth round by the rising young phenom from Detroit Joe Louis; Max Schmeling, who was in the audience to observe a future foe in Louis, said that Uzcudun went to the canvas "as though he was struck by a bullet." The Basque Woodchopper returned to his native Spain, joined the forces of General Francisco Franco in 1936, and after recovering from battlefield wounds served in Franco's government briefly before becoming a police chief in the town of Valencia.

The less than compelling result of the Baer-Uzcudun fight ended any hope that Reno would regain its stature as a lucrative location for major prizefights. The small western town located far from any major population center could not compete. When Tex Rickard had abandoned Nevada and assumed control of Madison Square Garden in New York City, the center of prizefighting automatically relocated three thousand miles to the east. It would be three decades before Nevada would reassert itself as home to major championship boxing. Reno, however, would remain largely shut out of the action, as the megacasinos in Las Vegas dominated the action.

Dempsey made the front pages in Reno when on August 17, as rumored, he sued his wife of six years, actress Estelle Taylor, for divorce. Six weeks later he spent thirty minutes in the Washoe County Courthouse to obtain the divorce he had previously denied seeking. Surprisingly nervous, he told Judge Thomas Moran and a packed courtroom that he was seeking the divorce due to "extreme mental cruelty" on the part of Estelle. After less than thirty minutes, William Harrison Dempsey left the courthouse a free man. Like thousands of other temporary Nevada residents that same year who came to town for the "Reno cure," he too had been "Renovated."

275

Start of Corbett-Fitzsommins Championship Fight March 10 97

Spectators watch the long-anticipated championship fight between Bob Fitzsimmons and Jim Corbett in Carson City on St. Patrick's Day 1897. Promoter Dan
Stuart of Dallas lost money at the gate, but royalties for the motion picture put
him in the black. Note the small wooden shack on the far side of the ring that
housed the delicate cameras that captured the fight on film. The edited film
became the first feature-length motion picture in history. Courtesy Nevada
Historical Society.

Larson Photo — The Worlds Greatest Champions — Nelson — Gans — Goldfield Nevada Sep 3rd 1906

THE WORLD'S CHAMPION
HEAVY WEIGHT — USES EXCLUSIVELY
Ratsch Peoples ATHLETIC GOODS MADE BY
CHICAGO SPORTING GOODS MFG. CO.

Reno businessmen eagerly anticipated a flood of tourists for the Fight of the Century on Fourth of July weekend, 1910. They were not disappointed, as this picture reveals fans departing one of the chartered trains hours before the fight. Courtesy Nevada Historical Society.

FACING PAGE:

Top: Getting ready to rumble: Battling Nelson (*left*) and Joe Gans shake hands before their three-hour, forty-two-round fight began on Labor Day 1906. This fight began Tex Rickard's spectacular career as the nation's first great promoter. The fight also served its primary purpose of luring out-of-state high rollers to Goldfield, where they bought large amounts of dubious mining stock. Courtesy Nevada Historical Society.

Bottom: Jack Johnson poses with a sparring partner before an appreciative crowd at Rick's Resort, located west of Reno on what is today Mayberry Drive. Unlike his opponent Jim Jeffries, who was sullen and withdrawn during the training period, a relaxed Johnson joked with and entertained spectators at his training site. Courtesy Nevada Historical Society.

Renoites were delighted when Jack Dempsey promoted a fight between two heavyweights eager to earn a shot at the heavyweight title held by Max Schmeling. The attraction of recently opened legal casinos turned out to be a bigger attraction than the fight between the "Livermore Butcher" and the "Bouncing Basque." Courtesy Neal Cobb Collection.

CLUB HOUSE

GRANDSTAND

JACK DEMPSEY ARENA, RENO RACETRACK
BAER-UZCUDUN
JULY 4TH-1931
RENO NEVADA

DEMPSEY
STANDING IN RING

To accommodate the anticipated twenty thousand spectators for the Baer-Uzcudun fight, investors commissioned Reno's celebrated architect Frederic DeLongchamps to design an arena. Local men eager for employment erected the elegant wooden arena in the middle of the racetrack at the fairgrounds. Jack Dempsey is standing in the ring in this rare photograph. Courtesy Colleen Rosencrantz Collection.

A capacity crowd of twenty thousand watches the action between Maxie Baer and Paulino Uzcudun under a blazing July 4 sun. Approximately half of the spectators did not buy tickets for the fight but were admitted after purchasing tickets to the horse races that George Wingfield was promoting. Courtesy Colleen Rosencrantz Collection.

FACING PAGE:

Top: Governor Fred Balzar was full of fight when he visited the Steamboat Springs training camp of Paulino Uzcudun in 1931. The governor was fresh off a major political victory when in March he signed legislation legalizing wide-open casino gambling. Posing with him is Hearst newspaper sportswriter Bob Edgren and his son. Courtesy Colleen Rozencrantz Collection.

Bottom: Jack Dempsey points to the location of the soon-to-be-erected arena while standing in the middle of the racetrack. With him are the major investors in the promotion, the notorious bootleggers, casino operators, and alleged associates of gangster Baby Face Nelson: Bill Graham (*left*) and Jim McKay. Courtesy Colleen Rosencrantz Collection.

GOV. OF NEVADA,
FRED BALZAR
BOB EDGREN, JR.
BOB EDGREN
STEAMBOAT SPRINGS - JUNE 13 1931
UZCUDUN TRAINING CAMP

It was not an auspicious beginning for prime-time boxing in Las Vegas when former Jack Dempsey manager Jack Kearns promoted a heavyweight fight at Cashman Field on May 2, 1955. Several cowboys watch from atop the cheap seats as Archie Moore wins a close decision over Niño Valdés. Kearns predicted a crowd of fourteen thousand, but fewer than six thousand bought tickets. Courtesy Las Vegas News Bureau.

Caesars Palace became the main focus of boxing in Las Vegas during the 1980s. On October 2, 1980, an overflow crowd estimated at twenty-nine thousand filled a wooden arena to watch Larry Holmes soundly defeat an inept Muhammad Ali. Because of Ali's physical condition, many experts said the much-anticipated fight should never have occurred. Courtesy Las Vegas News Bureau.

Joe Louis became a popular Las Vegas figure when he was employed during the early 1970s by Caesars Palace to interact with guests. His job included betting heavily at the tables with house money (which he routinely lost). He is pictured here in 1977 speaking to a group of admirers. Courtesy Las Vegas News Bureau.

Round 5

When the Crowds Went Away

There were abuses on all sides. Poorly conditioned "boxers"
appeared on cards. Some who fought in Reno had been KO'd
a few days before in California. There was seldom a doctor in
attendance. There were no pre-fight medical exams. And there
were frequent no-shows of advertised main eventers.
—Ty Cobb, sports editor of the *Nevada State Journal,*
on the state of boxing in Nevada in the 1930s

The departure of Tex Rickard for New York symbolized the fact that Nevada had been pushed to the margins of the boxing world. For the next four decades, prizefighting in Nevada essentially reverted to the informal pattern that had existed in the mining camps and small towns during the nineteenth century. Small crowds of dedicated fight fans bought inexpensive tickets to watch inconsequential bouts featuring aspiring local novices and struggling barnstormers. The fights were staged by saloon keepers or "sporting men" usually connected to the local gambling scene, but in Reno businessman Johnny Gammick, himself a veteran boxer of ninety-two bouts, attempted valiantly to put on a good, honest show. His efforts aside, the average boxing cards were crude affairs that did nothing to elevate the stature of the Nevada boxing scene. These were held in both Las Vegas and Reno and attracted only marginal local attention outside of the true boxing fan. They attracted sparse crowds drawn as much by the opportunity to gamble and drink as much as to watch a few desultory bouts of little consequence. The lure of the possibility of a good fight was sufficient to keep the spectators coming back because the flame of boxing in Nevada, while flickering, was never extinguished.

Prizefighting in Nevada during the 1920s until the years after the Second World War mirrored the problems that reformers had so often criticized elsewhere. The victims routinely included poor, uneducated young men who entered the ring to make a few bucks, and whatever dreams they had of hitting the big time were quickly extinguished. These bouts attracted men, many of whom worked in mines or on ranches where the days were long, the work arduous and often dangerous. These spectators found in boxing a logical leisure activity. In her authoritative history of western mining cultures, Mary Murphy concludes that during this period, "The West became a haven for prizefighting" and that the "gladiator atmosphere" of the ring attracted spectators who "wanted [to see] lethal punches and blood."[1]

In Nevada and neighboring states, itinerant young quasi-professional fighters moved from one mining town and one state to another in search of an opportunity to make a few dollars. In Nevada such boomtowns as Goldfield, Tonopah, and Ely were home to a lively prizefighting culture, although the larger city of Reno with its location on a major transcontinental rail line became the unofficial boxing headquarters. Sporadic matches were sponsored in Las Vegas by the American Legion post. On the south edge of Reno, Moana Springs Resort became a popular venue in regional boxing circles, and in the 1920s a second open-air venue called the Airdome was opened downtown on Third Street, with seating for nearly a thousand. Other smaller venues, such as the Coconut Grove on North Virginia Street, offered sporadic cards during the 1930s. When the legalization of gambling occurred in 1931, casinos began to hold prizefights on the stages of their nightclubs or in the middle of a dance hall.

"I Can Lick Any Sonofabitch in the House"

The life of these prizefighters was neither glamorous nor lucrative. Most practitioners were young men who were born into poverty and lacked either an education or a viable trade and turned to fighting as a means of survival. Others were drawn by a sense of adventure, a chance to prove their masculinity. Vulnerable and often naive, they were easy marks for unscrupulous managers and promoters. These young men were often forced to live on the streets or in dangerous hobo camps, taking menial jobs in order to buy food. Some resorted to hustling a few bucks by fighting all comers in impromptu matches in saloons.

When a husky 200-pound John L. Sullivan walked into a working-class bar during his formative years as a prizefighter and uttered his famous challenge that he could lick anyone in the place, most patrons at the bar studiously stared into their drinks and otherwise attempted to make themselves invisible. Those foolhardy enough to accept Sullivan's challenge soon rued their decision. Not so when a scrawny 130-pound teenager with a high-pitched voice and stringy black hair used the same ruse in Nevada saloons. Locals quickly lined up to take the youngster's money, but most ended up flat on their backs, victims of a devastating left hook that "rolled off his shoulder like a smoothly released baseball." On some occasions the teenager would not issue the usual challenge as he walked in the door, but instead would quietly approach the bartender, inquiring if there was anyone in the saloon that he and most of his customers would like to see knocked out. A match would speedily be arranged, the size and enthusiasm of the crowd roughly proportional to the level of latent hostility directed toward the town bully. The fight would typically last for only a few minutes before the teenager had flattened his surprised opponent, at which time the hat would be passed and appreciative locals would express their gratitude. On special occasions the hat would contain upwards of fifty dollars, the amount being split with the barkeep. But on some occasions, it would be the youngster who ended up on the floor, sometimes being forced to flee the town ahead of the jeering crowd.[2]

It was in this manner that a teenage Jack Dempsey launched his boxing career and initiated a relationship with Nevada that would last his entire life. Jack Dempsey's role in promoting the Baer-Uzcudun fight in 1931 had, in fact, been built upon his years as a fledgling boxer who appeared in many prizefights staged in various Nevada towns in the years immediately before World War I. He was well known among boxing fans for his all-out efforts in many a prizefight during that era as he learned the nuances of the fight game. In a real sense Dempsey prepared himself for a seven-year reign as heavyweight champion fighting in Nevada barrooms. Born to impoverished parents in the small Colorado town of Manassa on June 24, 1895, William Harrison Dempsey began fighting when he was ten, learning to jab and counterpunch from older brother Bernie. Determined to become a boxer, he soaked his hands in a putrid beef brine to toughen them for the rigors of bare-knuckle fighting and chewed resin from pine trees to strengthen his jaw, the better to absorb a punch. His family moved several times during his early years in search of work for his father. At the age of sixteen, his family now living in Lakeview, Utah, Dempsey decided the time had come to leave home for good. Penniless, he adopted the life of a hobo, traveling from town to town looking for work, oftentimes suffering from lack of adequate nourishment and forced to sleep in the dangerous environment of a hobo camp, where violence and sexual attacks occurred frequently. Uneducated and lacking a trade, young Dempsey resorted to what he did best: fighting with his bare fists in saloons with the hope that the onlookers would drop a coin into the hat when the battle was over.[3]

Biographer Randy Roberts estimates that the scrawny teenager fought several hundred times during these formative years as he moved from town to town across Colorado, Utah, and Nevada, searching for the next meal and a place to spend the night. He kept moving and, unable to pay for a train ticket, risked his life "riding the rods" by holding onto two narrow steel rods beneath fast-moving Pullman cars. Although he willingly accepted manual laboring jobs—mowing lawns, washing dishes, digging ditches, working in a mine—he discovered that fighting was more lucrative and, for him, much more enjoyable. Despite the danger and the pain, he simply liked fighting. As he gained experience, he became known for his aggressive style and knockout punches, especially a lightning-fast left uppercut. Although he was a pleasant and affable young man, when he entered the ring he discovered that he relished inflicting pain upon an adversary, even a hopelessly outclassed opponent. This cruel trait lasted throughout his boxing career. Even during what were announced as sparring exhibitions, an instinctive desire to destroy his opponent would frequently flare. Most top-ranked boxers routinely took things relatively easy on their sparring mates. Not so Dempsey. The popular sportswriter of the 1920s Paul Gallico wrote that Dempsey "treated each and every one of them as his personal enemy as soon as he entered the ring. He seemed to have a constant and bottomless well of cold fury somewhere close to his throat." In one memorable event, during the mid-1920s when Gallico himself donned the gloves in a charity event to (he thought) spar lightly with the heavyweight champion, Dempsey promptly knocked him out.[4]

Between 1911 and 1914, with no one considering him a future champion or even a potentially adequate club fighter, the young Dempsey barely survived. He took the name of "Kid Blackie" to enhance his pugilistic stature, learning the rudiments of the sport and gaining experience, much of it on the receiving end of punches. Once he surprised locals by winning a match or two, however, he had to move on in search of new and unsuspecting victims in another town. As his fistic skills improved, Dempsey found that he had to ride the rods more often. At the age of eighteen, with a long string of impromptu fights behind him that he estimated numbered well over a hundred, Dempsey decided to forsake his life as an impromptu saloon pugilist to concentrate upon becoming a serious professional. He took up residence in the disreputable neighborhood along Commercial Street in Salt Lake City that was home to saloons, brothels, gambling dens, and boxing clubs. It was an area that the dominant Mormon community abhorred but did not seek to eradicate. For a time he worked in a hotel while working out in a boxing club, finagling a few fights under the name of "Kid Blackie" for five dollars from a local club promoter named Hardy Downing, who put on Monday-night fight cards featuring both amateurs and semiprofessionals. Although at this level the opposition would be more experienced and formidable, he would no longer have to ride the rods and evade railroad detectives.

After a few bouts in Salt Lake City, he took the name of Jack Dempsey, a popular middleweight champion of the late nineteenth century, whose formidable ring skills had earned him the nickname of "the Nonpareil." Fighting under his new but familiar moniker, at the age of twenty, the reinvented Jack Dempsey landed in 1915 in Reno, where fight cards were being staged at Moana Springs. The *Nevada State Journal* reported that Dempsey, "a big, untried slugger," would meet a "colored boy," Anamas Campbell, in a four-round preliminary bout. Dempsey won by a knockout, although newspaper accounts and Dempsey's autobiography disagree on the round in which he sent Campbell to the canvas. The *Nevada State Journal* reported, "Dempsey showed great cleverness and aggressiveness and has a punch with either hand that makes him a dangerous opponent."[5]

A month later, Dempsey appeared in Goldfield, where promoter

Jake Goodfriend staged fights in the Hippodrome Theater. Dempsey's putative manager at the time, a drifter by the name of Jack Gilfeather, convinced Goodfriend that his young fighter would make a respectable opponent for Johnny Sudenberg, a native of Omaha who had established himself in the mining camps of central Nevada as a fearsome fighter who always put out an honest effort. Goodfriend had grown weary of local fighters who put on "brother-in-law" matches, "running and hugging" each other for ten rounds rather than slugging it out. Goodfriend guaranteed Dempsey a purse of $150—a stupendous amount for the young fighter—but he warned that if Dempsey did not put up a "good show," he would withhold the purse. He need not have worried, because Dempsey was excited to have such a substantial payday, and he and Sudenberg fought a crowd-pleasing ten rounds, throwing haymakers at each other in hopes of a knockout. Both men gave as good as they received, and when the referee, state senator Emory Arnold, declared the bout a draw, the appreciative crowd of a few hundred miners was satisfied. Dempsey had no quarrel with the decision and would recall in his autobiography, written fifty years later, that it was the most difficult fight of his career. "Sudenberg almost killed me. For two rounds it was a fight. For the next eight, I was a helpless, blood-soaked punching bag. It was the worst beating of my life. I don't remember going down once because I still don't remember the last three or four rounds."[6]

Exhausted and in considerable pain, Dempsey collapsed after the fight and by local legend was hauled in a wheelbarrow to the crude dugout in which he had been sleeping under newspapers because he could not afford a hotel room. The next morning, when he went in search of his manager to claim his first big payday, he learned that a drunken Gilfeather had gambled away the $150 purse in a craps game and skipped town. "I had been damn near killed for nothing," Dempsey ruefully recalled. "I was broke and starving. It was the lowest point of my entire life."[7]

His showing against the popular Sudenberg prompted calls for a rematch, and he signed on with Nick Ableman, a saloon owner who promoted fights in the Airdome in nearby Tonopah. He and Sudenberg provided the overflow crowd estimated at eleven hundred with another bloody brawl in which power superseded technique. Dempsey knocked his adversary to the floor three times in the first round, but he wilted in the later rounds, a problem he attributed to his lack of adequate nutrition. Once more the referee declared the fight a draw. Bad luck continued to plague Dempsey. After he and Sudenberg pocketed their $100 purses, they went to the Cobweb Saloon to discuss their fight over a few beers. Shortly after they arrived at the Cobweb, they and the other patrons were robbed at gunpoint. "They cleaned us and the others out. Completely. I was broke again." So went the life of a young, and desperate, Nevada prizefighter.[8]

Dempsey and Sudenberg, now flat-broke soul mates and in need of another payday, thereupon commandeered a railroad handcar and pumped their way to Mina Junction, some sixty miles distant. They arrived broke, exhausted, and hungry. They went to a saloon, offering to put on a boxing exhibition if the bartender passed the hat. Dempsey recalled that he and Sudenberg mixed it up bare-knuckle fashion for thirty minutes, and after the hat made the rounds, it contained only $3.60. Dempsey made his way to Reno, stopping in the crossroads village of Wabuska in Lyon County to earn a few dollars picking potatoes. In Reno he and Sudenberg signed on with promoter Jack Thurm for a July bout for the "Western Heavyweight Championship," with both men to receive $150. Dempsey trained hard for the fight, but for unknown reasons Sudenberg disappeared and the fight was canceled.

The two men did meet one more time, on February 5, 1916, at the Bijou Hall in Ely, but this time Sudenberg entered the ring obviously drunk. The "Big Swede," according to an Ely newspaper, "was in no condition for a fight and a gentle tap from Dempsey sent him to the mat to stay." Dempsey had seen the last of Sudenberg, but fortuitously remained in Ely for a bout in April with Joe Bond, who was under the tutelage of manager Jack Kearns of San Francisco. Kearns, duplicitous to the core but an experienced fight man, had connections to the major figures in the fight game. Dempsey won a grueling ten-round decision, and in so doing impressed Kearns with his potential. Dempsey returned to Ely in October to meet Terry Keller, a much-hyped bout that proved to be a huge disappointment to spectators because Dempsey, suffering from three broken ribs sustained in a fight in Salt Lake City, could not generate his usual aggressive style and fell back upon a defensive strategy. He was declared the winner to the disgust of the crowd.[9]

At this juncture, with the experience gained from hundreds of fights in the rough-and-tumble environment of western saloons and in makeshift rings in small arenas, the twenty-one-year-old signed on with Kearns. Although untrustworthy and a conniver of the first order, Kearns knew the boxing game. It was Dempsey who gave Kearns the famous nickname of "Doc." Under Kearns's guidance, within two years Dempsey quickly became a recognized fighter of national stature, considered capable of challenging for the heavyweight title. His rapid development was facilitated by the fact that he was able to obtain a deferment from the draft and did not serve in the Great War, an issue that would damage his public reputation when he became champion. In 1919, now bulked up to a hefty 180 pounds, the six-foot-one Dempsey won the heavyweight championship in Toledo, when he knocked out Jess Willard in a much-hyped fight promoted by Tex Rickard.[10]

Dempsey would soon become one of the most popular celebrities of the 1920s. The little-known saga of his experiences in Nevada would provide the foundation for his championship career. It was also the place where he learned the rudiments of his chosen profession. That oft-overlooked and difficult period of his life remains instructive as to the informal and ruthless culture of boxing in Nevada that existed at a time when the state still resembled life during its formative frontier stage. Dempsey became rich and famous, but most of the eager young men who sought their fortune in the dingy fight clubs and saloons in small Nevada towns soon learned to seek another line of work, their brief pugilistic careers erased from public memory.

Reforming Nevada's Boxing Culture

With the exception of the minispectacle of the Baer-Uzcudun fight of 1931, not much changed in the small-time Nevada boxing world during the decades between the two world wars. As the largest city, with a population hovering around twenty thousand, Reno became the hub of this small-time sporting culture. Bouts were held regularly at Moana Springs and upon occasion at other venues, wherever a few hundred seats could be assembled. In order to drum up a decent crowd, promoters found themselves resorting to staging less than professional events, such as a five-bout Moana Springs card advertised for December 2, 1921, that included a "battle royal" featuring an unknown number of youthful participants who would slug away at each other simultaneously. General admission for that curious event was listed at $1.65, with the best ringside seats selling at $2.75. Although the advertisement emphasized "a good card promised," it was a card of unknowns, because no individual participant was mentioned.[11] During the 1920s, prizefights were also held periodically downtown at the Chestnut Street Arena, actually located on the corner of Arlington and Commercial Row, and the South Side Arena, located a short distance south of the Washoe County Courthouse on Virginia Street. At these small venues, predominantly male crowds of a few hundred would drink, bet, and shout encouragement or disparagement at inexperienced fighters. After the Chestnut Street and South Side arenas closed, the action shifted in the 1930s a few blocks away to Plaza Street and the small Olympic Arena, but occasionally fights were also staged in casinos. The Reno sports pages sometimes reported on fight cards offered in Tonopah by onetime fighter Buddy Traynor. During the late 1930s, retired local boxer Johnny Gammick patched together cards of four or five fights, most of which he held outdoors on the baseball field at Moana Springs Park, where he could attract, on a good night, upwards of a thousand paying spectators.

These boxing cards, featuring inexperienced young fighters handled by managers of dubious knowledge or intent, readily invited corruption and chicanery. Spectators sometimes left a fight with the sense that the boxers had not put forth a notable effort, or, worse, that the outcome had been predetermined. Allegations of a "fix" had long been endemic in Nevada boxing circles—including all the early championship fights—and that dubious tradition remained alive and well during the 1930s. Mismatches were not infrequent, and sometimes a featured fighter did not appear the night of the scheduled bout, leaving the promoter with irritated paying customers demanding refunds. Fighters who had suffered recent knockouts (or more than one) in other states sometimes lied about their physical condition and would fight in Nevada with no one knowing that they still suffered from concussion symptoms. Physical examinations were not required, and sometimes fighters entered the ring in poor condition. Referees often lacked experience and training, and decisions rendered by volunteer judges raised suspicions. The result was that Nevada prizefighting lacked credibility and readily invited cynicism and healthy skepticism. To knowledgeable observers, Nevada's provincial boxing culture needed a strong government oversight commission. Such a commission, it was believed, would provide much-needed credibility and contribute to a healthier and more vibrant sport.

This view was made apparent to a young journalist as he began to report upon the local fight scene after assuming the position of sports editor (actually becoming the total sports staff) for the *Nevada State Journal*. Ty Cobb (no relation to the baseball player) was a recent graduate of the University of Nevada, where he had studied under the legendary journalism professor Alfred Higginbotham. A native of Virginia City, Cobb had been a student-body leader during his four years on the Nevada campus, and he was just beginning a distinguished journalism career that would make him a popular, iconic figure in the city.[12] His efforts would prompt a major reform of the questionable culture of Nevada boxing. He established himself as a leading Nevada journalist and sports authority, and although he covered all local high school and university sports, he always found a way to popularize his favorite sport of boxing. Although he had never pursued an amateur boxing career himself, Cobb was a boxing enthusiast from the time he was a youngster. Late in life Cobb recalled being enthralled watching the Uzcudun-Baer fight as a young boy while squirming uncomfortably on the wooden bleachers in the blistering Nevada sunlight. Throughout his long career, he gave the sport extensive coverage, contributing to its popularity among local sports fans. In his oral history, Cobb's contemporary University of Nevada athletic director Jake Lawlor referred to him as "a boxing nut."[13] As a sportswriter for three decades, Cobb was widely respected among his sportswriting peers across the western states. In 1978 he was inducted into the World Boxing Hall of Fame for his work in helping reform Nevada boxing and for his extensive coverage of the local boxing scene. He was inducted into the University of Nevada Wolf Pack Hall of Fame in 1982, one of only two inductees who were neither athletes nor coaches, and in 1986 the University of Nevada, Reno, and the Nevada Board of Regents named him a Distinguished Nevadan.

The young sports editor had been in his position less than eighteen months when he launched a campaign to establish a regulatory commission to oversee Nevada prizefighting. In that brief time, he had seen more than enough to make him cringe at what he was covering under the name of "competitive sports." Local promoter Johnny

Gammick joined in the effort, providing Cobb with information that helped advance the cause. Writing in his column "Inside Stuff" in February 1939, Cobb urged state legislators, then in session in Carson City, to establish a commission such as the one operating with considerable effectiveness in California. The need for such a body, he wrote, had been "readily apparent for a long time" and was necessary "to protect boxers, promoters, and fans alike" in order to "keep the fistic game from slipping into the same state which brought it such a black name so many times before." Actually, the status of the fight game in Nevada provided all the ammunition he needed: "No longer would fighters be able to come here to take dives if the house is small, would the promoters chisel athletes out of promised purses, would fighters run out on their scheduled bouts and force poor matches through substitutions. . . . A state athletic commission could require local promoters to put up a deposit of a few hundred dollars which would guarantee that their promised purses would be paid."

Cobb urged that the commission be authorized to establish close working relationships with the California Boxing Commission so that fighters would have to undergo a licensing process and secure physical examinations. "This would often prevent mismatches and injuries, as well as guarantee good fights." Fighters could no longer come to Nevada and fight under assumed names to hide previous injuries or their participation in fixed fights. He urged his readers to encourage legislators "who are interested in clean sports to make a progressive move."[14]

He enlisted his father, state senator Will Cobb from Storey County, to introduce a reform bill in the 1939 general session of the legislature. It passed without opposition, but Governor Edward P. Carville objected to some of the wording and did not sign it. In the summer of 1940, Gammick, who enjoyed a positive reputation for his promotions of local fight cards, suffered a substantial financial loss when prominent heavyweight Lou Nova backed out on the eve of a fight at Moana Springs, scheduled for Labor Day. At the time, Nova was the third-ranked challenger to champion Joe Louis. Nova, who would lose a title fight to Louis the following year, had been training in Carson City after recovering from a serious infection and signed on to fight Tom Jordan, who worked as a guard at the state penitentiary. For reasons that are not clear—Nova's manager cited a sparse advance ticket sale—Nova backed out, forcing Gammick to cancel the card, much to the irritation of his regular fans. Because there was no authorizing commission to punish Nova or his manager, Gammick joined in Cobb's campaign.

The legislature passed a comprehensive bill during the 1941 session that Governor Carville signed into law. It established a five-person commission to be appointed by the governor. The legislature was in its usual penny-pinching mode, however, and specified that "neither the members of the commission nor the inspectors . . . shall receive any compensation for their services or for traveling or other expenses." The bill vested substantial power in the unfunded body, giving it "sole direction, management, control, and jurisdiction" over all boxing and wrestling matches. The legislation limited bouts to fifteen rounds—by this time the established distance for championship bouts—and specified that only "duly licensed referees" could officiate a match. Further, all purses could not be paid until after the bout had ended. A referee could stop a match or order a purse withheld pending a commission review if in his determination, one or more of the participants were not "honestly competing." Boxers and their managers would be required to be licensed, greatly reducing the likelihood of chicanery.[15]

Without public comment, the bill also addressed the issue created by the 1919 legislature that had limited "glove contests" to those "between white men." By writing the legislation establishing the commission, Senator Cobb inserted the catchall wording that "all acts in conflict herewith are hereby repealed."[16] By this time the lingering resentment over Jack Johnson's defeat (and humiliation) of "Great White Hope" Jim Jeffries had faded, in large part because the popularity of heavyweight champion Joe Louis had ended resistance to interracial bouts. A few historical-minded Nevada boxing fans might have recalled that in 1923, an effort was made to convince Tex Rickard to promote a championship fight in Reno between Jack Dempsey and the talented black heavyweight Harry Wills; that bout would have been prevented by the existing legislation. (In the last analysis, although Dempsey apparently had no desire to avoid Wills, his manager, Doc Kearns, and promoter Tex Rickard, citing nebulous public opinion sentiment and opposition by unspecified "public officials," were not inclined to give the formidable Wills a match with Dempsey anywhere, anytime.)[17]

Governor Carville appointed William Lewis, warden of the Nevada State Penitentiary, to serve as the first chairman of the Nevada Athletic

Commission (NAC), apparently because he encouraged a supervised boxing program among inmates. During the 1960s, the commission became an important state agency when boxing became, once more, big business in Nevada. The commission established policies and regulations to prevent many of the excesses that had long plagued prizefighting. Referees and judges were required to undergo training in order to obtain a license. The commissioner assigned the referees to sanctioned fights, and their performances were evaluated. Fighters and managers now were required to obtain a license to practice in Nevada, and the financial books of promoters were subject to audits. Medical examinations were required of all fighters, and for major fights trained observers were required to be present in the locker room prior to the bouts and observe the fight in the corner of each boxer. The NAC also established a procedure to share records of fighters with other state commissions and made clear that it had the authority to penalize any fighter or promoter for misconduct, including denying them the right to practice their profession in Nevada. Over the years, although it endured its inevitable share of criticism after controversial decisions by judges or various unusual events, the commission became a national model for the way it conducted its business. With the emergence of Las Vegas as a major center for championship bouts during the 1960s, the NAC ensured that prizefighting in Nevada would be conducted in an ethical and honest fashion. This in turn contributed substantially to the financial bonanza that prizefighting proved to be over the next half century. As each governor discovered, despite the fact that commissioners remain unpaid (although they were now permitted to receive expense reimbursement and complimentary tickets since the 1960s), appointment to the NAC was considered a political plum, and it was made with careful consideration for the political implications. Implied in that fact was that some men who coveted a seat on the commission apparently believed it a prudent gesture to make a substantial contribution to candidates seeking the governorship.

Amateur Boxing Fills a Void

Journalist Ty Cobb noted at the time of his retirement that he covered "hundreds" of local fights, many of them involving amateurs. Among those fights were the popular amateur bouts conducted under the aegis of the Golden Gloves program that held tournaments in Carson City and Reno. Between the 1930s and '60s, Golden Gloves tournaments enjoyed substantial popularity across the United States, providing young amateurs the opportunity to test their mettle in the ring. Cobb worked to establish a novice division for high school boys that proved popular. The Golden Gloves competition provided a few days each year when boxing fans could watch competitive bouts featuring local youth and young adults. These annual tournaments also attracted entrants from neighboring states.

In May 1940 Golden Gloves fever reached an apex in Reno. On four consecutive evenings, a series of upwards of twenty three-round bouts attracted standing-room crowds in excess of three thousand. Sponsored by the local chapter of the Spanish War Veterans, this tournament attracted amateur boxers from the contiguous states of Arizona, Idaho, California, Oregon, and Utah, as well as Colorado, Nebraska, and Washington. The great majority of the entrants had little ring experience, and according to the newspaper accounts prior to the tournament, most began training (and learning the rudiments of the manly art) just a few weeks before the tournament. One hopeful applicant, the six-foot-six, 225-pound Fred Ater from Sidney, Nebraska, confessed that his only relevant experience was in local dance halls: "I have never fought in the ring," he confessed, "but have flattened plenty of bozos around dance halls and beer parlors. My last experience was ten days ago. I made a few passes, KO'd two or three and the dance hall was cleared out in a hurry."[18]

In one of several pretournament articles, Cobb promised that fans would see plenty of action in "15 to 20 wild fights each night." Predictably, the ballroom brawler from Nebraska, Mr. Ater, did not survive his first bout. The single-elimination tournament was held in the ballroom of the El Patio Casino, where three thousand seats were squeezed in around the ring. The tournament was divided into two groups based upon prior experience—novice and advanced—and many teenagers from Reno and neighboring Sparks, along with other northern Nevada towns, signed up for the novice section, many of them preparing for their first bout with only a few weeks of training. More than three hundred young fighters registered for the tournament, and enthusiastic sell-out crowds paid fifty cents for general admission and two dollars for ringside seats. Among the many entrants was a newcomer from Carson City whose athleticism had earlier in the year won him the state's high school tennis singles championship. Future governor and US senator Paul Laxalt, Cobb reported, "turned in some clever boxing in defeating by decision, 'grinning Frank Roylance' of Reno. Laxalt kept Roylance at bay with a left jab and met him coming in with right uppercuts." The future powerful national political figure did not make it past the semifinals on Friday night.[19]

Assimilating the Natives

One of the leading attractions at the Golden Glove tournaments during the years before the Second World War was the team from the Stewart Indian School located in Carson City. Unlike most of the entrants, the "Braves" participated in a year-round training program supervised by athletic director and coach Al Hawley. He founded the Stewart boxing team in 1935, and it captured the team title at the Reno Golden Gloves tournament in 1937. The well-coached youngsters became a favorite of northern Nevada boxing fans and routinely attracted a crowd of a thousand to the Stewart gymnasium when they hosted matches with older boxers from nearby army and navy bases. In 1940 they once again were dominant. Heavyweight Gardner Allen repeated his 1939 title by winning by knockout on Saturday night over Augie Lager of Scottsbluff, Nebraska. Hawley, and his successor, Joe Anderson, each year took the team to American Athletic Union (AAU) tournaments in Oakland, where they enjoyed considerable success and likewise were favorites of the spectators.[20]

That boxing was a "major sport" at Stewart was not the result of mere coincidence. During the early decades of the twentieth century, the Bureau of Indian Affairs (BIA) operated twenty-five boarding schools under an umbrella philosophy designed to assimilate Native American youth into mainstream American society. The philosophy of these schools derived from the leadership of Richard Henry Pratt, a military officer who had spent eight years dealing with Indian uprisings in the Oklahoma Territory during the 1870s. After considerable interaction with Native Americans on the Great Plains, including eight years engaged in sporadic military campaigns against local tribes, Pratt's goal in life became the assimilation of Native Americans into white society. Appointed the commander of the military base in Carlisle, Pennsylvania, which housed the first boarding school operated by the Bureau of Indian Affairs, Lieutenant Pratt designed a curriculum and residential life to civilize the perceived young "savages." The Carlisle Indian School opened its doors in 1879. Its stated objective was to remove young Native Americans from their families and tribal reservations and place them in a military-style environment to ease a process of cultural transformation under the direction of an all-white instructional staff. In addition to being subjected to a traditional instructional curriculum being offered in public schools, the students' process of assimilation also included the cutting of traditional long hair of males, daily military drills, rigid disciplinary codes, even the requirement that the students learn to play an instrument and participate in a marching band.[21]

Historian Scott Riney describes Pratt's underlying goal as "kill the Indian and save the man."[22] Central to the BIA school curriculum was inundating the students in the dominant white culture, with emphasis placed upon courses in English and American (white) history and culture. Technical education courses stood at the heart of the curriculum, with the intent of preparing boys for work in various manual trades and girls to be homemakers. As part of this overall philosophy to assimilate Native Americans into American society, organized sports for the boys were required. As a result, at Carlisle early in the twentieth century, one member of the Sac and Fox Tribe from Oklahoma, Jim Thorpe, was removed from his family at age twelve and would spend nearly a decade at the school, where he became an All-American football player and the Olympic decathlon champion at the 1912 Olympics, held in Stockholm. He also learned the game of baseball and played six years in the National League for the New York Giants, Cincinnati Reds, and Boston Braves.

During the Depression years of the 1930s, the BIA faced serious budget cuts, prompting director John Collier to encourage the elimination of expensive sports, such as football, and to emphasize less costly activities. Because one of the secondary objectives of the BIA was to encourage local community support for the schools, boxing was established at Stewart in 1935. This was in line with BIA policy, designed to demonstrate the effectiveness of its assimilation program by encouraging schools to provide activities, such as marching bands and sports teams, that could showcase the schools and their students to the larger communities in which they were located. Boxing also had a close link to the curricula offered at the nation's two military academies. Some critics within the BIA opposed boxing because they considered it a "savage" sport, but advocates of the robust philosophy of "muscular Christianity" countered by contending that, unlike professional prizefighting, the amateur version was a "sweet science" that emphasized agility and technique over brute strength and taught such valuable traits as self-reliance and good sportsmanship.

Thus did the coaches at Stewart emphasize that boxing was "a valuable part of the physical education program" and that the team was open to "all boys who are interested, and who are physically fit." Coach Hawley was a graduate of the Haskell Institute in Lawrence, Kansas, whose sports teams by the 1920s had become nationally prominent. Hawley had played in the 1927 East-West Shrine football game in San Francisco. Under his direction, the Stewart Indian School boxing team became a favorite across northern Nevada. A few graduates of the team, such as Ned Crutcher, a Paiute from Walker Lake, Nevada, went on to capture regional and national amateur boxing titles after leaving Stewart.[23]

One of the objectives of BIA boxing was to encourage the interaction of students with white society. In that regard, apparently the only non–Native American ever to participate regularly in the Stewart boxing program was Carson City teenager Robert Laxalt. In his early teens, Laxalt had suffered from a severe case of rheumatic fever and was forced to spend three miserable months in bed. For a few years he was restricted from participating in vigorous activities. By the time he reached high school, however, Laxalt sought to catch up on the sports he had missed. His father, Dominique, had long been an avid boxing fan, and it was a regular subject for discussion at home. He encouraged his sons to learn the manly art. Consequently, all four Laxalt boys participated in Golden Gloves.

Robert Laxalt took his interest to the extreme, however, when he convinced Hawley to let him work out with the Stewart team. Nevada's future prominent journalist, novelist, and editor would later admit that his experiences during workouts were often challenging. In the ring with the well-schooled Stewart boxers, he usually received more than he gave, but despite taking his lumps, he gamely persevered. As the future Pulitzer Prize nominee and founder and longtime director of the University of Nevada Press would later recall, "My real distinction in the fighting game was in being the only white guy on the

Stewart Indian School team. This distinction had its drawbacks, however. They happened during the training sessions at the old gymnasium at Stewart. What was supposed to be casual sparring turned into bloody brawls and for me at least, whether I was going to get out of the ring alive. It got so that I looked forward to the weekend fight cards as an escape from the training sessions." His planned participation in the Reno Golden Gloves tournament in 1939 was "cut short by my mother when I walked into the house [after practice at Stewart] with two black eyes and a broken nose. I calculated that I had been hit in the head one hundred thousand times."[24]

Following the Second World War, the BIA issued a directive to all of its schools that, although it did not forbid boxing as an interscholastic sport or physical education program, it nonetheless strongly discouraged its continuation. Thus, in 1948, the Stewart administration shut down the program. During the 1960s the emphasis upon vocational education was reduced, with a traditional academic and precollegiate curriculum put in its place. In 1980 the Stewart Indian School closed its doors. The aging buildings could not meet upgraded earthquake requirements, and the BIA no longer embraced the concept of separating youngsters from their families. Assimilation into white America had been replaced by the objective of reinforcing and promoting indigenous tribal cultures.

Boxing on Campus

Concurrently with the demise of the Stewart boxing program, amateur boxing gained a major boost with the development of the intercollegiate boxing team at the University of Nevada. A limited program was instituted in 1927 under coach Dick Wallace, director of the Reno YMCA and a former University of California boxer, but a lack of teams in other western colleges and universities led to its elimination in 1932. The student yearbook indicates that a modest program limped along during the late 1930s, with intramural bouts being held. During the Second World War, the program was mothballed, but under coach Richard Taylor it returned in 1946. One of the team members that year was returning veteran Robert Laxalt, who fought in the 132-pound classification, and another member was a star multisport athlete from Las Vegas High School, Bill "Wildcat" Morris, who would later enjoy a successful career as a prominent Las Vegas attorney and influential member of the University of Nevada Board of Regents. In 1948 Cliff Divine took over the coaching position, and the program gained a modicum of stability with a limited schedule that included Chico State, Sacramento State, California, and Idaho State. Athletic director Jake Lawlor provided the team a large room for its workouts in the basement in the gymnasium on Virginia Street that it called home until the mid-1980s.

In 1953 the coaching duties were assumed by Jimmy Olivas, who had attended the university in 1929 and 1930 and had been a member of the boxing team. He pursued a professional career on the West Coast but gave it up to work in Reno casinos. Olivas provided strong leadership for a program that had limited funding at a time of severely constricted intercollegiate budgets. The coaching position was part-time, and he worked as a pit boss in local casinos. His university salary was essentially symbolic, rising to ten thousand dollars at the time he retired in 1984. He forged a strong bond with his boxers that would result in an active alumni group that raised supplemental funds to support the program, enabling him to offer modest scholarships and pay for travel and equipment. Most of Olivas's boxers had little or no experience, but he welcomed anyone interesting in trying out for the team. His good friend Lawlor commented that Olivas "did a wonderful job." One of his former boxers during the 1950s, Reno attorney David Hoy, recalled that Olivas was above all concerned about the safety of his boxers: "He was always careful not to put someone into a situation in which he could not compete and defend himself."[25]

The boxing program under Olivas enjoyed a special niche in the relatively limited intercollegiate sports program at the university, and the few matches held each winter semester attracted a loud and raucous group of fans. When the team had a particular popular fighter or two, such as John Genasci, Skip Houk, Joe Bliss, Doug Byington, or Mills Lane, attendance exceeded that at basketball games; newspaper estimates often mentioned boxing crowds in excess of one thousand. The program made no pretense of preparing young men to enter the professional boxing ranks, although a few made such an effort without notable success. Under Olivas, it adhered to the guidelines established in the 1920s for intercollegiate boxing and adopted in 1937 by the National Collegiate Athletic Association (NCAA), when it began to sponsor national championships. From its inception on the campuses of the University of Pennsylvania and Penn State in 1919, the sport's founders sought to distinguish it from the professional fight game, although critics never acknowledged this effort, contending the college sport was nothing more than a pale imitation of the professional version. The emphasis was upon safety, with larger ten-ounce gloves and protective headgear required. Bouts were limited to three rounds of two minutes each, with the scoring system designed to emphasize "skill and science" rather than inflicting physical punishment upon one's opponent. Nonetheless, knockouts were not uncommon and, not surprisingly, created the greatest spectator reaction. The catalyst for college boxing was the founding coach at Penn State, Leo Houck, who had fought professionally for fourteen years as a flyweight between 1902 and 1916. He was the prime mover in the creation of the Eastern Intercollegiate Boxing Association in the early 1920s.[26]

Despite the emphasis upon technique and safety, intercollegiate boxing was never able to escape the negative image of professional prizefighting. Consequently, it never became a mainstream intercollegiate sport, but tended to exist on a relatively few campuses that had a charismatic coach and an established tradition. By the eve of the Second World War, it flourished at the two military academies and on several eastern campuses, most notably Virginia, Syracuse, Penn State, and the Virginia Military Institute. It also enjoyed a niche on the West Coast at Stanford, California, California at Davis, Idaho State, San Jose State, and Washington State, and in the Midwest at Wisconsin, Nebraska, Haskell Institute, and Michigan State. When the NCAA assumed control of the sport by sponsoring a national championship tournament in 1937, it established an important addition to the rules by emphasizing that no person could participate unless he met strict amateur standards as well as the usual academic requirements. By 1940 some forty colleges and universities fielded boxing teams. The number of participating institutions tended to fluctuate each year and never got much bigger. Dedicated boxing enthusiasts could never understand—or at least appreciate—the lack of interest at the great majority of colleges and universities.

Olivas soon had some of his top boxers competing for the national honors. Athletic director Jake Lawlor, a strong supporter of the program, lamented the lack of adequate competition among western schools. In 1955 a nineteen-year-old welterweight from Elko, Ted

Contri, lost a close decision in the national championship to defending
champion Herb Odum of Michigan State. In 1956 119-pound Sammy
Macias, who had yet to lose a contest, battled through the preliminary
rounds but lost by decision to Choken Maekawa of Michigan State in
the finals; in 1957, after winning the Pacific Coast tournament, Macias
once again lost a narrow decision in the finals to Idaho State's Dave
Abeyta, who had represented the United States in the 1956 Olympics.

Nevada claimed its first national champion in 1959 when lightweight
Joe Bliss, a native of Lovelock, Nevada, won a TKO over Bill Hartz of
the University of Virginia. A member of the Paiute Tribe, Bliss became
one of the most popular boxers in the history of the Wolf Pack program.
In the championship bout, he had the advantage of support from Wolf
Pack fans because the national tournament was held for the first time
on the Reno campus. An overly melodramatic *Sports Illustrated* article
captured the enthusiasm of the crowd that described Bliss's victory as
a "special treat for hometown spectators": "The crowd—mostly Nevada
partisans, naturally—had other wild moments on the three nights of
the tournament but none wilder than when it shook the gym, filled
to its 4,500 capacity, with hysterical roars as another Indian lad, this
time a Paiute, brought Nevada its first NCAA championship in history. Joe Bliss, a 139-pounder, outpressed and outslugged clever Darrel
Whitmore of Washington State and so became immortal in the annals
of the college."[27] The two-page article provided Olivas with his biggest
recruiting coup. Later in the summer of 1959, a marine corporal about
to return to civilian life was shown a copy. Seeking to continue his boxing experience as a marine and pursue a college degree, Mills Lane
sent a letter of inquiry to Olivas that resulted in his decision to attend
Nevada, although he had never visited the campus. He arrived in January 1960, and with Bliss returning for his senior year, boxing fans
eagerly anticipated the new season. They were not disappointed, and
while the team won the majority of its matches, most attention was
focused upon Bliss and the twenty-three-year-old freshman who had
amassed a boxing record of 19-1 in Marine Corps tournaments.

The team closed out a winning season with a 6-2 record against
Washington State and sent five boxers to the Pacific Coast Collegiate
tournament in Sacramento. A record four men from the Wolf Pack team
were invited to the NCAA national championships in Madison, Wisconsin: Joe Bliss, now competing in the 132-pound classification; the

crowd-pleasing Lane in the 147-pound division; Lonnie Tolano in the middleweight (156-pound) division; and heavyweight John Genasci. Tolano and Genasci lost their opening bouts, but Lane and Bliss fought their way to the championship round by winning their first two bouts. In the finals, before an enthusiastic crowd of 10,500 Wisconsin fans, Bliss lost a narrow decision to a local favorite, Brown McGee. It was a close bout, and Olivas contended that the cheers of the hometown fans had swayed the judges. Shortly thereafter, Lane faced another Wisconsin fighter, but he dominated the bout from start to finish, earning a clear decision over Gary Wilhelm.

During the posttournament awards ceremony, the two Nevada boxers were selected to receive the two top individual awards, Bliss receiving the DeWitt Portal Trophy that was awarded to the individual who best "exemplifies the spirit of collegiate boxing in skill," and Lane receiving the highest prize, the John S. LaRowe Trophy, for "the athlete whose sportsmanship, skill and conduct perpetuate the best attributes of collegiate boxing." Both men received standing ovations from the appreciative fans who were packed into the University of Wisconsin Memorial Gymnasium. It was the only time in the history of the tournament that members of the same team had received both awards. San Jose State, however, walked away with its second consecutive team title.

The awards ceremony, however, was not an uplifting conclusion to the tournament. What should have been a high point in the history of Nevada boxing was suddenly and tragically dampened. After Charlie Mohr of Wisconsin was defeated by TKO by Stuart Bartell from San Jose State in his quest to retain his 156-pound title, he walked to the locker room, pausing along the way to chat with supporters and sign autographs. Once in the locker room, however, he complained of a headache, collapsed, and fell into a coma. Rushed to the nearby university hospital, he underwent emergency surgery for a hematoma on the right side of his brain. When the Wolf Pack delegation departed Madison on Sunday, he was fighting for his life and would die seven days later, never having regained consciousness. The Mohr family declined to permit an autopsy be performed, and as a consequence some doubt lingered over the actual cause of his death. Defenders of college boxing contended that he had an undetected aneurysm that predisposed him to a massive hemorrhage, and that speculation gained widespread acceptance. It was not, however, based upon an autopsy or even comments by the surgeon who attempted to save Mohr's life. Ironically, the introspective young man had announced to his fiancée and his parents that same day that he had grown weary of the sport and that this would be his last bout.[28]

The death of a collegiate boxer received relatively little national media attention because of the limited interest that the sport enjoyed. It also reduced the attention that the victorious San Jose State team might have otherwise received, and it definitely deprived Mills Lane of relishing his moment of triumph. The leadership of the National Collegiate Athletic Association, however, definitely took note of the incident and quietly moved to drop boxing from its annual championships. At the annual NCAA national convention in Pittsburgh in January 1961, with little fanfare, it voted to drop the sport "because of the limited number of institutions conducting an intercollegiate program." Many other reasons were posited by supporters and detractors of intercollegiate boxing: the inherent danger of the sport, the large number of mismatches that led to quick and easy knockouts, the lack of qualified coaches, the strong undercurrent of antiboxing sentiment among college faculties, and the inability of the sport to distinguish itself from the negative publicity surrounding professional prizefighting.

In 1968 the legendary *Sports Illustrated* boxing writer Martin Kane concluded that the sport fell victim to its own success: "As [intercollegiate] boxing advanced in popularity and gates increased, ambitious coaches began to recruit highly experienced amateurs from the Golden Gloves and AAU clubs, some of the boxers with as many as 50 bouts or more behind them. Result: kids who wanted to take up boxing only after they entered college were sadly outclassed by the semiprofessionals—many of whom wanted to become full professionals after graduation." Kane quoted Art Lentz of the US Olympic Committee, formerly a University of Wisconsin sports publicist, who was present the night Mohr died: "The pool room element had come in and changed the atmosphere of college boxing. People talked about going to see the fights, not bouts, when they went to college matches." But in the hours immediately after Mohr had collapsed, two unnamed college coaches immediately anticipated the implications. "I think college boxing is now finished," one said; the other responded, "This will kill college boxing."[29] Indeed it did.

All of these factors undoubtedly contributed to the NCAA abandoning boxing as a sanctioned sport, but Charlie Mohr's death was most certainly the catalyst that made the decision uncontroversial at the organization's convention. The sport simply did not have sufficient support among the NCAA membership.

Those institutions that wanted to continue had the option of turning the sport over to student groups that could operate a program as a club activity. Only a few institutions did so, and they were in the West: California, Stanford, Sacramento State, and Nevada. The programs struggled because of the decline in competition, the absence of institutional financial support, and the lack of a national tournament. At the end of the decade, only students at one other institution, Chico State, had created a boxing club, and as Lawlor commented, the University of California program was "hanging on by a thread." On the Reno campus, the enthusiasm generated by the sensational season of 1960 overrode any possibility that the program would be dissolved. Lawlor, himself a strong boxing enthusiast, allocated the usual small amount within his budget to support a modest number of partial scholarships and help meet travel expenses. He also continued to provide a small stipend for Olivas and permitted the team to continue its use of the space in the basement of the gymnasium.

In the mid-1980s, with the pressures for space mounting resulting from the university's efforts to properly fund its women's programs under the dictates of Title IX that mandated gender equity for female athletes, the limited financial support provided by the Department of Athletics was ended. The team was forced to abandon its space and relocated in a storefront location near downtown Reno. The program continued, supported by donations from boosters, including a sizable number of former Wolf Pack boxers. Mike Martino, who was active within the Nevada Athletic Commission and had boxed for the team in the 1970s, assumed the duties of head coach, volunteering his time and expertise and continuing up until the writing of this book. Martino and his few athletes were bound by a love of the sport, but their exploits received only brief and occasional mention in the local newspaper. Even those athletes who won a national championship received little, if any, publicity from the Reno media or even the campus newspaper.

In 1976 Olivas joined with Al McChesney, the coach at West Chester State in Pennsylvania, to establish the National Collegiate Boxing

Association (NCBA), completely independent from the NCAA. The emphasis was upon providing truly amateur college student boxers an opportunity to compete on an equitable basis. The organization grew slowly until thirty-five schools were involved in 2012. The program emphasizes safety within an educational setting, requiring twelve-ounce gloves, headgear and mouthpiece, regular physical examinations, the use of qualified referees, and essentially the same academic eligibility requirements as stipulated by the NCAA. Referees are instructed to stop a bout if there is any indication that an athlete is injured or cannot defend himself. The possibility that a boxer has sustained a concussion requires the calling of a match.[30] The rules of the NCBA are intended to encourage true amateurism. No scholarships are permitted, and participants must be novices. Participants joining a team cannot have had more than ten amateur bouts or experience in Golden Gloves or AAU tournaments. (Such a requirement would have precluded many former Wolf Pack boxers, including both Mills Lane and Joe Bliss, from participating.) The NCBA has no full-time paid administrative staff and relies heavily upon volunteers; consequently, it has been forced to rely upon the integrity of each boxing club to self-enforce the rules.

The NCBA has held national championships since its founding in 1976. The University of Nevada, Reno, team captured the first national team championship that year and repeated in 1991 and 1993. However, the championships were dominated by the military academies, which have coaches who are part of the regular instructional staff and have a large number of cadets interested in boxing. As of 2012, the Air Force Academy had won twenty-five titles, while the army and naval academies have claimed a total of nine titles between them.

In 1996 a former Olympic boxer, Skip Kelp, created a boxing club at the University of Nevada, Las Vegas (UNLV). He secured financial assistance from a local beer distributor and other interested Las Vegans and soon had a team competing on equal terms with the club in Reno. A large storage room was converted to a gym on the edge of campus. Kelp and his sponsors were quick to note that the club was intended to highlight the fact that Las Vegas had become the "boxing capital of the world." In 2006 Kelp's team won the NCBA championship, breaking a thirteen-year domination by the military academies. Like the volunteers who kept the program going at Nevada, Reno, so too did Kelp and his assistants. "It's a labor of love for me," said assistant coach Frank Slaughter, himself a former air force boxer. "I've never asked for money. My satisfaction has always come from seeing these kids come into the gym and learn, work hard, and then see them graduate."[31]

Glimmerings of a New Era

Several disparate forces in the world of amateur and professional boxing seemed to converge about the time of the death of Charlie Mohr. The NCAA's decision to abandon boxing as a sanctioned sport was but one small part of a much larger scenario. On the national level, professional boxing entered into a period of decline due to the oversaturated television coverage that effectively served to undercut hundreds of boxing gyms and clubs that had provided the pipeline for young professionals. Investigations into the power structure controlling boxing revealed that those who controlled the sport were often closely associated with organized crime families. By 1960 very serious questions about the integrity of professional boxing remained unanswered. The result was that boxing suffered an enormous loss of prestige, and its popularity as a spectator sport declined. The avalanche of negative publicity severely affected the prizefight business in New York City. Radio and television networks abandoned the sport. One of the attractions of boxing for many fans was its affinity for gambling, but America's sports bettors, enamored with the point-spread concept, were now turning to professional and intercollegiate football and basketball.

Boxing clearly needed an overhaul, a new beginning, for the emerging new era dominated by mass marketing and extravagant commercialism. That did not happen overnight, of course, but during the 1960s prizefighting entered into a period of transition in which Nevada, with its hotel-casino industry expanding rapidly, once more became the place where prizefighting was welcomed as part of a much larger entertainment and commercial endeavor.

Boxing's golden era had passed when such charismatic fighters as Rocky Marciano, Jake LaMotta, Joe Louis, and Sugar Ray Robinson ended their careers during the 1950s, but the sport would find a natural new home on the booming Las Vegas Strip. In the final four decades of the twentieth century, Nevada would once more become home to a sport that had never been able to shake its renegade image and now was burdened with a new wave of negative publicity. With public attitudes toward divorce and gambling having moderated considerably since the Second World War, Nevada was no longer subject to the fusillade of moral condemnations that had labeled it "America's Disgrace" and the "Sin State." The state's embrace of wide-open casino gambling and its historical toleration of the foibles of human nature led to the logical conclusion: prizefighting, with its rough edges and visceral appeal, would fit right in among the slot machines and green-felt tables. It was only natural that Nevada would once more reclaim its reputation as a good place to hold a big fight.

Round 6

"Let's Get It On!"

God help me, I love boxing. It is the discipline upon which my
entire life has been built. —Mills Lane, 1998

Mills Bee Lane III was a Nevada original, even if he was a native of
Georgia and grew up on a South Carolina plantation. In his autobiography he emphasizes that as a young man, he had been attracted
to Nevada and his adopted hometown of Reno because "it's a no-
nonsense city in a no-nonsense state. People here are built of solid stuff—
uncompromising on ideals and values. Most of all they stand tall on
their own two feet without the aid of artificial props."[1] It was boxing
that initially attracted this scion of a southern aristocratic family to
Nevada, and he would become a major figure in its boxing culture and
use the sport as a launching pad for a remarkable professional career.
Lane became a popular young man in northern Nevada when he won
the NCAA welterweight championship in 1960, and he went on to a
brief and modest career as a professional fighter in northern Nevada
and California boxing venues before earning a law degree at the University of Utah, ultimately becoming a prominent prosecuting attorney
and district court judge.

His professional boxing career was short-lived because he recognized all too soon that he was not possessed of adequate skills. He thereupon launched a career as a referee, becoming well known throughout Nevada and eventually the United States for his talents as the
third man in the ring. Before he retired in 1998 at the age of sixty-
four, he had refereed a record ninety-seven championship fights, the

most famous being one of his last, the 1997 bout in which Mike Tyson chomped off a portion of Evander Holyfield's ear. Lane's decisive handling of that bizarre situation made him an instant national media sensation that led to a three-year run of the syndicated television reality show *Judge Mills Lane*. His aggressive style as a boxer and his command of the fierce action in the ring as a referee did much to shape his approach to the law. Mills Lane—boxer, referee, prosecutor, judge—was indeed a Nevada original. His life story is central to an understanding of the special niche that boxing has enjoyed in Nevada history.

An Evening of Triumph and Tragedy

The evening of April 9, 1960, was a special moment of achievement and vindication for the twenty-three-year-old welterweight from the University of Nevada. It was one of those events that become central to an individual's entire life. Before 10,500 raucous, partisan fans in the University of Wisconsin Field House, Lane won the national NCAA championship by a clear-cut decision over a local University of Wisconsin favorite, Gary Wilhelm, who was the defending national champion in the 147-pound classification. The victory gave Lane an automatic entry into the Olympic Trials in May, and he believed he had a good shot at representing his country in Rome later that summer. For this proud marine, now a freshman at the university, it was supremely gratifying that the countless hours spent conditioning his body and learning the finer points of boxing had led to a national title. When the evening's boxing card had been completed, Lane was announced as the winner of the John S. LaRowe Trophy, an award given by the NCAA at the national championships for "the athlete whose sportsmanship, skill and conduct perpetuate the finest attributes in collegiate boxing."

His elation, however, was short-lived, due to the tragedy that occurred less than an hour after his moment of triumph when he learned that University of Wisconsin middleweight Charlie Mohr had collapsed in his locker room after losing the championship fight to Stu Bartell of San Jose and had been rushed to the university medical center with life-threatening symptoms. Lane recalled his shock and horror when the news of Mohr's collapse filtered through the field-house crowd, and he ran to the locker room to console a fellow boxer. Forty years later he would recall Mohr as "tall and good-looking and a pleasure to be around," a "great boxer . . . who knew how to operate in the ring" by utilizing his jabbing and counterpunching skills because he lacked a knockout punch.[2] The Mohr tragedy put a damper on Lane's special night of triumph, and he would never forget the tragic turn of events that night.

The death of a collegiate boxer also meant that Lane would never again have the opportunity to defend his NCAA title because at its annual convention in January 1961, the organization quietly announced that it was discontinuing boxing as an intercollegiate sport "for lack of interest." The Associated Students at the University of Nevada and athletic director Jake Lawlor decided to provide modest funding to keep the program alive as a club activity, but all formal ties other than a modest budget line to support a part-time coach with the Department of Athletics were cut. With his athletic scholarship no longer available, Lane decided to turn professional in order to earn money to help pay his college expenses.

Taking a "Road Less Traveled"

In his autobiography Lane observes that for a young man who had been born into a wealthy and influential southern family, his path to becoming a prominent judge in Nevada was most unusual: it was "a road less traveled . . . considering my family background and fortune." The grandson of Mills Bee Lane, a prominent banker from Savannah who in 1887 had founded what became one of the largest banks across the southern United States, the Georgia Citizens & Southern Bank, young Mills spent his formative years on his father's eleven-thousand-acre timber and cattle plantation located fifty miles north of Savannah, near the small town of Yemassee, South Carolina. His father expected him to learn the importance of hard work. During the summers until he left for the military, Mills spent his summers wrestling hay bales, herding cattle, and cutting timber. When he was twelve, his parents sent him off to an elite New England prep school that he detested. He nonetheless persevered, eventually receiving his diploma from Middlesex School in Concord, Massachusetts. According to his own words, he spent six miserable years there because he "disliked schoolwork in any form or fashion" and, even worse, chafed under traditional rules designed to produce polished gentlemen that, among other things, required him to wear a coat and tie to class and meals. His only fun was "knocking guys flat on their butts" on the football field as an undersize linebacker and on the hockey ice (where he lost a tooth to a fast-flying puck). The short, wiry guy with the southern drawl spoken in a high-pitched, raspy voice that evoked images of Bugs Bunny could not skate with the proficiency of his New England teammates, and so he was often relegated to the position of goalie. He also got his first introduction to boxing in gym class, but was disappointed when the headmaster refused to approve his request to enter the Boston Golden Gloves tournament ("because it would be demeaning"). Football and hockey, along with a touch of boxing in gym class, provided him with a much-needed release from the stuffiness of the "masters" who taught his classes. As he later recalled, "I flat-out loved hitting people."[3]

The young Mills put up with Middlesex because he was determined to please his father, but at this juncture of his life, he had all the formal education he could take. His father, Remer Mills, apparently had his son's future well mapped out. After Middlesex he would attend the University of Michigan, where he would major in business and forestry to prepare himself to take over Combahee, the family's sprawling plantation. Years of hard labor in the fields and among the stands of white pine trees had convinced him that such was not the life he wanted. "In essence, my daddy had farmed all the farming out of me."[4] Before departing for the fall term at Ann Arbor, a future he did not relish, Mills convinced his father that he wanted to take that road less traveled, and after weeks of discussion and argument, and apparently some downright pleading, he received his father's reluctant permission to join the marines. He immediately hustled to Savannah and enlisted before Remer changed his mind, and in short order, on August 16, 1956, Mills Lane was at Parris Island getting his head shaved and thrust into the rigors of thirteen weeks of a special form of hell—marine basic training. Although he never mentions it, the quid quo pro of obtaining his father's permission to join the marines was predicated upon the understanding that he would no longer have access to his daddy's bank account. His was a pivotal decision of a young man determined to set his own path as he entered young adulthood.

The Education of a Boxer

He might have escaped the classrooms of Ann Arbor, but Lane got a serious education during his three years in the Marine Corps. "The Corps teaches you to stand on your own two feet," he liked to say, and throughout his lifetime he drew analogies from the psychological demands placed upon a marine to the emotions a boxer feels when he climbs through the ropes into the ring to face his opponent. At that moment, he says, "the battle was mine alone. . . . Either you kick his ass or he kicks yours. When the bell rings, there's nothing [anyone] can do to help you."[5] "The most valuable and enduring lessons I've ever learned were taught in a boxing ring," he told a journalist at the peak of his legal career, "courage, honesty, integrity, responsibility, persistence, and loyalty, to name just a few."[6]

After completing basic training, he was shipped off with the Third Corps to Camp Sukiran on Okinawa, where he spent his time training for possible combat. When his regimental colonel announced that he was seeking volunteers for the battalion boxing team, he was quick to sign up. He developed into a promising club boxer under the tutelage of two sergeants, Colston Donahue and Harold Williams. He was initially surprised by their expectations that their boxers attain a level of physical conditioning far beyond that of a regular marine. They demanded that he run five miles a day, in addition to the three miles or so he put in during his daily training regimen. "Simply being a Marine was tough enough," he recalled. "But being a boxer on top of it was pushing endurance to the max."[7] At their suggestion, he maintained his weight at 145 pounds in order to meet the welterweight division maximum of under 147 pounds. It was a weight that he would proudly maintain throughout his lifetime. He learned the fundamentals of the sport, developing an aggressive style that was based upon defensive skills. As a left-hander, he became known for his ability to counterpunch and wear down his opponents by a swarming style that took advantage of his superior conditioning. He was able to take a punch and often said that he had no fear of being hit. The ability to take punishment, he apparently told himself, was part of the price he had to pay to become successful in "the sport that I love."

His reward for his dedication was a 19-1 record in formal Marine Corps competition, but he estimated that he probably entered the ring three hundred times to mix it up with other marines. In 1958 he won the welterweight All-Far East Marine Championship. Clippings from a marine newspaper indicate that he was a favorite of the several thousand marines who watched the championship tournament: "Mills Lane connecting often . . . hard dropped a tired Joe Guadia in the third round before it was stopped." "Mills countered nicely and began banging away late in the second round." "In one of the evening's top bouts, Mills Lane stopped veteran Brooks Stewart." "Fast swinging Mills Lane cut loose with a two-fisted attack that sent Ron Tollivar sprawling through the ropes at 1:29 of the first round." In the finals against Irval Hamm, Lane met a seasoned fighter and won a decision in a tough bout: "An aggressive Mills Lane battered a back-peddling Hamm for five rounds in a great exhibition of in-fighting which saw both boys banging away to the middle. Lane jolted Hamm in the final round with two wicked left hooks but couldn't land the big blow." The one loss in Lane's career as a marine boxer occurred as a result of a facial cut that required the match be stopped.[8]

Finding a Home in Reno

When his three-year enlistment was up, Lane decided that the time had come to move on with his life. He loved the corps but recognized that without a college degree, his potential for advancement was minimal. Perhaps he felt a pang of regret that he had not followed Remer Lane's advice and enrolled at Michigan, but he was also proud of his service years and what he had accomplished. "I had boxed myself in. Because I did not have a college education, becoming a Marine officer was out of the question. . . . I sure as hell did not want to be a corporal all my life."[9] Thus, in August 1959, he was honorably discharged. Boxing was still very much in his blood, and he applied to a western university that he had never visited after he had read a laudatory article on college boxing in *Sports Illustrated* that had reported on the NCAA national championships held on the University of Nevada campus.[10] He had never been to Reno but immediately decided to enroll without so much as a campus visit. But there was the matter of his anemic academic record at Middlesex to contend with; a semester at Armstrong Community College in Savannah after his August discharge was the solution. He was determined to use the discipline instilled in him by the Marine Corps to overcome any obstacles that he might encounter as he reluctantly but with a seriousness of purpose became a college student. At Savannah he applied himself diligently and enjoyed for the first time a semester of academic achievement. He was admitted to Nevada for the spring semester that began in January 1960. As he put it, "I chose business administration as my major, and subsequently minored in left hooks and right crosses."[11]

He was declared eligible for the boxing team and, because of his marine experience, became a star performer as a freshman. He had learned his lessons well under Sergeants Donahue and Williams and continued to refine his skills under the guidance of Jimmy Olivas, who was in his seventh year as the Nevada coach. During the four weeks before the season began, he impressed with his speed, his mastery of fundamentals, and especially his dedication and enthusiasm. A pre-season newspaper account identified him as "a hard-fighting little welterweight from South Carolina, who Olivas labels as sure to be 'the greatest crowd-pleaser in Nevada history.'" Olivas was also quoted as saying that he believed his newcomer "could be the best boxer in Nevada's history." Despite an early draw and defeat as he became acclimated to collegiate rules, Lane lived up to that lofty prediction when the team opened the season at Idaho State on February 6: "The flashy new welterweight from South Carolina threw everything but a Rebel Yell at Dale Trumbo," a Reno newspaper reported. Although the veteran Trumbo was fighting over the weight limit, Lane "dug into his reserve strength and came up with a fine third round to salvage a standoff." Lane began a string of victories a week later when the Wolf Pack traveled to meet a Sacramento State team that had a squad loaded with returning lettermen. He outpointed George Waggoner, who had previously defeated Nevada's returning national lightweight champion, Joe Bliss. He lost when the Wolf Pack visited the defending national champion, San Jose State, on February 18, when Charlie Brown staggered him in the first round with a right-hand punch. Although Lane "battled back strongly in the last two rounds," he lost on a decision.[12]

Despite his mixed early-season record on the road, his enthusiastic style inspired considerable anticipation among Reno boxing fans when Sacramento State came to town: "Action-hungry ring fans are expected to swarm into the University of Nevada gymnasium," a local sportswriter enthused, "spurred by a desire to see the home debut of Wolf Pack Boxer Ellis Lane [sic]. The sturdy little ex-Marine from South Carolina has been a crowd-pleasing welterweight walloper in his first three bouts." *Reno Evening Gazette* sports editor Rollan Melton was unrestrained in his enthusiasm: "Western Nevada people have been reading about Mills Lane, sophomore [*sic*] from South Carolina the past month. They get their first look tomorrow. They'll like the view. Lane can really fight! In the gym he takes them all [on]. Lane and [Joe] Bliss have staged a couple of real 'wars' on campus while tuning for 'real' competition. Lane is by far the most aggressive fighter we have seen on a University of Nevada team. He is short, weighs about 146, crowds constantly, weaves, and is tireless." Melton, himself a former heavyweight on the Wolf Pack team, went on to point out that when he faced San Jose State two weeks previously, George Waggoner "staggered to his corner and was heard to mutter: 'God, he's tough.'"[13]

And indeed he was when the Sacramento coach sent a marine, George Walker, into the ring against another leatherneck. The crowded gymnasium exploded with cheers when Lane shook off a second-round bombardment from Walker to storm back with a ferocious attack upon his opponent's midsection that sent him to the canvas. Partisan Nevada fans thought that the referee's count had reached ten, but Jack Tighe ruled that a low blow may have occurred, and he ordered the fight to continue for the final third round, his decision prompting a cascade of boos from the crowd. Lane left no doubt who was the better fighter when he came out "full of business, firing both hands to the body," as Walker "wilted visibly" and then received "a lightning combination" that "resulted in a ten count that no one could question." After the fight Walker said that the alleged low blow was "a fair shot." The hustling newcomer from South Carolina had become the favorite of Wolf Pack fans along with two returning lettermen, lightweight Joe Bliss and heavyweight John Genasci.[14]

By the time the season closed with the Pacific Coast Intercollegiate Tournament in San Francisco in mid-March, Mills Lane had become, according to a newspaper headline writer, "A Sensation," winning his bouts against boxers from the University of Wisconsin, the US Naval Academy, and Washington State. Lane was one of five Nevada boxers who qualified for the NCAA championships scheduled for early April at the University of Wisconsin, home to one of the most successful programs in the history of intercollegiate boxing. At Madison he knocked out Harry Long of the College of Idaho in the quarterfinals and won a unanimous decision over "husky" Dale Trumbo of Idaho State in the semifinals the next evening. He and lightweight Joe Bliss were the two remaining Nevadans in the finals. Bliss lost a split decision to a

Wisconsin boxer, and two bouts later Lane handily defeated another Badger, former Texas Golden Gloves champion Gary Wilhelm, to win Nevada's second national title in history. According to ringside reports, Lane "battered Wilhelm from gong to gong and frequently had his stylish opponent hanging on as he worked to close quarters and jolted the Badger with short lefts to the body and jaw." Upon returning to Reno with a bloodshot eye suffered in the semifinals, Lane said that he "knew for certain" he had defeated Wilhelm, but "I wasn't so sure in the Trumbo fight. I was really sweating out the decision."[15]

Lane returned from Madison to prepare for the US Olympic try-outs scheduled for mid-May in the Cow Palace in San Francisco. His NCAA championship gave him an automatic qualifier, and he furiously prepared under the tutelage of Jimmy Olivas. He was among eighty Olympic hopefuls who did battle in the trials, eight of whom were in the 147-limit division. News reports, however, tended to focus upon one of the 178-pound contenders, a high school student and national Golden Gloves champion from Louisville by the name of Cassius Clay. Already well known for his loquaciousness, Clay was, the Associated Press reported, "a better prospect than Joe Louis when the Bomber was a simon-pure [amateur]." In his first elimination bout, after Bliss won his opening bout, Lane outpointed navy champion Victor Lopez by using "his potent left uppercut" and a "battering attack to the body." Both Nevada boxers, however, came up short in the semifinals, losing by decisions. In his match Lane met another left-hander, Phil Baldwin from Muskegon, Michigan. For reasons that he later regretted, after watching his opponent win his first-round match, Lane decided that he could outpoint Baldwin with a style he seldom used—by seeking to score style points by boxing rather than launching his usual all-out physical assault. When he told Olivas, who was in his corner, that he thought he could outthink and outbox Baldwin, his coach "nearly had a heart attack." He told Lane, "For Christ's sake, Mills, forget that boxing shit. Fight your fight. Just jump on him and kick his ass." Lane discovered too late that Olivas was right. "I came down with a bad case of stupidity," and "the reality was that no matter what I did, Baldwin did it three times better." After losing the first two rounds decisively, he resorted to his normal swarming style, but it was too late. Baldwin won by decision and went on to win the coveted Olympic slot. It was a chance of a lifetime, and Lane blew it. In his memoirs written nearly forty years later, he said that in reflective moments he still heard his coach's postfight lament: "Dammit, Mills, if you would only have listened . . ."[16]

He did well in the classroom—*Nevada State Journal* columnist Ty Cobb reported that despite Lane's boxing exploits that won him the university's Athlete of the Year award as a freshman, he also "made an outstanding scholastic record last semester with all As but one B." He later told a journalist that he spent considerable time reading and annotating the copious notes he took in classes because he believed those more important than the assigned texts: "There ain't a professor who ever lived who didn't spout off what he thought was important."[17]

Fledgling Club Professional

The death of Charlie Mohr led to the immediate demise of the small and struggling enterprise that was intercollegiate boxing. With Joe Bliss having used up his eligibility, Lane was the leader of the Wolf Pack team—now relegated to the status of club activity—when it opened its truncated 1961 schedule in January. The loss of some traditional foes and a national tournament at season's end put a damper on the enthusiasm surrounding the team. Lane was further disappointed when Chico State demanded that he be held out of its meet in Reno because "he is too tough"; with the exception of Cal Poly, the other teams on the schedule followed suit. When the new California association announced its rules for its postseason tournament, he was once more disappointed to learn that he would be excluded because he had participated in too many amateur bouts.

Disappointed that he was withheld from several matches, Lane began looking ahead, announcing that he had set a goal of attending law school. He still had a gnawing itch for the ring, however, and decided to turn professional, in part because he relished the challenge, but also because he needed the money. As one Reno sportswriter observed, "The personable South Carolinian turned pro with still a year of eligibility left because he simply ran out of college-type competition." In March 1961 he announced that he had signed a professional contract with Reno manager Bill Dickson, who declared that Lane would make his professional debut in a four-round bout on April 7 in the State Building in downtown Reno against a seasoned fighter, just released from the state penitentiary in Carson City, Artie Cox.

Ringside tickets were upped to $3.25 in anticipation that Lane would attract a large following.

Lane's many fans were to be severely disappointed, in fact were dealt "a stunning surprise," when Cox nailed him with a strong right hand in the first minute of round 1. He went down and became entangled in the ropes, managing to beat the count when he was pushed back into the ring by some friendly fans. He staggered to his feet and was overwhelmed by a flurry of "rapid-fire punches" and hit the canvas again. Although he managed to reach his feet by the count of nine, the twenty-four-year-old fledgling professional was clearly unable to defend himself. According to newspaper accounts, at this point referee Ted Contri stopped the fight, but Lane (his memory obviously clouded) recalls that he was counted out. The clock stood at thirty-eight seconds of round 1 as he wobbled back to his corner, and angry protests from a group of university students engulfed the crowd of one thousand. But he was through for the night: "I saw the punch coming, from 'way back,'" he told a reporter, ". . . and yet . . . I just can't believe it," he mumbled time and again.[18]

"It isn't the end of the world," Jimmy Olivas told him in the locker room afterward, but his quick exit at the hands of a more experienced fighter was not the auspicious beginning that Lane had anticipated, and it probably stimulated further his sometime ambition to become a lawyer. The university junior had, it seemed, chosen a tough way to pay for his education, but he was undaunted. After taking a full year off to concentrate on his studies and to further his demanding physical training regimen, he made his return before a cheering group of fellow students at the State Building. Asked why he was continuing to pursue his passion after the pasting administered by the experienced Artie Cox, he simply confessed, "I can't stop fighting. I don't know why, but I can't." He came out swinging against a veteran of several professional preliminary bouts, Carlos Loya, and in a furious first round battered his opponent with both hands to the body before unleashing a left uppercut that gave him his first professional victory. The fight had lasted less than ninety seconds. That win propelled him to ten straight professional victories in Reno and Sacramento. Seven of those wins were by knockout, and he began to gain attention as an up-and-comer.[19]

Sixteen months after Lane's ignominious loss to Cox, manager Dickson finally got the rematch that his twenty-five-year-old novice wanted.

"The loss to Cox seems to have spurred him," Dickson matter-of-factly told the press. Indeed. As the August 7, 1962, return bout with Cox scheduled for the Civic Auditorium in Sacramento neared, Lane made no effort to disguise his desire for revenge. Cox "was as mean as ever," Lane recalled in his memoirs. The fight was advertised as the premier preliminary bout on the evening's card and was scheduled for eight rounds, the longest yet of Lane's career. Both fighters came out swinging, Cox hoping to replicate his early knockout and Lane determined to avenge "something that happened that night I've tried to explain a million times." Cox almost carried out his plan, as he nailed Lane with a right hand to the nose that shattered the cartilage as blood spewed out. Another punch knocked out Lane's bridgework, a relic of his hockey days in Massachusetts. A flurry of Cox punches raised a welt under his eye and a large bruise above it, as he bobbed and weaved to avoid his aggressive opponent. In the second round, however, control of the match switched, when Lane connected with his favorite left uppercut and Cox went down for a count of eight. Before the round ended, Lane had knocked his dazed opponent to the canvas two more times. Cox staggered to the nearest corner and plopped down on the stool. "Go over to your own corner," Lane growled.

Cox attempted to rush Lane as round 3 began. That was a mistake. The determined university honors student sent him down for the count with a vicious left hook to the stomach. The fans were on their feet cheering, and then, as Lane recalled, "one of the damndest things I ever saw" occurred. They showered the ring with coins and dollar bills! He scooped up the money and returned to the locker room to celebrate. In the aftermath boxing writers talked about his potential to reach the national welterweight rankings, and the *Sacramento Bee* informed local fight fans that Lane's performance was "the best thing that's happened to boxing around here in years." Beyond the loose change he picked up off the canvas, he pocketed $150 for the Cox fight, the largest payday of his professional career. For some he seemed to be a promoter's dream: a white boy with a southern pedigree and a college education who could speak intelligently and with good humor. But, according to experts, he lacked sound defensive skills and was too easy to hit and had never developed a strong right-hand punch.[20]

He knew that he had no future in professional boxing. His nose was flattened, and his entire body hurt from the punishment Cox had administered. "Regardless of what ringside observers thought, I realized two very important things. I would never be able to beat Emile Griffith, the welterweight champion, and I was getting hit far too often." He fought three more times, all decisive victories, over local opponents in Reno clubs. His last fight was his only ten-round main-event bout, fought at the small venue of Mathisen's Hall in Reno on February 17, 1963, against the experienced journeyman Dave Camacho, a native of Mexico and veteran of fifty-eight professional fights. Lane won a unanimous decision by dominating the fight, although the ring-savvy Camacho pressed his advantage in the final rounds as Lane visibly tired. Manager Dickson was elated: "Mills proved himself beyond any doubt" and predicted that he was ready to move up the West Coast rankings.[21]

Such was not to be. After his victory over Camacho, in which he had once more absorbed a substantial bruising, Lane announced his retirement. His professional record stood at 10-1. He graduated with honors from the university three months later with a major in business administration—he was rightfully proud of his 3.64 grade point average—and took a position with the Security National Bank of Nevada as a loan officer in the downtown Reno office. Perhaps he had dreams of becoming a prominent banker, just like his namesake grandfather, Mills Bee Lane, but his initial assignment was not all that prestigious: repossessing automobiles. According to a former senior deputy district attorney, the young banker's enthusiasm for his task allegedly prompted him to sometimes become overly aggressive in his work. After receiving several reports in 1966 alleging physical intimidation from those in arrears on their payments, District Attorney Bill Raggio instructed Bob Berry, one of his chief deputy district attorneys, to handle the matter. Berry called Lane into his office and issued a warning about his alleged pugnacious tactics with delinquent payers. When the reports continued, Berry repeated his warning with the addendum that should future complaints be received, a felony assault and battery indictment would be issued that would "severely impact your future career." According to Berry, Lane initially responded with his usual colorful language, but promised to be more circumspect, adding for good measure that the warnings had convinced him that it was time for him to apply to law school.[22]

He applied to the University of Utah School of Law and was one of 85 selected out of 450 applicants. He knew that some extra money would be useful, despite being eligible for the GI Bill for law school, and he agreed to return to the ring for a five-round prelim bout at the recently opened Reno Convention Center. His love of the ring prevailed over common sense, and at age thirty he entered the ring against veteran Bobby Knox on May 6, 1967, in the worst condition of his entire boxing career. "I don't know how to explain it," he later wrote, but "all of a sudden those pugilistic juices started to bubble. I found myself bouncing on my toes . . . and a voice began whispering to me, 'Dammit, Mills, you've gotta go for it. Just one more fight—just one more fight.'"[23]

Fortunately for him, the well-worn Knox was at the end of a lackluster career, but he and Lane slugged away at each other for five rounds, after which the referee raised Lane's hand in victory. But it had been a close match against a mediocre Bay Area professional in the last stages of his career, and Lane knew it. The next day he did not hesitate: he reretired for good because he was wracked by "aches and pains." He pulled no punches in his announcement: "I think I just found out that I'm not good enough. And I'm a little old." He admitted that he had returned without having sparred with a live opponent and had worked out on punching bags for only two weeks. "I hurt all over," he told a reporter. "I have a couple separated ribs. He hit me there. It hurt so bad, I didn't know if I could make it." In his memoirs he is even more critical of his decision to fight after more than four years of inactivity, saying Knox "made me pay for my stupidity. . . . I kept reliving the fight, kept seeing Knox's punches coming at my head, kept seeing his face as my own punches impacted into flesh and bone. And then I drifted off to sleep, dreaming of the man who once was, watching myself age before my very eyes. . . . When I awoke the next morning, the harsh reality of my own half-truths was abundantly clear. It stared back at me from the bathroom mirror—a brutal, battered reflection of my own simplemindedness."[24]

A few weeks later, in September 1967, he announced his resignation from the Security National Bank and, on the eve of his thirty-first birthday, set out for Salt Lake City. He was now set upon a course that would propel him to a distinguished career as a prosecutor and jurist. His greater fame, however, would come unexpectedly because his zest for boxing would open doors that he never could have anticipated.

"Let's Get It On!"

After completing law school and passing the Nevada State Bar examination, Lane returned to Reno. He had stated with emphasis upon his departure for law school that he "loved" Reno and planned to return after obtaining his law degree. He stayed only briefly with a private firm, deciding within months that his real calling was in criminal prosecution. He signed on with newly elected Washoe County district attorney Bob Rose, who was delighted with his new hire. In a statement to the press in his first morning on the job, Deputy District Attorney Mills B. Lane, Esq., was quick to make the connection between his boxing career and law enforcement: "I thought my fighting days were over, when I just got too old for it, that the thrill would be gone forever. But, you know, when you go into the courtroom, it's the same feeling all over again [as entering the ring]." He acknowledged that the pay would be less than in private practice but that the district attorney's office "is one corner I've always wanted to fight in. I tell you, as long as I can remember, I've always wanted to be in law enforcement." And with a sharp prescience about his future image as a political figure and prosecutor, "I guess you could say that I stand somewhere to the right of Louis XIV when it comes to law and order."[25]

His new career soon had him investigating criminal cases and determining which ones should proceed to trial. Those activities often brought him into contact with less than sterling members of the community, and he wisely accepted the advice of his peers and followed standard departmental procedure and obtained a license to carry a concealed firearm. Thereafter, when he was interviewing defendants and witnesses in cases that included armed robbery and murder, his snub-nosed Colt. 38 went with him. His work was demanding but exhilarating, and he knew that he had found his special niche.

The work schedule, however, made it possible for him to continue his passion for boxing. In his scrapbook his first referee's license, no. 580, is neatly pasted. It was issued in 1964 and signed by the executive director of the Nevada Athletic Commission, Jim Deskin. Lane had previously refereed a few fight cards for the university boxing team, and Jimmy Olivas encouraged him to pursue this avocation. During his time with Security Bank, he was assigned to officiate preliminary bouts at Lake Tahoe casinos, where monthly fight cards had become popular, and he discovered that he not only enjoyed the experience but was good at it. By the time he departed for Salt Lake City, he had handled main events at clubs across Nevada and Northern California, sometimes making as much as a munificent fifty dollars for an evening's work.

Like referees who call high school and college basketball and football, Lane was pursing an avocation that kept him in touch with a sport that he had participated in and loved. It was not a full-time job. Although the fees helped pay the bills, money was largely secondary in importance to simply staying involved with the sport he loved. He requested feedback from experts so that he could improve his skills and advance to more challenging matches. The boxing referee has a difficult task. The action is often fast and furious, requiring that the referee have the instinctive ability to anticipate the movement of the fighters in order to be in a position to see every punch. The emotions of the fans and the cornermen for each boxer add to the pressure, especially when a fighter has been hurt: when to stop a fight or to permit it to continue? Always lurking in the back of the referee's mind is the possibility that at any moment, a fighter's health, indeed his life, could be at risk. The position calls for split-second decisions based upon experience and instinct, any of which could easily be second-guessed by the two fighters and their managers, the state commission, and, of course, the spectators who have bet money on the outcome. Stop a fight, and the battered boxer and his manager will protest that he still had a fighting chance; permit the bout to continue, and risk condemnation for endangering a man's life. At the end of each fight that goes the limit, the referee's round-by-round grading of the bout has major financial, career, and sometimes title implications. As in other sports, the common sentiment in boxing is that when the event is over, no one should remember who the referee was. He wanted to officiate fights in an unobtrusive manner that permitted the two fighters to decide the outcome themselves.

Lane had just completed his third month as a fledgling deputy district attorney when he got the call that all sports officials yearn for—news that he had been selected to officiate a major sports contest. In October 1971, Lane got such a call, when Nevada state athletic commissioner Jim Deskin asked whether he was interested in refereeing a world championship fight. He would receive a hefty stipend of five hundred dollars plus air travel and other expenses. Deskin had received an inquiry about assigning a referee from José Sulaimán on behalf of the World Boxing Council. The bout would feature defending featherweight WBC champion Erbito Salavarria against challenger Betulio González and was scheduled for November 20 in Luis Aparicio Stadium in Maracaibo, Venezuela. Salavarria was a native of the Philippines, while González would be fighting in his native country. Lane was naturally excited: he had hit the big time much sooner than he could have hoped. Not only would he have a chance to referee a world title fight, but he would get to travel to a part of the world he had never visited. And the five hundred dollars was a tidy sum for a young lawyer just out of law school. As he later said, "I would have flown into the heart of the Vietnam War for such an opportunity."[26]

At the Miami airport en route to Maracaibo, he met up with the head of the Filipino delegation that included one judge assigned to the fight. It did not take long for him to recognize that this would be no ordinary title bout, because he was subjected to not-so-subtle pressure. He was informed by his travel companions that Salavarria was not only a decent man who respected law enforcement officials, but also up against terrible odds, fighting in his opponent's backyard. In Maracaibo the situation quickly turned ominous. He had gotten himself smack in the middle of a fight with strong nationalistic emotions. The prefight rules meeting, usually a brief and routine affair, turned into a four-hour shouting match between the handlers of the two fighters, each alleging that the judge from the other country had already predetermined the winner. A local newspaper account alleged that the Filipino judge had said he thought Salavarria was the better fighter! Lane was aware of the nationalistic intensity that was often exhibited at Venezuelan soccer matches, and when he entered the ring before six thousand rabid González fanatics, he knew that he was in a difficult situation, especially if González did not emerge victorious.[27]

The fight itself went well and was a clean, hard-fought battle between two evenly matched fighters. By all accounts, Lane's performance was polished and professional. As was the policy for the WBC, the referee scored the fight along with the two judges. When he called the two men to the ring and held their hands as the announcer read the three scorecards, his heart suddenly fell when the Spanish-speaking announcer informed the chanting crowd that the Filipino judge had awarded the fight to his fellow Filipino and that the Venezuelan judge had judiciously decided it in favor of his own countryman. Lane suddenly felt his stomach contract because his verdict was about to be announced—147–146 in favor of Salavarria! As he raised the Filipino's hand in victory, "all hell broke loose." Then the announcer shouted over the crowd to Lane (in Spanish, a language he did not speak) that the outcome, somehow, was a draw! So he thereupon raised both fighters' hands, which still meant that the Filipino would retain the title. The announcer and González's cornermen rushed Lane, but he was already busily ducking beer bottles and chairs heaved his way. He used his own pugilistic talents to duck several punches thrown at him by irate fans who had stormed into the ring to get a piece of the Yankee. Fearing that he was about to be the victim of a mob lynching, he was relieved when a flying squadron of state police came to his rescue, several of whom used their nightsticks to club Lane's assailants. As he was half carried by the police from the ring, one punch landed squarely on his face along with the saliva from several hostile Venezuelans. He was hustled out a side door of the arena to an unmarked car and taken to a new hotel, where he spent a sleepless night, nursing a few beers and counting his blessings that he was still in one piece.[28]

Secretly transported to the airport the next morning, he felt the euphoria of having escaped serious danger. But not so fast. At the customs station, he was escorted to a sealed room, where he was angrily berated—in Spanish—but quickly grasped the gist of their fury: their man had lost and he was the reason! But then he perceived that they had decided that he was illegally carrying a handgun—his trusty Colt .38 he had brought from Reno—although he had presented his law enforcement credentials and license to carry the weapon to the same officers when he entered the country. Finally, an English-speaking official came to his side and was able to assure his associates that Lane had every legal right to carry his pistol. A relieved Lane was permitted to board his aircraft but had to leave the firearm behind. When the wheels were up, Mills Lane contemplated the fact that no matter how long he would continue to referee boxing matches, he would never become involved in such a confusing and dangerous situation again. Or would he?

Lane left Maracaibo not knowing the complete story. Venezuelan boxing officials entered the ring after he was escorted to safety to—

surprise!—"discover" that Salavarria had consumed "colored water" during the fight and was therefore disqualified. They declared González the winner on that tenuous and obviously fabricated basis. To further complicate matters, the other judges' cards had apparently been altered. The matter was eventually submitted to the WBC, which deliberated for months before declaring González the winner and official champion; Salavarria continued to fight, winning back the title in 1975, only to lose it on his first defense. Lane's future as a referee was blemished by this bizarre and confusing episode. He would not be assigned to another championship fight until 1978.

Reno Reality Show: Judge Mills Lane

Unfazed by the controversy in Maracaibo, Lane continued to referee while he learned the ropes as a prosecuting attorney. In 1973 he was assigned the Bob Foster–Muhammad Ali fight at Stateline, Nevada, along the shores of Lake Tahoe. He had gotten to know Ali during the 1960 Olympic Trials in San Francisco. With the experience gained from each fight he officiated, he continued to refine his skills as the third man in the ring. With few individuals willing to take on the role, Lane quickly became recognized by promoters, managers, and fighters as someone they could trust to be both competent and fair. But Deskin did not assign him to a title fight.

Although the confusion that surrounded his first title fight resulted from many complex emotions that were well beyond his control, he had erred when he held up the hands of both fighters, indicating the fight had ended in a draw after he had previously declared Erbito Salavarria the winner. But his scoring of the fight was sound, as was his ability to control the close contest. He understood that he had to overcome the lingering questions before he could once again be assigned a championship fight. Thus, he felt both relieved and anxious when he got the call that he was being assigned to the heavyweight championship fight scheduled for Caesars Palace in Las Vegas between Ken Norton and Larry Holmes on June 9, 1978. The fight was for the World Boxing Council version of the heavyweight title, and Lane's old nemesis, José Sulaimán, vigorously protested Lane's selection because he was still upset about the confusion that occurred at the end of the 1972 featherweight title fight in Maracaibo. Never one to avoid a controversy that would help sell tickets, promoter Don King joined in the protest, but Deskin held firm.

Lane entered the fight knowing that in all likelihood, his future as a main-event referee hung in the balance. The two fighters battled ferociously, entering the final fifteenth round even, at which time Holmes prevailed to win the title. Lane was gratified that Sulaimán came by his dressing room afterward to congratulate him on his performance, and King never again protested his assignment to one of his megapromotions.

His two careers thereupon took off, each reinforcing the other. As a prosecutor, he often drew upon his boxing experiences, and especially the blunt and simple imagery it projected, to make his case when addressing juries or the press. Boxing metaphors were liberally sprinkled in his public presentations. Just as he was known as a boxer for relentlessly pursuing his opponent in the ring, he similarly stalked those who were accused of a major crime in the courtroom.

He not only became well known for his rigorous pursuit of criminals, but also spoke out long and loudly that society was coddling the criminal element. He became outspoken in his support of the death penalty. His blunt comments made for great headlines and considerable criticism from left-leaning Nevadans, but he never hesitated to speak his mind. The American legal system, he often said, had been undercut by the Warren Court, which he believed had stepped over the line to protect the rights of criminals to the detriment of society and law-abiding American citizens. In the sentencing phase of criminal trials, he routinely pushed for severe punishment, engendering the nickname around the Washoe County Courthouse of "Maximum Mills." Once convinced that he had sufficient evidence, he prepared for trial with a fierce determination. He was a compelling courtroom presence, wielding his evidence like a blunt instrument. Juries were often mesmerized by his command of the facts and his compelling presentation as he paced around the courtroom, speaking simply but with dramatic effect in a relentless pursuit of the accused. He succeeded in convicting twenty-two men for murder and in the process became as well known as his popular superior, District Attorney Calvin X. Dunlap. Disagreements with Dunlap led to Lane's resignation in 1979, at which time he became a criminal investigator for the Washoe County Sheriff's Office.

Lane became a popular speaker, making the rounds of service clubs and fraternal organizations. His talks often included vigorous attacks upon the left-leaning Ninth Circuit Federal District Court, located in San Francisco. In particular, he was vocally critical of the so-called exclusionary rule that prohibited prosecutors from using in trial evidence that was not lawfully obtained by law enforcement officers. Such rulings, he believed, were often based upon very narrow and "tickytacky" interpretations of constitutional law and severely undermined the ability of prosecutors to put dangerous persons behind bars. He often colorfully labeled these as "bullshit" decisions. Such commentaries often drew standing ovations from his enthralled audiences, making him a highly visible and enormously popular political figure in northern Nevada. His endorsement in local political races was the equivalent of solid gold.[29]

In November 1982 Dunlap moved on to private practice, and Lane easily won election as district attorney. It was his dream job. His growing national reputation as a boxing referee reinforced his image as a strong advocate of rigorous law enforcement, and in 1986 he ran unopposed for reelection, the first time in the twentieth century that this important position was not contested in Washoe County. "He is the best prosecuting attorney I've ever seen operating in a courtroom," popular Reno television news anchorman Tad Dunbar said in 1990, "and I have been covering trials for 29 years."[30]

In 1989 he became incensed when Department 9 district judge Robert Schouweiler excluded evidence that Lane believed clinched a high-profile criminal case. Just as he did in the ring during his own boxing career, he instinctively counterpunched and went for the knockout. And he did it in the most public way possible. On January 2, 1990, the first day permissible, with the press notified well in advance, he filed his papers as a candidate to oppose Schouweiler in the November general elections. He was determined to make his point that the judge had become soft on crime, but that confrontation did not come to fruition. Schouweiler decided not to fight to hold his current seat and instead filed for an open seat in a newly created Department 10 of the Washoe Court. It was a move widely perceived to avoid what most observers saw as certain defeat before the enraged defender of law and order. But Schouweiler still lost his election, while Lane captured his adversary's old seat by a whopping two-to-one margin.

Lane's elevation to the court was cause for concern among members of the Washoe County Bar who made their living as criminal defense attorneys. It was widely rumored that many feared he would be inclined to side with the prosecution in criminal cases. That worry was soon put aside because he became recognized for his equanimity in applying the law. Lane remained the same gruff, blunt-spoken person, but attorneys who appeared in his courtroom came to appreciate that he had read the relevant case law and found his rulings to be fair and well grounded in the law. He tempered his public remarks in a remarkable display of self-control, but remained true to his basic values that placed great importance upon individual responsibility: "When someone comes into my courtroom and says, 'Yes, Judge, I'm a thief. But it's because I have this drug problem,' I tell him, 'Son, the problem isn't drugs, the problem is you.'" As he explains:

> Let's say that you have a problem with booze and you go to a doctor and he or she tells you that you are an alcoholic. In the abstract, if you buy into the word *addiction,* that gives you an excuse for doing everything that's a producer of addiction, whether it's beating your wife or becoming a thief to support the craving. Once you accept the premise of addiction, you've accepted an excuse for losing. And once you've done that—believing the proposition that drugs or booze is bigger than you—then you've set yourself up for failure. When you buy into the idea that the problem isn't your fault, that it's the fault of the booze or the narcotics, then you're whipped. You're tossing in the gloves without a fight, which is bullshit.[31]

Thus, in his roles as boxing referee and judge, Lane saw close parallels: "In both instances I am an arbiter, a mediator between right and wrong." His reputation with the general public continued to grow as he became a highly respected jurist, recognized for his equitable application of the law and his fair sentencing; no longer was the bulldog reputation of "Maximum Mills" that he had deservedly earned as a prosecutor deemed appropriate by those who closely followed the Reno justice system.

It was a curious combination, the distinguished jurist and the third man in the ring prying apart two hulking heavyweights intent upon doing their opponent serious bodily harm. When he entered the ring, he also felt that he was serving a noble cause of protecting the (oft-criticized) integrity of the sport. He viewed his role as referee as comparable to presiding over a capital murder case: "I am as comfortable standing between two brawling prizefighters as I am on the judicial bench," he said. In an interview with the *Oakland Tribune* in 1993, he said, "As a judge I don't favor either party. As a ref you don't favor either party." The image of impartiality was also important: "Don't get close to the promoters, don't get close to the fighters, and do the best job you can." In 1993 *Ring* magazine, recognized as the "bible of boxing," named him the "world's best referee."[32]

Lane's ascendancy as a referee fortuitously occurred simultaneously with the emergence of Las Vegas as a popular location for championship fights. Following his successful handling of the Holmes-Norton fight, other choice assignments readily followed. In 1979 he handled two championship fights in Las Vegas, and prestigious assignments continued to roll in. He became widely recognized—indeed a national celebrity—as the seemingly ubiquitous third man in the ring, the short, trim man with the bald head and high, squeaky voice now recognized for his patented prefight instructions to the boxers of "Let's get it on!"

He would make the one-hour flight from Reno to Las Vegas the day before the fight to conduct the required rules meetings, check into a hotel, and perhaps sit in on a casino poker game for a few hours as a means of relaxation. He became widely recognized by boxing fans around the world who appreciated his ability to enforce the rules while allowing the fighters to settle the match themselves. In 1986, in one of boxing's dramatic and historical eras, he counted Trevor Berbick out in the second round in the outdoor arena erected behind Caesars Palace and held aloft the glove of the new heavyweight champion, Mike Tyson. Thus, he was unknowingly present at the beginning of a new and, as it turned out, disastrous era for prizefighting.

In addition to working the fights of Iron Mike, he officiated those of such ring luminaries as Evander Holyfield, Thomas Hearns, Sugar Ray Leonard, Gerry Cooney, Ray Mancini, Héctor Camacho, Marvin Hagler, Leon Spinks, James "Bonecrusher" Smith, James "Buster" Douglas, George Foreman, Riddick Bowe, Michael Carbajal, Oscar De La Hoya, Lennox Lewis, and Pernell Whitaker. Boxing experts were amazed that he could handle large and powerful heavyweight fighters despite the fact that he weighed just 145 pounds. "He was respected by the fighters. When he told them to break [a clinch], they broke." Between 1978 and 1998, Lane made the trip to Las Vegas for seventy-four title fights, but he also traveled to other major American cities to ply his trade. Sometimes he could stay home and work a major bout, refereeing twelve championship bouts in Reno and six at Caesars Palace at State-line on the shores of Lake Tahoe. His last heavyweight championship fight was held on June 28, 1997, and proved to be the most memorable: he disqualified former champion Mike Tyson for twice biting the ears of Evander Holyfield. His decisive role in resolving that fiasco greatly enhanced his status as a national celebrity, and it even led to major changes in his long-term career planning.

He traveled to Detroit to referee his last fight in November 1998, counting out Jay Snyder, who was flattened by forty-year-old former light-heavyweight champion Thomas Hearns in the first round. By that time his life had been changed dramatically. As he wrote to an acquaintance in Wisconsin, "When Mike Tyson bit Evander Holyfield my life went crazy."[33] Overnight, he became a national celebrity, and the Monday after he disqualified Tyson, his judicial office was swamped by calls from national media companies seeking interviews. He accepted an invitation to appear on *The Tonight Show with Jay Leno* and had to sift through a raft of speaking invitations to determine which ones to accept. Random House sent an advance for his autobiography that had previously received rejection notices, and then came the difficult decision, whether to accept a lucrative offer from a television production company to star in his own reality court show or to serve out the four years remaining on his second term as a district judge.

Such lucrative opportunities do not come to many individuals, no matter how successful they have been in their lives. He opted to start a new career and resigned his seat on the bench, which disappointed some Nevadans, but the great majority of residents supported his decision. His popularity, if anything, increased. Before departing for New York City to launch the tapings of his television show, he accepted a position as senior partner in the new Reno law firm of Lane, Fahrendorf, Viloria, and Oliphant. He also incorporated a new boxing promotions firm, the Let's Get It On Corporation, that he intended would eventually improve the dubious culture of professional boxing by promoting fights that treated the fighters fairly. At some distant point, he planned to turn over the firm to his teenage sons, Terry and Tommy.

The producers of his television show hoped it would displace *Judge Judy* in the national ratings. He initially attracted a substantial daytime audience as he dispensed justice in his inimical way, mixing wry comments with sometimes cutting observations—"Millsisms," his producers called them—as the parties who had agreed to air their differences over minor legal squabbles before a national television audience presented their cases. He soon found himself at home before the television cameras, but like several other television judges, he was unable to catch *Judge Judy* in the all-important ratings game. *Judge Mills Lane* lasted three years before being canceled.

Lane returned to Reno and his new law firm. But in March 2002, his seeming magical lifestyle ended suddenly, and with crushing finality. He was alone in his home in a secluded Reno neighborhood when a massive stroke left him paralyzed, unable to speak, unable to move. His wife, Kaye, was out of town, and his two boys were away at college. He lay stricken in an upstairs hallway for an indeterminable time, probably in excess of twenty-four hours, before Kaye became alarmed upon being unable to reach him by telephone and sent friends to check. Ironically, Lane had maintained excellent physical condition throughout his lifetime. He still weighed the same 145 pounds that was his fighting weight in the marines. Even after becoming a television celebrity, he had continued his vigorous exercise routine that including running three miles several days a week and, for old time's sake, punching a bag that hung in his basement. During his television taping stints in New York City, he became a familiar sight to early risers as he briskly ran along the near-deserted midtown streets as the sun was just beginning to cast its first rays of light upon the Big Apple. At the relatively young age of sixty-five, Lane's very public life was sidelined. He seldom appeared again in public and was cared for and protected by his devoted wife and sons. An endless quest to find a cure led to many clinics and physicians, but all proved futile.[34] In 2006 he made a rare public appearance in downtown Reno for the dedication ceremony of an ultramodern new county courthouse, the Mills B. Lane Center for Justice, and in 2013 he was inducted into the International Boxing Hall of Fame.

Round 7

Las Vegas
Embraces Prizefighting

This is the biggest thing we've ever had. We've had some big
New Year's here, but I think this fight will do five-fold of those
weekends. —Harry Wald, Caesars Palace executive,
on eve of Ali-Holmes fight, October 2, 1980

Following the epic 1910 confrontation between Jim Jeffries and Jack
Johnson, Nevada lost its ability to attract major prizefights. With legalization occurring in several states, the epicenter of prizefighting moved
eastward, leaving Nevada boxing fans with only occasional lackluster
fight cards featuring local novices or down-and-out itinerant fighters looking for a small payday. New York City emerged as the center
of American boxing during the 1920s and maintained its dominance
for the next three decades, but during the 1960s Las Vegas began to
attract major fights as part of its rapidly expanding gaming economy.

New York developed an integrated boxing subculture. It was home
to several training gyms, essential incubators for new pugilistic talent, in particular the famous Stillman's Gym on Fifty-Seventh Street
that opened in 1910. It was there, in a nondescript building, that generations of boxers, from novices to champions, trained in a large room
in which the windows were nailed shut and cigar smoke blended with
the fragrance of liniment and yesterday's sweat. Management actually
took pride in the fact that the floors were seldom cleaned. Gene Tunney refused to train there because of what he considered "unsanitary
conditions."[1] Over the years, spectators paid a modest fee to watch such
famous ringmen as Jack Dempsey, Georges Carpentier, Primo Carnera,
Joe Louis, and Rocky Marciano prepare for their big fights alongside

rank beginners. New York City was also home to the men who exerted great influence over the sport: promoters, trainers, gamblers, sportswriters, and mobsters.

New York was where Tex Rickard relocated after having made Nevada his home for more than a decade. By the time of his death at age fifty-nine in 1929 from complications following an appendectomy, Rickard had become a celebrity in the Big Apple, where he presided over the new iteration of the Madison Square Garden. He promoted all sorts of events to draw a crowd, including circuses, track meets, and bicycle races, but he refused to have anything to do with professional wrestling. Always a boxing man, he was proud of the weekly boxing cards that drew large crowds. The professional hockey team he created to compete in the National Hockey League in 1926 was an instant success, and sportswriters provided the team nickname of Tex's "Rangers." He outdid himself as a fight promoter when he put on the second Dempsey-Tunney fight on September 22, 1927, in Chicago's Soldier Field. An estimated 145,000 jammed the football stadium, producing the first two-million-dollar gate in history.

Rickard would have been delighted that boxing remained popular in New York City throughout the 1930s. Championship fights were held with predictable regularity. The enormously popular Joe Louis fought many of his major fights at Madison Square Garden, or outside at the Polo Grounds and Yankee Stadium. National radio networks carried live blow-by-blow accounts of his fights that generated enormous listening audiences. The crisp, unique voice of Clem McCarthy became familiar across the United States as he described the ebb and flow of championship matches. On the evening of June 22, 1938, an estimated 100 million Americans, including President Franklin D. Roosevelt, hovered by their radios listening to McCarthy describing that magic moment when Joe Louis avenged an earlier loss by knocking out Max Schmeling in the first round at Yankee Stadium.

In 1939 NBC began its popular radio broadcasts of Friday-night fights from New York, with Don Dunphy providing rapid-fire descriptions of the main event from ringside at Madison Square Garden or at the converted aging ice rink up on Columbus Avenue, St. Nicholas Arena. During his long career, the popular Dunphy broadcast an estimated two thousand bouts. Those weekly broadcasts were labeled the *Gillette Cavalcade of Sports* and sponsored by the Gillette Safety Razor

Company, touting its distinct "blue blades." These popular broadcasts firmly established New York City as boxing's capital in the minds of American sports fans. The city was the media capital of the nation and at the end of the Second World War seamlessly made the transition from radio to television.[2]

Television and the New Boxing Culture

Following the Second World War, boxing returned with a flourish that some fans have considered boxing's "golden era." Between 1946 and 1960, many of the greatest names in boxing made their careers largely in the city: Sugar Ray Robinson, Jake LaMotta, Rocky Marciano, "Jersey Joe" Walcott, Kid Gavilán, Carmen Basilio, and Willie Pep. Largely hidden from public view, however, was the infighting going on behind the scenes, as the fight game was taken over by individuals beholden to kingpins of New York's organized crime families. This was the time when Joe Louis came to the end of his ten-year reign as heavyweight champion; his decline was a sad spectacle that nonetheless fascinated the American people. Although his skills had diminished during the four years he served in the army, the Brown Bomber successfully defended his heavyweight title against Billy Conn on June 9, 1946, in a much-anticipated rematch resulting from Conn's near defeat of the champion on June 8, 1941. The venue once more was the infield of Yankee Stadium, where the ring was engulfed by a crowd of 45,000 that produced a two-million-dollar gate for promoter Mike Jacobs. The match attracted an enormous radio audience, but this time it also was televised to a small number of taverns in the city and select NBC locations on the East Coast. This early sports telecast, little noticed at the time, was a harbinger of boxing's future. The face of prizefighting was about to change forever, as the first generation of twelve-inch black-and-white television screens invaded living rooms across American.[3] In 1948 Gillette moved its *Friday Night Fights* from radio to NBC-TV, where it would become the longest-running sports show during television's early years until it was canceled in 1960.

By 1952 prizefights were carried each week on all three major television networks, reaching five million American homes, a figure that doubled by 1956. Most Americans had never seen a boxing match in person, but because of television, overnight millions of men and women became enthusiastic fans. The brightly lit, compact square "ring" made for excellent viewing during television's formative years when the technology was primitive and picture quality often of dubious quality. In 1954 Arthur Daley of the *New York Times* wrote, "The ring is small enough to always be in focus. The contestants are the absolute minimum of two. It's the ideal arrangement because every seat in front of a video screen is a ringside seat. The price is perfect—free."⁴ Soon television stations in major cities began hosting their own fights (as well as wrestling exhibitions) in their studios to supplement network fare. The cumulative effect resulted in an oversaturation of the market, which inevitably produced within a few years a steady decline in public interest. Sharply lower viewer ratings led advertisers and television executives to look elsewhere for programming. In 1951 one-third of the nation's television sets were tuned to the Friday-night fights; by 1960 that figure had declined to less than 10 percent. In 1960 NBC pulled the plug on its once-popular Friday-night programming, and other networks soon followed. Boxing would find a new home on closed-circuit productions for major fights and, during the 1980s, on cable networks.

Television executives and commercial sponsors liked the numbers generated during the early 1950s. Production costs were low, and ratings remained high for several years. For example, the Rocky Marciano–Jersey Joe Walcott fight in 1953 captured 69 percent of viewers, and the welterweight championship fight between champion Kid Gavilán and the charismatic young challenger Chuck Davey attracted 68 percent. Gavilán crushed the overmatched Davey, who spent a week in the hospital recovering from a brutal ten-round beating administered by the ring-wise Cuban. Davey was a graduate of Michigan State, and his blond hair and stylish left-handed style made him a favorite with the unsophisticated television audience. His stunning demise served as a metaphor for the ways that television adversely influenced prizefighting. At a technical level, television had a crippling impact upon the traditional structure of professional boxing. Sluggers, rather than skilled boxers, were popular with viewers, and therefore by advertisers seeking high ratings. As Randy Roberts and James Olson have written, television "failed to capture much of the nuance and subtle violence of the sport," because it was not capable of conveying to viewers "the thin, red trickle of blood and the red and blue color of a pummeled body . . . nor could television capture the force of a stiff jab or cross." Few viewers in the television audience, they point out, had ever "sat at ringside and witnessed the power and awesome brutality of professional boxing. . . . Consequently, their demand for frantic action was greater than that of an experienced fight fan."[5]

With fights readily available on network television, attendance plummeted at fight cards staged in cities large and small. These club fights had been a staple of the fight game ever since the 1920s. It was in these venues that promising fighters honed their skills and prepared for their opportunity to become a mainliner in New York City. Fans now opted to watch prominent boxers on television rather than pay to see lesser-known fighters in local arenas. Television advertisers demanded high-profile fighters to produce acceptable ratings, but that meant that those with even a few losses were no longer acceptable; in the pretelevision era, professional fighters spent years working their way up the ladder, which often included several defeats, as they learned the nuances of their profession. Joe Louis, for example, fought 46 times as a professional before getting a shot at the heavyweight title, and one of the all-time great light-heavyweights, Archie Moore, fought 170 professional bouts before having the opportunity for a title fight. After the advent of television, a boxer who had lost a main event, especially on television, was damaged goods to advertisers and promoters.

As a result of the impact of television, nearly half of the urban boxing clubs and training gyms closed during the 1950s. By 1960 the number of cities that hosted fight cards had fallen from three hundred to just fifty. These developments essentially cut off the pipeline of new fighters, creating a new environment in which the splashy championship fight carried over network or closed-circuit television took center stage. The overall impact was that the foundation of the boxing culture—its traditional pipeline of training gyms and club fight cards that produced major talent—was severely impacted.

A Matter of Integrity

Television was not the only factor that contributed to a restructuring of the fight game during the 1950s. Shortly after the war, the newly formed International Boxing Club (IBC) of New York, a powerful operation headed by two multimillionaires originally from Chicago, Arthur Wirtz and James D. Norris, effectively consolidated its domination of the sport. The two men had previously gained control of the six-team National Hockey League through their ownership of the Chicago Blackhawks and the Detroit Red Wings and the arenas in which they played. They also controlled 40 percent of the stock of the New York Rangers through their positions on the governing board of Madison Square Garden. Norris and Wirtz had major investments in a wide array of businesses, ranging from agricultural commodities, motion picture theaters, arenas, and radio stations to thoroughbred racehorses, real estate, banks, and liquor distribution. As a major stockholder in Madison Square Garden, Norris gained control of the promotion of fights and was able to control the careers of fighters by determining whom they would fight and when. He was cozy with influential gambling interests and powerful organized crime moguls. In 1947, when Joe Louis first announced his retirement, the rights to promote a series of fights to determine the new champion passed from Madison Square Garden's general manager, Mike Jacobs, to Norris and the IBC.[6]

With Wirtz staying in the background, Norris became the public face of professional boxing throughout the 1950s, facilitating his control of the sport in close association with organized crime figures. Norris especially worked closely with the notorious John Paul "Frankie" Carbo, a feared underworld figure who shunned the spotlight, but sported a lengthy arrest record. As an up-and-coming hoodlum during the Prohibition era, Carbo was widely believed to have been a hit man for the infamous "Murder, Inc." During the 1930s Carbo was arrested seventeen times and charged with larceny, robbery, conspiracy, and five murders. Conviction, however, was elusive for federal prosecutors. Potential witnesses tended to commit suicide, accidentally fall from hotel windows, or suffer acute amnesia on the eve of trials. During the 1940s Carbo moved into the New York boxing scene, becoming the unofficial "czar of boxing." He controlled many of the leading fighters, especially welterweights and middleweights, through his connections with prominent gamblers, promoters, and managers. He also became a close associate of key members of the New York State Athletic Commission. Carbo and his associates were later exposed for fixing prizefights, including infamously forcing the popular middleweight Jake LaMotta to throw a fight against a nonentity, Billy Fox, in return for a promise for a later opportunity for a title fight, a goal that Carbo had repeatedly denied him.

Carbo's power was on display before the antiracketeering hearings conducted by US senator Estes Kefauver in 1950, when more than a dozen key witnesses maintained a "code of silence" regarding Carbo's behind-the-scenes control of the New York fight scene. During most of the 1950s, Norris and Carbo had forged, in the words of boxing historian Randy Roberts, "a classic monopoly" over the sport that now reeked of corruption and Mob control.[7] In 1957, after a five-year inquiry, the Securities and Exchange Commission ordered Norris to disband the IBC, which had become a widely recognized corrupting influence on the always-suspect fight game. The IBC was stripped of its power and influence, but by this time boxing in New York was suffering from an acute negative image. In 1958 Carbo was sentenced to two years at Rikers Island for managing boxers without a license and the following year was indicted for extortion and conspiracy. In 1961 Attorney General Robert Kennedy involved himself in the prosecution of this high-profile case that resulted in Carbo being sentenced to twenty-five years in federal prison and incarceration on Alcatraz Island.

The convergence of the impact of television and public revelations of widespread corruption contributed to the decline of New York's dominance of boxing. The Friday-night fights disappeared, and New York sports fans, many of them seasoned gamblers, turned their attention to professional football and basketball, where the Giants and Jets, along with the Knicks, complemented the always-popular baseball Yankees to provide New Yorkers year-round sporting excitement—and gambling opportunities. Boxing's decline in New York City was swift, if not spectacular.

These developments provided an opportunity for the state of Nevada to reassert itself in prizefighting. The Silver State would again become a place where prizefighting flourished. This time, however, it was the rapidly growing city of Las Vegas and not Reno that dominated the action. Prizefighting, with all of the attendant hype and glitz that only Las Vegas could provide, would thrive once more in the Nevada desert, where gambling was legal and entertainment had become the state's primary business.

Establishing a New Boxing Tradition

Traditions often begin in small and inauspicious ways. So it was with the establishment of Las Vegas as the boxing capital of the world. In 1955 Las Vegas was a rapidly growing city struggling to come to grips with its new gaming economy. Now home to about fifty thousand residents—the 1940 census had reported fewer than ten thousand— the image of the emerging metropolis in the desert seemed caught between its cowboy past and metropolitan future. Although the city had been home to several small gambling operations after legalization in 1931, the new order began the day after Christmas in 1946, when transplanted New York City mobster Benjamin "Bugsy" Siegel opened the trend-setting Flamingo Hotel and Casino. The low-slung structure was located south of the city limits on the two-lane highway that led toward Los Angeles. It was an open secret that eastern crime syndicates financed the six-million-dollar adult playground. In the next few years, the Thunderbird, Desert Inn, Sahara, and Sands were constructed along what was now being called the Las Vegas Strip. In 1955 the Dunes and Riviera opened, as Nevada's new industry began to pick up steam, and the new era was fully embraced with the opening of Caesars Palace in 1966.

Siegel's arrival, and subsequent gangland-style murder on June 20, 1947, when he was gunned down in Hollywood, signaled the beginning of a steady influx of gang members from around the country to the only state in the Union where gambling was legal. Investigative reporter-historians Sally Denton and Roger Morris have correctly concluded that this immigration turned Las Vegas into a city "largely operated by and for organized crime" that was part of a much larger conspiracy to enable "criminal forces and their collaborators in business to magnify their investment and control far beyond the Strip."[8] With local banks unable to lend the sums necessary to build the large hotel-casino complexes that began to sprout up along Las Vegas Boulevard South, beyond the city limits, large loans were funneled from the Teamsters' Central States Pension Fund by Allen Dorfman, who himself dealt with allegations of close ties to the Chicago Mob. He died in 1983 in a gangland-type execution in suburban Chicago, shortly before he was prepared to turn state's evidence in a high-profile federal trial. By the mid-1950s, the emissaries of powerful organized crime families—from Miami, New York, Chicago, Detroit, Kansas City, and elsewhere—had firmly gained control of gaming operations and used them to launder vast sums of drug money while they simultaneously engaged in sophisticated skimming operations to avoid taxes. The notorious Meyer Lansky, who was connected to crime organizations across the country, never obtained a gaming license, but he had his hand in the operations of most Las Vegas casinos. The entrepreneurs who were constructing Nevada's gaming industry had names that resonated with law enforcement agencies: Siegel, Moe Dalitz, Frank "Lefty" Rosenthal, Moe Sedway, Johnny Roselli, Gus Greenbaum, and Tony "the Ant" Spilotro, among others.

Even Ross Miller, the father of future and highly respected governor of Nevada Bob Miller, was a former small-time Chicago gambler with ties to the Mob. The elder Miller arrived in Las Vegas in 1955 and became a pit boss at the Desert Inn, eventually rising to become the general manager with an equity holding.[9] In November 1950 infiltration of the Mob became the focus of five days of hearings by the US Senate Committee on Organized Crime. Under the chairmanship of Estes Kefauver, the committee exposed the truth that leading Nevadans already knew but studiously avoided: Nevada's burgeoning new economy was grounded upon the money and power being funneled into the city by the most powerful of the nation's crime families. It was no coincidence that prizefighting found a new home in Las Vegas, given its long association with crime bosses back east.[10]

By this time the presence and influence of organized crime figures had become the elephant in the room for concerned Nevadans. Everyone knew of the growing influence of shadowy figures who arrived with questionable reputations from across the nation to assume prominent roles in the casinos, but no one wanted to publicly discuss the issue. Many national newspaper and magazine articles alluded to this fact, however, and in 1963 Nevadans were stunned by a blunt and forceful book by investigative reporters Ed Reid and Ovid Demaris, detailing the extent of the penetration of organized crime families into Nevada's casino industry. *The Green Felt Jungle* would abruptly lift the veil of silence that Nevadans had attempted to maintain.[11]

In 1955 Governor Charles Russell urged the state legislature to respond to revelations revealing that out-of-state crime syndicates effectively controlled most hotel-casinos. The state was still facing negative publicity from five days of sensational testimony in Las Vegas before the US Senate Committee on Organized Crime in 1950. Governor Russell convinced legislators that a major overhaul of the lax licensing and oversight of Nevada's flourishing new industry was essential. Although libertarians opposed Russell's plan to create a three-member board that would have far-reaching power over the licensing and operation of casinos, the legislature overwhelmingly passed the legislation. It was, in fact, an act of self-preservation on the part of state lawmakers. The governor and the legislature acted in order to prevent the very real possibility of a federal takeover of casino regulation. Moving with unusual haste, the state's political establishment acted boldly to retain control of Nevada's promising future.[12]

In that same pivotal year of 1955, with little fanfare, another significant development occurred that would portend the return of big-time prizefighting to the Silver State. On Monday, May 2, Jack "Doc" Kearns promoted a fifteen-round prizefight in Las Vegas between an aging Archie Moore and Niño Valdés, a promising newcomer from Cuba. The winner was promised a shot at the heavyweight title held by Rocky Marciano. It would be the 170th professional fight for the popular thirty-eight-year-old Moore, but it was also the first major prizefight in the city's history. *Las Vegas Sun* publisher Hank Greenspun enthusiastically proclaimed that the fight would be "the greatest event for the town since the government started using the area for atom bomb tests." Kearns, now seventy-two, had been around the fight game for much of his life. He was a onetime popular West Coast fighter who later became famous as Jack Dempsey's manager. Kearns was determined to demonstrate that Las Vegas could become home to major prizefights, just as had been the case for Reno, Carson City, and Goldfield a half century earlier.[13]

During the 1920s and '30s, an occasional low-profile fight card had been sponsored by the Las Vegas American Legion. In one 1936 bout, welterweight Ernie Duarte knocked out Domingo Lopez, who never regained consciousness and died seventeen days later after being transported by train to a Los Angeles hospital. That somber event tended to put a damper upon boxing in Clark County for years afterward. Las Vegas prizefighting had long suffered from a lack of good bouts and general ineptitude on the part of local promoters. As sports entrepreneur and boxing aficionado Arne Lang writes, between the 1920s and 1960, the most consistent aspect about prizefighting in Las Vegas was that many announced fights were never held and those that occurred often disappointed the small number of fans who purchased tickets. Befitting the sunny optimism endemic with fight promoters, Kearns predicted that 14,000 fans would fill the minor league baseball park

Cashman Field. This lofty prediction prompted local sportswriters to scoff because they had been stung too often by the unfulfilled promises of promoters. After Kearns announced the fight, writers suggested that a crowd of 7,000 was more likely . . . if the fight actually took place.

Kearns scheduled the fight for a Monday evening, hoping that some of the fans in town for the Tournament of Champions golf tournament being staged at the recently opened golf course at the Desert Inn would stick around to attend. The Desert Inn management had audaciously put up $37,500 prize money, which was the second-largest purse in golfing history. The purse was ostentatiously displayed in the hotel lobby in the form of a closely guarded wheelbarrow overflowing with silver dollars. The large purse had attracted such leading professionals as Sam Snead, Doug Ford, Billy Maxwell, and Julius Boros. Gene Littler won the tournament and pocketed the first-place money of $10,000. Kearns also hoped to attract some of the several thousand curiosity seekers and military personnel who were in town to observe an aboveground atomic bomb test at Yucca Flat, some eighty miles to the north in the Nevada desert. The blast was scheduled, weather permitting, sometime the same week.

Kearns managed to raise $100,000 from the casino operators so that he could guarantee the fight. "The casinos are going right down the line with us," he enthused to the press. This subsidy created a template for the future, in which hotel-casinos would put up crucial front money in hopes of luring big spenders to their properties with the lure of a major prizefight. Kearns offered ringside seats at $30 with distant bleacher seats priced at $5. Kearns knew that he was wading into treacherous waters because he had attempted to promote a fight in Las Vegas three years previously between Joey Maxim and Moore, but could not raise the required $150,000 guarantee and ended up moving the fight to St. Louis. As he made the rounds soliciting pledges this time, he told reporters, "This is Las Vegas's first, last, and only chance to become the sports capital of the world."[14] Kearns's prediction of a gate of 14,000 proved hopelessly optimistic; pictures of the fight revealed vast stretches of empty seats. One photograph captured the changing image of Las Vegas from a small western town into an internationally famous urban icon: a cluster of cowboys, with their ten-gallon hats and tight-fitting blue jeans, intently watching the battle from the cheap seats.

It was an inauspicious beginning for the opening of a new era of Las

Vegas prizefighting. Kearns drew plenty of guffaws when he announced the crowd at 10,800. Reporters were probably much closer to the actual paid attendance when they estimated the crowd at half that number. Not surprisingly, the fight was conducted on a more or less ad hoc basis. Kearns openly defied the rules of the Nevada Athletic Commission that the bout be scored by two judges and the referee. Kearns had never liked the use of judges and announced that the referee alone would judge the fight, although he agreed to employ the commission's system of ten points per round. The fight itself was not much of a crowd pleaser, but it provided sufficient action to keep the spectators' attention. In the early rounds, Valdés opened up cuts on Moore's face, but the Cuban received a series of blows that obscured his vision (Moore apparently hit Valdés with three left-hand shots above the eye when Valdés was temporarily blinded by rays from the setting sun). The fight seemed about even until the final three rounds, when Moore took control. Valdés, barely able to see through swelling around both eyes (his right eye was the "size of a hen's egg," the *Las Vegas Review-Journal* reported), managed to hold on until the final bell. The referee, former heavyweight champion Jim Braddock, apparently found the official point scoring system too complicated to fathom and simply awarded the fight to Moore, eight rounds to five, with two even.[15] Three days later, just before dawn, the skies north of Las Vegas were brightly illuminated with bright green and orange flares as thousands of cheering men and women sipped early-morning cocktails and watched an enormous mushroom-shaped cloud rise above distant Yucca Flat while the ground beneath their feet trembled.

The following September in Yankee Stadium, Moore, having earned his shot at the heavyweight crown, was decked four times by Rocky Marciano before being knocked out in the ninth round. At age thirty-nine, he would lose a second title fight in November 1956 to new champion Floyd Patterson. The promoters never considered holding either fight in Las Vegas.

Disappointed with the small crowd, Kearns ended his career as a Las Vegas promoter, and no one seemed willing to fill the void. It would be five years before professional boxing returned. Las Vegas hosted its first title fight in the spiffy new Convention Center on May 27, 1960, when Benny "the Kid" Paret won a fifteen-round decision over Don Jordan to claim the welterweight crown. The crowd, however, was announced at a disappointing 4,805. Promoter Tom Brenner of New York, however, was nonetheless pleased because more than 1 million fans watched the fight on NBC Television, and the network was pleased because it did not have to black out New York City.

Sometime in the early 1950s, St. Louis native Johnny Tocco arrived to see a fight and stayed until he died in 1997. A boxing lifer, the tough-nosed Tocco opened Ringside Gym just south of downtown Las Vegas at the corner of Main and West Charleston. It became a mecca for anyone associated with the fight game when they came to Las Vegas, and over the years many of the headliners who attracted enormous crowds on the Strip trained at Ringside. Sonny Liston, Michael Dokes, the Spinks brothers, Larry Holmes, and Marvin Hagler, among other notables, were seen there working out, sometimes beside a teenage neophyte attempting to learn the basics of the sweet science. The place was reminiscent of Stillman's Gym in New York City and many of the hole-in-the-wall training gyms in American cities that were essential to the fight game during its heyday. It was never air-conditioned, and the irascible Tocco reportedly had the windows nailed shut. Its ambience was of last year's sweat and yesterday's cigar smoke, with a touch of liniment. Tocco was a fount of knowledge about boxing lore as well as conversant with the current rumors. Tocco's Ringside Gym was the place to visit if you were a serious boxing aficionado. He sold the gym shortly before his death at age eighty-seven, and it has remained open under a series of owners, each of whom has maintained the ambience for which it was famous. Johnny Tocco and his Ringside Gym, in a real sense, were as much a part of Las Vegas boxing as were the championship blockbusters held a few miles away on the Strip.[16]

The first star boxing attraction in Las Vegas was middleweight champion Gene Fullmer, who attracted large crowds of supporters from his native Utah. Fullmer had captured the title in 1957 in an upset of Sugar Ray Robinson, but five months later was knocked out in a rematch. He recaptured the title in 1959 in a decision over Carmen Basilio and successfully defended his title at the Convention Center in 1961 with a decision over aging Sugar Ray. Reporters duly noted that the audience, dominated by enthusiastic Utah fans, provided the champion with a pronounced "home field advantage." The following year, once more in the friendly confines of the Convention Center, Fullmer successfully defended his title by knocking out Benny Paret in the tenth round. The following year Paret would absorb a frightful beating in Madison Square Garden at the hands of Emile Griffith; after being knocked out in the twelfth round, he became comatose and died shortly thereafter.

Boxing in a Neon Oasis

The idea of Las Vegas becoming the location for major prizefights struck boxing traditionalists on the East Coast as either absurd or at least an extreme oddity. On the eve of the city hosting its first heavyweight championship fight in July 1963, sportswriters from the East poured into the city as wide-eyed as any first-time tourist. Typical of these seasoned journalists was senior columnist for the *New York Times* Arthur Daley, who was visiting Las Vegas for the first time. A native New Yorker, Daley joined the *Times* in 1926 after graduating from Fordham University and established himself covering the city's sports beat. He began writing his popular column in 1942 and was the first sportswriter to win a Pulitzer Prize, in 1956. "This sinful city" left him both bemused and confused: "Las Vegas has to be seen to be believed," he wrote on the eve of the rematch between Floyd Patterson and Sonny Liston. "Even then it defies belief. Not since those ancient days when men fought on barges in the Mississippi River has there been a stranger site for a boxing extravaganza." After a couple of days touring the sights, the New York native remained unenthusiastic: "Las Vegas is a neon oasis dropped in the middle of the desert. The sun beats down with a pitiless intensity day after day, and the temperature wings over the 100 mark with appalling regularity." As for the fight itself, Daley compared the former champion with the "suckers" who jammed the casinos in which "the clang of slot machines is the only background music" to be heard. The decidedly underdog Patterson, he wrote, seemed like the tourists who "stream in here with greed and money, and depart with both dissipated."

Daley noted that the fans assembled in town for the fight were hoping against hope that Patterson would find a way to upset the brooding, unpopular Liston. Like those who flooded the casino floors, Daley observed, "Most of the experts here are doing considerable wishful thinking themselves. The majority will be rooting for Patterson, yet when a guy stays in this gambling capital long enough, he develops a profound respect for the percentages. And the percentages dictate

Liston. That's why Sonny will have to be the reluctant choice of this observer." Daley's prediction proved correct. The next evening, a crowd of seventy-eight hundred filled the Rotunda at the Convention Center, producing a gate of three hundred thousand dollars, and saw Liston bludgeon Patterson to the canvas three times in the first round in what was considered a devastating display of power by a seemingly invincible champion.

Daley might have been unimpressed with Las Vegas as a place for a serious prizefight, but the casino managers were giddy with excitement as they contemplated holding future fights as a means of attracting flush clientele to their establishments. Ticket sales for the Patterson-Liston mismatch were the largest in Nevada history since the epic 1910 battle between Jim Jeffries and Jack Johnson. The great majority of those who filled the hundred-dollar ringside seats had been flown in from distant cities by the casinos—many of them beneficiaries of "comps" provided by their hosts. They got to witness a mere 130 seconds of one-sided action before a seemingly petrified Patterson was counted out. As it was, Patterson lasted four seconds longer in this rematch with Liston than he had ten months previously in Chicago. One reporter said that Liston "simply bullied and battered Patterson into the canvas like a street-corner tough smacking down a dreamy schoolboy."[17] Liston may have been the winner that evening, but the real winners were the casinos when the fight fans jammed the tables.

By the late 1960s, the fight cards at the Convention Center had established Las Vegas as an important venue for prizefights, its steady rise paralleling the sport's decline in New York. Managers of the major hotel-casinos had yet to figure out how to fully capitalize upon the potential of hosting a major championship fight by hosting the events on their own premises, but they were willing to contribute to the coffers of promoters seeking guaranteed money for an upcoming fight. By 1970 Las Vegas had hosted several championship fights as well as other high-profile bouts, most of which were carried across the United States by one of the commercial television networks or, as increasingly became the case, on a closed-circuit television feed to theaters across the country. These events occurred with increasing frequency, creating the impression that Las Vegas was a place where visiting fight fans had many other options for exciting action beyond the prizefight itself.

Two of those early title bouts were for the heavyweight championship.

The first was definitely not a memorable moment in the history of prizefighting, but it got the attention of Las Vegas's hotel-casino executives. It took place in the Convention Center on July 22, 1963. The fact that Liston, an ex-con who had been convicted of a felony in Missouri for armed robbery and assault, was licensed for a championship fight by the Nevada Athletic Commission symbolized the transition taking place within the hierarchy of boxing. Although onetime czar of the fight game James D. Norris had been stripped of his once near-monopolistic International Boxing Commission by the federal courts, he was determined to maintain his influence indirectly. Through associates Frank "Blinky" Palermo and Frankie Carbo, he became a silent partner in a new company, Inter-Continental Promotions, Inc. Although Carbo and Palermo were behind federal prison walls, they nonetheless controlled Liston through the shady personage of Jack Nilon, who became Liston's de facto manager. Behind the scenes, however, the ailing Norris and friends still called the shots. These widespread allegations of the Mob's control of Liston did not deter the commission, which by now was fully attuned to the economic advantages of sanctioning major fights in Las Vegas.[18]

The crowd resoundingly booed Liston as he left the ring after demolishing Patterson's title hopes, some fans apparently protesting his grisly public image as a violent ex-con, others irritated that they did not get to see much of a fight for their money. But the many attractions at the major hotels seemed to mollify out-of-town visitors, who happily bet large sums at the green-felt tables. Most important, however, was that the buzz surrounding the fight made for great newspaper copy and created an excitement that locals and visitors would come to expect from a major Las Vegas prizefight.

In this instance, however, considerable media attention was focused upon Liston's sullen, often angry behavior that he exhibited toward patrons and employees at the Thunderbird, where he trained. Word of his churlish behavior spread like a prairie wildfire across the small city, and a great majority of the spectators who paid their way into the Convention Center were hoping for an improbable Patterson upset. Liston's surly demeanor alienated nearly everyone who came in contact with him at the Thunderbird. Robert H. Boyle of *Sports Illustrated* devoted more of his coverage of the fight to Liston's criminal past rather than the fight itself, highlighting Liston's association with such Mob figures as Carbo and Palermo. He described Liston's boorish behavior in Las Vegas hotels and restaurants: "He has carried into his public life the bullying and cockiness that he uses to intimidate opponents in the ring." The angry, unsmiling champion even irritated African Americans who worked in the Thunderbird. A busboy caustically told Boyle, "Sonny Liston is just too mean to be allowed around decent people. They ought to ship him back to Africa. No, make that Mississippi!" A bellhop, who had encountered Liston upon several occasions, told Boyle: "He's mean. Why? Because he's just mean."[19]

The Greeter at Caesars

The impact of a big fight impressed casino and hotel managers, who noticed a large uptick in revenues during the days surrounding a major fight. One of the more observant casino executives in this regard was Irving "Ash" Resnick, who had begun a colorful casino-management career at the Thunderbird shortly after he was discharged from the army in 1946. His initial title at the Thunderbird was officially "director of sports," but in reality he kept an eye on the counting room for his New York City associates. The Genovese organized crime family had allegedly sent him to Las Vegas to look after their investments. Resnick was known as an associate of notorious Mob figures Meyer Lansky and "Fat Tony" Salerno. He was widely regarded as a pioneer casino executive who figured out how to lure high rollers as well as everyday grinders to the Thunderbird by organizing complimentary bus trips from California and chartered flights from the Midwest and East Coast. Resnick got in on the ground floor of Caesars Palace when it opened in 1966 and spent much of the rest of his career there as a senior member of its management team. At Caesars Resnick was known as the "boss of the casino," although he officially held the title of vice president of gaming operations.[20]

Resnick had long been close to the fight game. He became a close confidant to the retired Joe Louis, who now lived much of the time in Las Vegas. Resnick provided Louis with a public relations position known as "greeter." Louis did what came naturally, chatting amiably with guests, answering time and again the same questions about his major fights. He was a regular at the craps table, where he lost heavily, but he was playing with house money. His presence was bound to generate a crowd. According to Resnick, he and Louis went back a long way, having first met by coincidence when they found themselves standing together in line in early 1942 to take their preinduction army physical exams.[21]

By the time Louis hired on at Caesars Palace, he had become a familiar face about town, living with wife, Martha, an attorney whom he married in 1958. They lived in a condominium just off the Strip. Res-nick paid Louis $50,000 a year and provided the condominium. He made certain the former champion could play all the golf he wanted and provided the house money for him to lose at the tables. The position at Caesars enabled Louis to live out his remaining years with dignity because he was hopelessly in debt to the Internal Revenue Service. In 1957 the IRS claimed Louis owed back taxes amounting to $1,243,097. After years of negotiations between his lawyers and the IRS, an unofficial settlement was reached when the IRS quietly acknowledged that Louis would never be able to pay his back taxes and tacitly agreed to back off its relentless crusade demanding payment. Because the IRS would not forgive the debt, however, the interest compounded, and Louis officially owed the US government an estimated $2 million when he died in 1981. Louis's friends viewed the IRS position as mean-spirited and wrongheaded. They pointed to the fact that Louis donated two title defense purses in 1941 to military relief organizations and spent four of his prime fighting years in the army. As a spokesman encouraging the purchase of war bonds, the Brown Bomber had been, they pointed out, one of the military's most effective spokesmen on behalf of the war effort.[22]

By the mid-1970s, Louis's public appearances at Caesars became less frequent. Martha confided to friends that he had become severely paranoid, repeatedly expressing fear that "they" were coming to kidnap him. At one point he even called the White House in an attempt to persuade President Richard Nixon to order the FBI to protect him. On other occasions he tore hotel rooms apart in an attempt to find the source of poisonous gases he believed were seeping into the room. He began sleeping in his street clothes so that he could flee unknown assailants at a moment's notice. He often seemed sluggish, probably the result of the impact of the medications prescribed by physicians intended to deal with his hallucinations. Until 1977, when his heart began to fail, Louis put in his time shaking hands, playing blackjack, and shooting craps at Caesars. He suffered a stroke following heart surgery, and doctors inserted a pacemaker. He needed a wheelchair to get around.

Louis was still a familiar figure at ringside for major fights. On April 11, 1981, he was loudly cheered by the crowd at the outdoor Sports Pavilion before the heavyweight title fight between Trevor Berbick and Larry Holmes. The next morning Louis died from a heart attack at the age of sixty-six. A memorial service was conducted in the same ring before an assemblage of three thousand fans and boxing personalities along with a cluster of celebrities that included Frank Sinatra and Sammy Davis Jr. The audience heard a stirring memorial by the Reverend Jesse Jackson, who praised Louis as a man who had gone from "Alabama sharecropper to champion." Jackson concluded his upbeat message by urging the crowd to stand and cheer the former champion one more time as his casket was removed from the ring. He was later buried with military honors in Arlington National Cemetery. One of the silent donors who helped pay his funeral expenses was German business executive Max Schmeling. In the decades that followed his death, a seven-foot marble statue of Louis stood guard outside Caesars' sports book. It has ever since been a popular spot for visitors to have their pictures taken beside the marble likeness of the great champ.[23]

The Big Fight Night

Joe Louis added a celebrity presence to the steadily expanding Las Vegas prizefight culture. During the 1980s the era of the big fight arrived. In addition to a steady diet of prizefights that occurred on almost a weekly basis, between 1970 and the present, Las Vegas was home to more than two hundred championship fights. Although the endless parade of champions and challengers temporarily captured the headlines, the real stars of Nevada's prizefight culture were the thousands of fans who poured into the city for a long weekend in anticipation of enjoying the varied pleasures and amenities to be found in the city of a million lights. Although most fight venues accommodated upwards of fifteen thousand, with ringside seats selling as high as two thousand dollars, a big-name fight would draw visitors in far greater numbers than could actually attend the event. "There was nothing like a big fight to generate a level of excitement and anticipation that is simply difficult to describe," recalls sportswriter John Trent, who wrote for the *Las Vegas Review-Journal* during the 1980s. "There simply was nothing like a big championship fight." With boxing in decline in New York City, it was relatively easy for Las Vegas, even with its organized crime connections of the 1970s and early 1980s, to become the new capital of American prizefighting. The city offered big-name entertainment, a wide range of restaurants and bars, and, especially, legal sports gambling books located within the casinos. It was an ideal package that attracted those who loved the excitement of a big fight.[24]

The Nevada Athletic Commission kept the crime bosses at bay and enforced rules and regulations that established a reputation for honesty and propriety that benefited a sport that had long labored under a dark cloud of suspicion. Casino managers knew that many of the high rollers who streamed into town would bring upwards of a million dollars with them that they would happily bet at the tables, where they would be, for the moment, the center of attention. The atmosphere of a big fight blended perfectly with the gambling and partying for which Las Vegas had long been famous. A big fight produced brief periods of bonanzas for the casinos, restaurants, bars, strip joints, escort services, and other purveyors of Vegas-style amenities.

As the day of a big fight approached, restaurants and bars geared up for anticipated overflow crowds, with bartenders and food servers anticipating the influx of big tippers. Showrooms touted big-name performers and were sold out days in advance, and rooms at the hotels all along the Strip and in downtown Las Vegas were booked solid at premium rates. Pit bosses scheduled full crews to handle the crowds that jammed casino floors. Sports-book managers sharpened their pencils to set the most attractive betting line, eagerly anticipating the influx of those willing to bet the house limit on the fight. Pimps and their stable of prostitutes made plans for long working hours, knowing that fight crowds included a bounty of eager customers. Law enforcement and private security agencies went on high alert to handle the anticipated increase in public drunkenness; undercover officers prowled the streets and hotels seeking to deter pickpockets and burglars. The entire city seemed to take on an even greater sense of excitement and vibrancy during the few days before and during the fight. Sportswriter Tim Dahlberg got it right when he wrote, "There was something special about the odd confluence of gambling, boxing, and partying that was beginning to take place on a regular basis in a town just starting to flex its muscles." Las Vegas became "the only place for a big fight . . . [because] a Vegas fight was like no other."[25]

A Superstar Among Superstars: Muhammad Ali

One person, above all, provided the spark needed to enable Las Vegas to become recognized as the new capital of boxing. During a professional career that spanned two decades, Muhammad Ali fought in Las Vegas just eight times, but his electric personality had the ability to turn a prizefight into a red-letter event. Las Vegas had long become accustomed to the presence of megastars on the stages of its oversize showrooms. But no media celebrity, not even such superstars as Frank Sinatra or Dean Martin or Barbra Streisand, could generate the same level of excitement as Muhammad Ali. He trained at either the Stardust or Caesars Palace, and his afternoon training sessions were the hottest ticket in town. Although many of his most famous championship battles occurred elsewhere—New York, Zaire, Manila—it was in Las Vegas that his star seemed to shine the brightest.

Ali's Las Vegas narrative began inauspiciously enough when he still was known as Cassius Clay. He won a less than impressive ten-round decision over the tall and lanky Hawaiian (six-foot-six, 200 pounds) Kolu "Duke" Sabedong, on June 26, 1961. Clay was just nineteen, only a few months away from having won the Gold Medal as a light heavyweight at the Rome Olympics. This was his seventh professional fight and his first scheduled for ten rounds. The *Las Vegas Review-Journal* enthused that Clay was "the most promising and refreshing young heavyweight to come along since Joe Louis" and said his fancy footwork equaled the "finesse of Fred Astaire." His handlers were in the process of systematically developing him as a professional, and the experienced Sabedong was a logical next step; the Hawaiian had become a main-event attraction on the West Coast in a career that began in 1954 and sported a modest 15-11 record, and he had lasted several rounds with Zora Folley before being knocked out. A slender crowd of twenty-five hundred turned out to witness a fight that proved an important learning experience for the young professional. Although he took several solid punches from the Hawaiian, Clay dominated the action and won a lopsided decision. When Sabedong died at the age of seventy-eight, his obituary in Honolulu newspapers duly noted that he had won a round from the future champion. In his Las Vegas debut, Clay impressed his trainer, Angelo Dundee, who told the press, "The kid can go 10 rounds and can take a punch to the chin and the midsection."[26]

In his postfight press conference, for the first time, Clay proclaimed himself "the Greatest." He likely picked up that gimmick, as he later told Thomas Hauser, when he appeared with the consummate self-promoter Gorgeous George on a Las Vegas radio interview prior to his Sabedong fight. After listening to the wrestler in long blond curls praise himself and witnessing a sold-out crowd at the Convention Center cheering and jeering the perfumed grappler, Ali concluded, "That's when I decided I'd never be shy about talking [about myself]; there was no telling how much money people would pay to see me."[27] A few months later, young Clay began adding simplistic poetry to his prefight routine by predicting the round in which he would knock out an opponent in a simple four-line rhyme. Sometimes he was correct, as in 1963 when he fought an aging Archie Moore in Los Angeles: "Don't block the aisle and don't block the door / You will all go home after round four." Sure enough, he knocked Moore down three times in the promised round in an impressive performance. He later expanded his prefight hype by saying outrageous things about his opponent, calling Sonny Liston an "ugly bear" and a "chump." Later, in an unfortunate descent into crude racial stereotyping, he referred to Joe Frazier as a "monkey" and an "Uncle Tom." In these prefight charades, which became part of his Las Vegas mystique, Clay was merely drawing upon a rich oral tradition that had thrived in urban black neighborhoods in which young males frequently exchanged rhythmic insults. Although his act initially attracted favorable attention from journalists, it soon grew old, but not in Las Vegas. "Maybe I'm old fashioned," one veteran reporter groused prior to Clay's first fight with Sonny Liston, "but I always thought a fighter had to prove himself with his fists, not with his mouth."[28]

In Las Vegas, however, Clay's juvenile act was accepted as merely part of the Vegas hype . . . part of the show. On July 22, 1963, having won a series of fights over increasingly better opponents, the undefeated Clay returned to Las Vegas to watch champion Sonny Liston defend his title against Floyd Patterson. He sat at ringside in the Convention Center and loudly ridiculed Liston, despite his impressive first-round victory. Immediately after Patterson was counted out, Clay jumped into the ring and pretended to chase after Liston, as if to challenge him right then and there to a fight. While Clay garnered plenty of attention for himself, few experts gave him any hope of defeating the ruthless Liston when their title fight was announced for Miami in February 1964. Some observers thought he was a little nutty, if not downright unhinged.[29]

That 1963 evening in Las Vegas, however, Liston had dispatched Patterson in ruthless fashion in the city's first heavyweight championship bout, further enhancing his image of cold-blooded invincibility. No one seemed to disagree when he said that he would destroy Cassius Clay just as easily as he had Patterson. Liston snarled, "Clay can't lick a Popsicle. All he knows is how to fight with that big mouth." Even Cus D'Amato, Patterson's veteran manager, suggested that Liston was the equal to Joe Louis in his prime, and it became commonplace for so-called experts to suggest that Clay actually risked possible death if he entered the ring with Liston. *Las Vegas Review-Journal* sports editor Ron Amos agreed, concluding a column with the observation that "Clay must be terrified under his cocky shell," because Liston seemed a "giant, terrifying indestructible man." A beat writer for the *Review-Journal* was even more decisive in his analysis: "Clay is the next man up to be knocked down" and predicted that "after Liston knocks out the loudmouth Clay, there won't be many contenders left, which might result in a ten year moratorium on heavyweight title fights."[30]

Although boxing commissions in New York, California, and Pennsylvania refused to approve the Liston-Clay fight, reportedly because of Liston's association with Mob figures, the athletic commissions in Nevada, New Jersey, and Florida announced they would grant a license. Florida won the bidding contest with $625,000 for promotional rights. Clay, of course, won that fight when Liston failed to come out for the seventh round, claiming a mysterious injury to his shoulder. The only evidence of Liston having received punishment was a modest mouse under one eye; although Liston was no match for Clay's quickness and was losing on points, he seemed in no immediate physical danger. Rumors of a "fix" swept the boxing world, but an investigation by the Florida attorney general and hearings by a US Senate committee found no evidence to support the allegations.[31]

Las Vegas's second heavyweight championship bout proved to be a memorable one. After Ali defeated Liston in Lewiston, Maine, on

May 25, 1965, with what many believed to be a "phantom punch," he turned his attention to former champion Floyd Patterson, who was demanding a shot at the new champion. On the evening of November 22, 1965, a capacity crowd of seventy-eight hundred was on hand at the Convention Center, the great majority hoping for a Patterson victory. The fight attracted considerable attention because of the political and religious issues that now surrounded the champion, who had taken the name of Muhammad Ali and declared himself a Black Muslim in the days after the first Liston fight.

Patterson was on a mission to reclaim the title. His public criticism of the champion placed the fight into a contentious religious context. Like most members of the crowd who had lustily booed Ali when he entered the ring, Patterson had been angered by Ali's public embrace of the teachings of the Nation of Islam. A devoted Catholic, Patterson refused to use the name Muhammad Ali, continuing to refer to the champion as "Cassius Clay." In an oft-quoted comment, he said, "I have nothing but contempt for the Black Muslims and that for which they stand. The image of a Black Muslim as the world heavyweight champion disgraces the sport and the nation. Cassius Clay must be beaten and the Black Muslim scourge removed from boxing." Patterson framed the fight as a symbolic battle between the Crescent and the Cross: Clay (or Ali) was "disgracing himself and the Negro race."[32]

Having been the recipient of unrelenting criticism for his embrace of the Black Muslims, Ali was not in a good mood when he entered the ring to a loud chorus of boos and catcalls. He was determined not only to win, but to make Patterson pay a steep price for his comments. The sellout crowd at the Convention Center watched in dismay as Ali humiliated Patterson with his taunts, as he banged away with impunity at the brave but outclassed former champion whose mobility and punching power had been diminished by a back injury suffered during training. Those sitting near ringside cringed as Ali peppered Patterson at will with a wide assortment of punches, all the while maintaining an angry and disparaging commentary. Many at ringside believed the champion toyed with Patterson for most of the fight so that he could inflict the most punishment possible. *Life* called the mismatch "a sickening spectacle," but having witnessed Ali's speed and technique, most fans also had to agree reluctantly that perhaps Ali was, as he liked to proclaim, "the Greatest."[33]

On that rainy November evening in Las Vegas, as Ali put on his impressive performance before a national television audience, Las Vegas became firmly identified in the sporting world as a place where important prizefights took place. One of its special advantages over such traditional boxing cities as New York City was its comparatively small population of 170,000. Television ratings (and advertising rates) would not be adversely affected by a local television blackout, as in New York City or other major metropolitan centers. Emanuel Steward, a veteran trainer of major fighters, first visited Las Vegas in 1964 with a group of AAU boxers and recognized the symbolic importance of a boxer becoming a headliner in Las Vegas: "It's the heart of boxing," he said in 1979. "New York is a big city, but Las Vegas is the big city of boxing."[34]

It was seven years before Ali again fought in Las Vegas. In the interim he had become the center of a raging national controversy over the Vietnam War when he refused induction into the army in 1967, famously explaining, "I ain't got no quarrel with them Viet Congs." He was sentenced to five years in federal prison for his stand based upon his religious faith, but Ali's lawyers somehow managed to prevent him from going to prison, despite a wave of anti-Ali sentiment that swept across the country. The Nevada Athletic Commission, joining in the denunciation, stripped away his title, and other state commissions quickly followed. His passport was seized so he could not fight abroad. For nearly four years, he was unable to pursue his professional career at the time he was at the height of his physical powers. In 1971 the US Supreme Court (apparently having observed a seismic change in public opinion regarding the war) reversed Ali's conviction with a tortured interpretation based upon an obscure legal technicality. He resumed his boxing career that year, losing a classic fight in an effort to reclaim the heavyweight title from Joe Frazier in New York City on March 8, 1971. This first of three epic battles with Frazier is considered one of the greatest fights of all time. Ali returned to Las Vegas to defeat Jerry Quarry on June 27, 1972, and after knocking out Bob Foster in November at Stateline, Nevada, on the shores of Lake Tahoe, he returned to the Convention Center, where he won a unanimous decision over Joe Bugner on February 14, 1973.

Ali regained his World Boxing Council title on October 30, 1974, in Zaire (now the Democratic Republic of the Congo) that the new promoter Don King hyped to closed-circuit television viewers as the "Rumble in the Jungle." Against George Foreman Ali unveiled his unique strategy of "rope-a-dope" by permitting Foreman to flail away at him while backed against the ropes as he covered up and deflected most of the hundreds of blows thrown his way. The "rope-a-dope" lured Foreman into exhausting himself in the hot and steamy outdoor arena, setting him up for an eighth-round knockout. Highlighting Ali's comeback were his two defeats of Joe Frazier in New York City in January 1973 and on October 1, 1975, in Manila. The third and final bout between the two warriors resulted in Ali winning a TKO when Frazier did not come out for the fifteenth round. In what Don King billed as the "Thrilla in Manila," both men displayed incredible courage, as they absorbed almost indescribable punishment. Ali had successfully defended his title in Manila, but it took him weeks to recover. This time Ali did not engage in his usual hyperbole, later admitting, "It was the toughest fight I've seen in my life. It was the closest I've come to death." The Boxing Writers Association appropriately declared both men its Boxer of the Year for 1975.[35]

By 1978, when Ali returned to Las Vegas at the age of thirty-six to defend his title against a young and inexperienced Leon Spinks, he had clearly lost some of the dazzling speed that had characterized his early career. But his box-office appeal remained high. He appeared overweight and not in top condition. Astute observers took note of his lackluster training sessions and attributed it to the fact that he did not take Spinks seriously. Ali apparently believed he was in for a big payday against an inferior opponent. The inexperienced Spinks had an unremarkable 6-0-1 record since winning the light-heavyweight Gold Medal at the 1976 Olympics; few experts believed he belonged in the same ring with the champion. Spinks and his entourage kept quiet the fact that ten days before the fight, he suffered a severe muscle pull in his rib cage that made use of his right hand extremely painful. A crowd of just 5,000 turned out at the Las Vegas Hilton to watch the fight on February 15. They were not treated to a spectacular bout. Spinks fought through intense pain every time he threw a right hand, and Ali was sluggish as a result of his lackluster training effort. Ali's early strategy of employing the "rope-a-dope" did not tire the young and energized (if unpolished) challenger, and by the time Ali launched a late offensive flurry, the fight had been lost. One judge gave the fight to Ali by a narrow score, but most observers believed that the other judge and referee had handed down a fair decision. This was the only instance in which Ali actually lost the heavyweight crown in the ring.[36]

Ali regained his title from Spinks in a unanimous decision in September in New Orleans and thereupon announced his retirement. But like many athletes well past their prime, he could not resist one last moment in the spotlight. After nearly two years of inactivity, and much to the dismay of friends and experts but to the delight of Las Vegas hotel and casino managers, he agreed to challenge Larry Holmes, who would be defending his title for the eighth time since defeating Ken Norton two years previously in the new indoor Pavilion at Caesars Palace. True to form, Ali loudly predicted that he would defeat the heavily favored Holmes and capture the heavyweight title for a fourth time. The fight was scheduled for an enormous new outdoor arena erected on the parking lot behind Caesars Palace, and on the evening of October 2, 1980, 24,570 spectators paid top money to see what promoter Don King was hyping in his usual over-the-top manner, calling the fight "the Last Hurrah" in anticipation that this would be Ali's last title bout. It was estimated that Caesars expended five million dollars to build the arena and to fly in hundreds of high rollers and comp them with suites, meals, tickets, and other amenities.[37]

King knew that Ali's return to the ring would virtually guarantee him an enormous profit. And indeed it did, with ringside tickets going for a record five hundred dollars and the distant seats high above the ring at fifty dollars. King knew closed-circuit television revenues would generate much more than the six million dollars he raked in at the gate. Much of the prefight hype revolved around whether Ali would be able to regain his form after shedding 35 pounds off a body that he had permitted to balloon up to a blubbery 256 pounds. In Holmes he faced a former sparring partner, and so he repeatedly told the media that he had taught Holmes "everything he knows, but not all that I know." As Ali put it in one of his less elegant prefight ditties, "Holmes's behind will be mine in nine."

That was pure bluster, and Ali knew it, as did his longtime trainer, Angelo Dundee, who had watched Ali being unable to fend off his sparring partners. In the weeks leading up to the fight, Ali was perpetually fatigued, unable to run his usual four miles each morning. Dr. Ferdie Pacheco, who had served as Ali's physician and cornerman since 1962, had recognized Ali's declining physical condition in 1977 following his near loss to Earnie Shavers. In a letter he wrote to Ali and his advisers, Pacheco urged him to retire, but was rebuffed. Unwilling to be associated with exposing Ali to serious injury, Pacheco left the Ali camp. As the fight with Holmes approached, Pacheco issued a public statement, urging the fight be canceled: "Ali should not attempt to come back. At his age, with the wear and tear he's had as a fighter, there's no way for him to escape the attrition his body has undergone. All the organs that have been abused will have to work harder. His heart, lungs, kidneys, liver. Even Muhammad Ali is human and subject to the laws of nature." Dr. Pacheco's voice was one of many that were raised questioning the propriety of the Nevada Athletic Commission's authorizing the fight. Others noted that Ali's words were occasionally slurred, his voice noticeably quieter, his speech patterns markedly slowed. In response, the Nevada Athletic Commission decided to require Ali to undergo a medical examination at the Mayo Clinic in Minnesota. He complied and apparently received a routine physical examination, not one administered by physicians experienced in the world of professional boxing.[38]

Having received a report signed by several Mayo Clinic physicians that confirmed Ali was in normal physical condition, the commission licensed the fight. Much later Dr. Pacheco suggested that the NAC had erred grievously by not requiring Ali to be examined by physicians experienced in boxing. "Just because a man can pass a physical examination doesn't mean he should be fighting in a prize ring. . . . Anybody in the gym can see it before the doctors can, because doctors, good doctors, are judging these fighters by the standards of ordinary people and the demands of ordinary jobs, and you can't do that because these are professional fighters." On the eve of the fight, Pacheco unleashed a powerful statement, contending that Ali could be "damaged for life." He asked rhetorically, "Have you ever heard of a fighter hit so often that his brain develops tiny hemorrhages that can render him squishy for life?" He continued his impassioned critique: "This fight is insane. The only way Ali can win is if Holmes drops from a diabetic coma or the fight is fixed. Holmes can only beat himself. Ali has not trained well for the fight."[39]

Ali and his handlers should have listened to Pacheco, but they all had bought into an unfounded faith that Ali could pull off one more comeback. That miracle did not happen. From the first bell, Holmes dominated his aging (within a few months of his thirty-ninth birthday) opponent, scoring with sharp jabs and then, near the end of the round, a powerful left uppercut to the temple and sharp right to the face. The tempo for the fight was firmly established, and at the bell Ali slumped onto his stool and said to himself, "Oh God, I still have 14 rounds to go, and I have nothing. Nothing." As the rounds went by, Ali was forced to defend himself from the relentless onslaught while abandoning any effort at launched a counterattack; he seemed unable to connect with his own feeble punches. In round 3, the *Las Vegas Review-Journal* reported, he did not even throw a single punch, as he sought only to avoid Holmes's onslaught. With the crowd continuing its support with the resounding cry of "Ali! Ali! Ali!" he rushed out for round 7 and fired off a flurry of jabs at Holmes. Of the eighteen jabs that he threw, only one landed. For the remainder of the fight, he did not score a single meaningful punch. After the ninth round, referee Richard Green contemplated stopping the fight. Ali was now absorbing a ferocious pounding but somehow managed to stay on his feet. In the tenth round, Holmes scored on a series of sharp jabs followed by a powerful hook to the kidneys and a flurry of punches thrown so fast that they defied description. Ali's fans had grown silent, and some began calling for the fight to be stopped. Somehow, Ali never went down, but after the bell trainer Angelo Dundee informed Green that the fight was over. Green later said that had Dundee not stopped the massacre, he would have. In the postfight analysis, reporters calculated that Ali had landed on average one or two punches per round, while Holmes connected with forty per round. Ali, the *Review-Journal* sardonically concluded, was "nothing more than a catcher of blows."[40]

Ali was so badly hurt that one of his aides requested a limousine to transport him the few hundred yards back to his suite in the hotel. Holmes, who had always admired his childhood hero, went to Ali's suite later that evening and asked the man he deeply admired, "You OK champ? I didn't want to hurt you." "Then why did you?" Ali responded with a smile that he forced through his battered face. Holmes told reporters that he felt "no joy" but only "sadness" for what he had done to Ali. Even the typically unsentimental Don King later admitted that although he reveled in an enormously profitable night, "It really broke my heart. Even I had to shed a few tears at the end." The *Las Vegas*

Review-Journal reported that while Ali had predicted he would work a "miracle" by defeating Holmes, the "only miracle was that Ali was not seriously hurt."[41]

It was later revealed that Ali entered the ring a seriously debilitated man. A *Sports Illustrated* writer, after observing Ali during training, predicted that he would be "in better physical and mental condition than at any time since he battled George Foreman. His face is slim and firm. So is his body. It's as if he turned the clock back to 1971, when he was twenty-nine." But the writer had been fooled by Ali's rapid loss of weight. Ali had aged, and his body's strength and resilience had been depleted by more than twenty years of amateur and professional fighting. Worse, he had been misdiagnosed and subjected to dangerous medications by a physician recommended by manager Herbert Muhammad. Three weeks before the fight, Dr. Charles Williams diagnosed Ali with a hypothyroid condition and put him on a heavy dosage of Thyrolar, a powerful medication that speeds up the body's metabolism and slows the normal cooling functions. The drug had the effect of reducing his strength, making him extremely vulnerable in the ring. His longtime publicist, Gene Kilroy, became worried during training sessions that Ali was suffering from dehydration and general lethargy: "He couldn't run; he was losing weight like mad. And the closer the fight the worse it got." In less than three months, Ali had shed thirty-five pounds, but despite his fit appearance, he was essentially a lamb being prepared for the slaughter.[42]

These revelations came to light after the fight, and they raised serious questions about the judgment of the Nevada Athletic Commission in permitting the fight to take place. It was easy, of course, to second-guess the decision after the fact, but at the time there was no compelling evidence to justify not issuing a license. The Las Vegas business community anticipated a huge influx of high rollers, and the NAC recognized that fans everywhere wanted this fight to take place. The commission had in hand a medical report from physicians at the famed Mayo Clinic stating that, although some slurring of his words was evident, Ali was in good physical condition. The Mayo Clinic examination had included a neurological examination that did not reveal any discernible damage to the brain. The report concluded, "There is no specific finding that would prohibit him from engaging in further prize fights." The commission had no way of knowing that in the weeks immediately prior to the fight that Ali was taking Thyrolar, a drug Dr. Pacheco said was the equivalent of Ali playing Russian roulette.[43]

These ethical issues, however, were far from the concerns of pro- moter Don King, the executives at Caesars Palace, and the managers of hotels and casinos on and off the Strip. The fight produced the most lucrative weekend in Las Vegas history up to that point. The casinos were overflowing with gamblers, and reporters noted lines of several persons deep patiently waiting their turn at the high-stakes blackjack and craps tables. These "high rollers" were individuals, according to casino executive Harry Wald, "who like to gamble and have the means to do so. . . . We have 3,500 people [registered in the hotel]. It's not just the number of people, it's the caliber." Many were flown in by the casino for the fight from all parts of the United States, but also South America, Asia, and Europe. In the baccarat room all tables were busy with gamblers betting the eight-thousand-dollar limit on each hand. All across Las Vegas, the constant clanging of slot machines produced a cacophony that brought joy to the hearts of casino managers.[44]

Fight Night had arrived in the City That Never Sleeps.

Round 8

Las Vegas,
"Boxing Capital of the World"

Every one of my big fights was in Las Vegas. I loved it there.
—Sugar Ray Leonard

The high rollers were there. Oh, the little rollers were there too,
but they were watching the high rollers smoke their foot-long
cigars, show off their big, sun-tanned bellies and their dollies at
poolside. —Paul Peters, *Las Vegas Sun,*
on the Gerry Cooney–Larry Holmes fight
at Caesars Palace, June 12, 1982

Between 1960 and 2010, Las Vegas was the site of more than two hundred championship fights. Although these contests attracted sizable crowds and served the underlying purpose of creating high demand for hotels, restaurants, and other Las Vegas amenities, they also increased significantly the action at the sports books and on the casino floors. These fifty years spanned an era that was marked by major changes in American race relations and state and national law. The substantial entry of black fighters into American boxing during the 1940s and '50s anticipated and accelerated the civil rights movement that would crest during the 1960s. The in-migration of Hispanics to the American Southwest and California that intensified in the 1970s and continues to the present time contributed to the sharp increase in Hispanic fighters—especially fighters of Mexican heritage—who became prominent in Las Vegas during the 1980s and thereafter.

Two promoters, as different in style and temperament as possible, provided the catalyst for making Las Vegas the capital of prizefighting.

Operating in a mass media–dominated marketplace, Bob Arum and Don King followed the same template that Tex Rickard had established nearly a century earlier, seamlessly melding the inflated hype of their promotions into an age of cable television and digital technology. Like Rickard, they also responded to, and sometimes manipulated, racial and ethnic stereotypes. As such, they were important catalysts, encouraging changes in both the racial and ethnic composition of prizefighters and the audiences who watched their matches. Although both men worked with boxers from all racial and ethnic backgrounds, King tended to concentrate his attention upon black fighters. In so doing he benefited from, and contributed to, the growing attention being paid in the sports world to the civil rights movement. By the 1980s, when most of King's stable of boxers were black, a new generation of affluent African Americans—including some of the leading figures in the entertainment industry—became prominent among the wave of high rollers who flocked to Las Vegas for big fights. They patronized high-end nightclubs and resorts, and they were seated prominently at ringside. Unlike King, Bob Arum's stable of boxers included many Hispanic boxers, and their appearance in main events and championship fights, beginning in the 1980s, reflected the growing Hispanic population in the United States. This diversity at the fights had not occurred during the 1960s, when Las Vegas remained predominantly an attraction for affluent whites. Until 1960, in fact, the casinos steadfastly maintained racial policies that excluded blacks from registering at hotels, eating in hotel restaurants, and gambling at the tables.

Both Arum and King were supercompetitive and became contentious rivals, happily loathing one another. For more than three decades, they sought to outmaneuver the other, but upon a few notable occasions managed to sublimate their animosity to join forces for a mutually rewarding promotion. Born just four months apart in 1931, they came from sharply different backgrounds.

Bob Arum was raised in an Orthodox Jewish family in the Crown Heights section of Brooklyn and, after graduating from New York University cum laude, earned a JD degree at the Harvard School of Law. He worked for a time as a tax attorney on Wall Street and in the New York City district attorney's office before joining the US Department of Justice. In 1966 he promoted his first fight in which Muhammad Ali obliterated Cleveland Williams before thirty-six thousand fans in the

Houston Astrodome. In 1973 Arum formed Top Rank Boxing, built it into a multimillion-dollar powerhouse, and in the early 1980s moved its headquarters to Las Vegas.[1]

Arum's major competitor was Don King, who grew up on the streets of Cleveland's east side. He was given to saying that he was a "summa cum laude graduate of the Ghetto," and journalist Budd Schulberg described him as "the prize student of the University of the Street who earned his Masters in Self-Promotion in the Ohio penitentiary." His was a life that included a career as a young numbers operator, killing two men, and serving four years for manslaughter. He received a full pardon from Ohio governor James Rhodes in 1983. Determined to stand out in any crowd, he wore colorful jackets, smoked expensive cigars, and applied gel to his hair so that it stood straight up as if he had just stuck his finger in an electric socket. His penchant for mangling the English language became legendary. His malapropisms were part of the flamboyant public persona he carefully cultivated, but however muddled his words might be, they were always crystal clear as to their intent and meaning.[2]

When he left the Ohio Correctional Institution at Marion in 1971, King was forty years of age and claimed he had never attended a boxing match. Personal connections led to his promoting a boxing exhibition featuring Muhammad Ali to benefit a Cleveland hospital in 1973; the following year he audaciously pulled off the improbable promotion of the "Rumble in the Jungle" in Zaire between Ali and George Foreman. He spoke the street language of urban blacks with fluency and as the first prominent black promoter was able to assemble a large stable of black boxers. By 1980 Don King Productions had become a competitor with Arum's Top Rank in the rapidly evolving boxing game at the time cable television networks and pay-per-view were gaining a foothold. King's ability to cut a sharp deal and insert murky language in legal documents became legendary. He was often sued by the fighters who had trusted him by signing binding long-term contracts. Such luminaries as Mike Tyson, Muhammad Ali, Larry Holmes, and Tim Witherspoon all filed legal actions alleging fraud or other nefarious schemes regarding their share of a fight's proceeds. An exasperated Holmes, who alleged that over his career King had managed to connive him out of millions, said at one point: "Don looks black, lives white, and thinks green. I was loyal to Don for ten years but he was never loyal to me. . . . After every fight he would say, here's ten dollars for you, here's twenty for me." Referring to Don's unique hairstyle, he jabbed: "When I see Don, I see the devil. The reason he wears his hair so funny is to hide the horns."[3]

By the early 1980s, King had signed most of the leading black fighters, especially heavyweights, to long-term contracts and had made himself incredibly wealthy by astute promotions that included maximizing the profit potential in pay-per-view television. King's many critics, and they became legion as the years passed, maintained that he had no compunction about ripping off those fighters he controlled. One of those many critics, journalist Jack Newfield, quotes King: "My philosophy is that all fighters are two-dollar whores. Never fall in love with your fighter. . . . Never let the fighter become bigger than the promoter."[4]

In his ultranegative account of what he calls "the life and crimes of Don King," Newfield concludes that, unlike Arum who created in Top Rank a highly sophisticated professional organization, King was a loner who never felt comfortable delegating authority to anyone. He was, Newfield claims, above all, a "con man."[5] This self-made man, who loved to exult, "Only in America!" when asked about his good fortune, was named by the *New York Times* as one of the top one hundred African Americans who helped shape the history of the United States during the twentieth century.

Arum and King routinely, seemingly instinctively, feuded with each other, looking for an extra cut of the take, sometimes seeking only to squeeze the other out of the limelight. Only late in their careers did they begin to reach a tacit cease-fire. That occurred much to the delight of cynical journalists when they jointly promoted a fight in Las Vegas at the MGM Grand Garden Arena in 2011 between two of their prizefighters. Arum's Miguel Cotto won a twelve-round TKO over King's Ricardo Mayorga. By this time, both men had made millions of dollars many times over and tacitly recognized that they had, in fact, benefited from the tough competition posed by the other. Although Arum and King walked in the path that Tex Rickard had established more than a half century earlier, neither man probably ever gave Rickard a moment's thought as they wheeled and dealed amid the glitter of the bright lights of Las Vegas.

The first fifteen years of the emerging prizefight culture in Las

Vegas (1960–75) was essentially a community-wide cooperative affair, with several hotel-casino properties contributing to financial packages to help put on a fight at the Convention Center. That began to change, however, on January 24, 1976, when King promoted a nontitle bout between heavyweights Ron Lyle and George Foreman at Caesars Palace. Individual casinos now began maneuvering to gain an advantage over their competitors by luring high rollers to their properties by hosting fights. In the first major prizefight held on the grounds of a Las Vegas casino, Lyle and Foremen met in a nondescript building erected behind the tennis courts. They put on a good show for several thousand fans (Foreman won on a fifth-round knockout), but most important the event filled the sprawling casino floor. Soon, several competing casino properties began to offer their own boxing attractions, although occasionally they sponsored matches at the Thomas and Mack Center on the University of Nevada, Las Vegas, campus, located just a couple blocks off the Strip. Throughout the 1980s, Caesars Palace was the leader in hosting fights, but during the 1990s its arena was torn down to make way for an elaborate pool and garden. The bulk of the action then moved south a few blocks to the MGM Grand and Mandalay Bay.[6]

Caesars established the new standard on October 2, 1980, when its management invested an estimated six million dollars to stage the much-ballyhooed comeback of the temporarily retired Muhammad Ali. His opponent was one of his former sparring partners, now undisputed champion, Larry Holmes. Caesars executive Cliff Perlman sensed a new era was at hand when he signed on with Don King to host the bout. A huge wooden arena—reprising the structures that Rickard erected in Goldfield and Reno—contained 24,570 seats and was located in the hotel parking lot. Officials announced that, with spacious standing-room sections located on the periphery, 29,210 spectators including those in the standing-room-only section had wedged their way into the place to witness Ali's last fight in Las Vegas. Caesars executive Harry Wald estimated that the wooden arena, which some nervous types feared would collapse under the load of the capacity crowd, cost an estimated $750,000. Additionally, several thousand freeloaders looked down from a closed freeway off-ramp west of the property, and untold thousands took in the one-sided Holmes victory in hotels and bars across the city via closed-circuit television. A huge American flag draped from atop a hotel tower put a patriotic touch on the event. One visitor from Detroit aptly summarized the sense of excitement surrounding the fight: "Nothing could be bigger than this fight. This is Ali! Maybe if God himself were fighting, then it would be bigger."[7]

The mark of a successful championship fight in Las Vegas was partially signaled by the number of celebrities who were on display in the high-priced $500 ringside seats. For Ali-Holmes the list was long and impressive and included such celebrities as Frank Sinatra and Jack Nicholson, along with an assemblage of major political figures. As far as the casinos were concerned, however, the real celebrities were the high rollers who poured into town from across the United States and four continents. These were individuals of considerable wealth who came expecting VIP attention from their casino host and, in return, were prepared to wager large sums at the tables. Their willingness to lose a million dollars or more during their stay was deemed a fair bargain in return for a passel of "comps"—air travel, luxurious hotel suite, gourmet dinners, ringside tickets. Caesars Palace executive Wald told the *New York Times* that these special guests were "people who like to gamble, and have the means to do it."[8] These high rollers, or "whales," as casino executives referred to them, were drawn to Las Vegas and a big fight as a moth is to a lighted candle. Wald estimated that the Ali-Holmes fight would bring $50 million to the city; all of the hotels were booked. When the executives at Caesars ran the numbers, they calculated that the cost of putting on the fight to harpoon their whales was well worth the investment. During the month of the fight, their "take" on the casino floor was reported at $30 million, more than two and a half times the norm for that time of the year.[9]

As the years rolled by, the purses claimed by the fighters (and their handlers) escalated to the point where Mike Tyson could command $30 million as his share of the purse for a single fight. For Oscar De La Hoya and other headliners in the early years of the twenty-first century, their paychecks would be substantially higher. Although ticket sales and the presence of high rollers on casino floors remained the primary objective, the promoters increasingly derived the bulk of their revenue from television. Cablevision offered customers the fight on its special pay-per-view, priced in the neighborhood of $50. Ticket prices to watch the bouts in person escalated. By the time of the first Mike Tyson–Evander Holyfield fight on November 9, 1996, at the MGM Grand, which had a seating capacity of 16,325 in its indoor venue, ticket prices began at $400 for the nosebleed section and increased to $1,500 for seats near the ring. It was estimated that Don King's promotion of that fight alone netted his company something in the neighborhood of a cool $100 million—$15 million for the live gate and an estimated $85 million from nearly 2 million subscribers who purchased pay-per-view to watch the bout in their homes.

Death in Las Vegas

The appeal of Las Vegas boxing was made apparent when even the "unfortunate" death of a boxer in the ring at Caesars Palace during a lightweight championship fight did nothing to deter public enthusiasm. The powerful appeal of two men in a ring seeking to wreak serious damage upon the other was evident on November 13, 1982, when 6,500 spectators in the new indoor arena at Caesars Palace and a national CBS-TV audience of several million looked on. The defending champion was Ray "Boom Boom" Mancini, a popular twenty-one-year-old from Youngstown, Ohio, who was following in his father's footsteps as a professional boxer. His father had become a leading welterweight contender, but wounds suffered during World War II had ended his chances of becoming champion. In May 1982 his son had fulfilled his father's dream by winning the World Boxing Association (WBA) lightweight championship when he knocked out Arturo Frias in the first round. On a Saturday afternoon in November, Mancini once more was in the same ring at Caesars, this time taking on an unknown but potentially serious challenger, the son of rice farmer from a South Korean village. Duk Koo Kim had risen to the ranking of number-one challenger, but he was unknown to American fans. He had never before been in the United States. When Arum announced the fight, many fans scoffed. Mancini, they said, was much the better man, but the young champion from Ohio knew he was in for a battle.

The fight more than lived up to the hype, as each man pounded his opponent with hundreds of blows. For thirteen rounds they repeatedly brought the fans to their feet, cheering as both men handed out and absorbed serious punishment. Almost incredulously, they kept coming back for more. Blood splattered across their faces, and dark purple and blue bruises blotched their faces and torsos. From the first round on, both fighters went for a knockout. This was a slugfest, not an exhibition of the finer points of the manly art of self-defense. In the third round a Kim right hand ripped Mancini's ear, and his seconds spent the rest of the evening seeking to stanch the flow of blood. In the eighth round the flesh around Mancini's right eye turned a frightfully discolored purple; by the end of the fight, the eye had swollen shut. In the eleventh round, Mancini began to turn the tide, as he buckled Kim's knees repeatedly. The champion's left hand had been seriously bruised, and by the end of the fight it had swollen to twice its normal size. "It was murderous," Mancini's manager, Dave Wolf, said after the fight. "It was like Ray was fighting a mirror. I hope the people who said Kim was nothing are impressed now."[10]

In the thirteenth round, Kim's courage was manifest, despite the exhaustion and dehydration that had sapped his strength and stamina. At one point, according to ringside record keepers, Mancini hit his opponent with forty-four consecutive punches without a blow being thrown in response. After a clinch Mancini rained another seventeen unanswered blows upon the young Korean. Kim's jaw bulged in a weird sort of way, and spectators feared it might be broken, but just before the bell he managed to recover and cut loose with a flurry of punches. After watching the Korean bravely hang on at the end of the round, the CBS announcer prophetically commented as the camera honed in on Kim while his seconds furiously attempted to revive their man: "This is the challenger, Duk Koo Kim. You may not have heard of him before. You will remember him today." A few moments into the fourteenth round, Mancini caught the exhausted Kim with two right hands to his unprotected chin. The brave Korean backed away from a glancing left hook, but did not see the next right hand that smashed into the side of his skull. He collapsed backward onto the canvas. Mancini quietly hoped he stayed down: "My left hand was killing me, and I felt that first right all the way up my arm." But Kim, improbably, did not stay down. He rolled over, looked at the timekeeper through dilated eyes, and stood up to face his opponent, but referee Richard Green took one look at Kim's unfocused stare and stopped the brutal fight.[11]

A few moments later, Kim collapsed. A stretcher was called, and he was carried from the ring. Kim "had been lifted out of obscurity on a stretcher," one reporter wrote.[12] He was managing only four breaths a minute as an ambulance rushed him to Desert Springs Hospital, where Dr. Lonnie Hammargren, a prominent Las Vegas neurosurgeon, awaited. Kim underwent a two-and-a-half-hour surgery, during which

Dr. Hammargren removed one hundred cubic centimeters of blood that had clotted on the right side of the brain. That was enough blood, he told a newsman, "to fill four shot glasses." Hammargren noted that the clot was of fresh blood, prompting him to conclude that it had resulted from one powerful blow. He absolved referee Green of negligence by stating that the blow had not been caused earlier in the fight, despite the terrible punishment Mancini had delivered. "They tell me he fought like a lion in the thirteenth round. Well, nobody could fight like that with a blood clot on his brain." The damage, however, was more than even a skilled neurosurgeon could repair. Hammargren told the press afterward that Kim was "very critical, probably terminal," and that he had suffered "terminal brain damage" due to extreme swelling. He had been placed on life support. "There is no sign of brain function. I expect the pressure in his head will go up and up and that will be it."[13]

The fact that several million Americans watched the fight on television naturally intensified public interest. Kim was kept on life support for four days so that his mother could fly to Las Vegas. Through her tears Sun-Yeo Yang spoke broken English, urging her comatose son to "open eyes." He did not, of course. Kim was taken off life support and soon thereafter pronounced dead. His mother returned home with his twenty-thousand-dollar guarantee, promising to give it to his pregnant girlfriend whom Kim had planned to marry when he returned home. The tragedy did not end there. Three months after returning to Korea, Kim's mother committed suicide by drinking a bottle of pesticide, and the next year referee Richard Green, who reportedly had become despondent despite the fact that he had been exonerated for the fight's outcome, committed suicide.

Mancini suffered from remorse, although his supporters told him that he was not to blame. In boxing, they said, such things sometimes happen. "I'm very saddened, very sorry it happened. It hurts badly to know you are a part of it," the downcast champion told the press the next day. Family members reported that he went through a period of depression, although he resolved to fight again. Mancini had received a quarter-million dollars for his day's work, but that large payday was small consolation. "Every time a fighter goes into the ring," he said, "he puts his life on the line. People always say, 'Give me $10 million and I'll get in there. That's a cheap price for a life.'" Mancini resumed his career, defending his title successfully three times before losing it in a violent bout in Buffalo against Livingstone Bramble. He lost by TKO after the fourteenth round and needed seventy-one stitches to close a gaping gash near an eye.[14]

Kim's death produced the usual wave of speculation that boxing might be legislated out of existence and calls for wide-sweeping reforms, but of course neither occurred. The WBA did announce that all future title bouts would be scheduled for a maximum of twelve rounds instead of fifteen, and various state boxing commissions dutifully announced more stringent medical testing before a fight. Newspapers reported that Kim's death was the 120th to occur in the United States since 1945, at least as best could be determined, because many ring-related deaths occurred in obscure places involving unknown boxers. *Ring* magazine weighed in with a story that its records indicated 439 men had died from injuries suffered in the ring since 1918. The Nevada Athletic Commission increased its medical-review process, limited championship bouts to twelve rounds, and mandated that a licensed physician be present at all sanctioned bouts. In addition, observers assigned by the commission would be present in the dressing room and corner of each main-event fighter. Its recommendation that the rest periods between rounds be increased from sixty to ninety seconds was not implemented. In 1919 the legislature had mandated by statute sixty-second breaks between rounds, and therefore new legislation would be necessary; the legislature did not act.[15]

For boxing fans, however, the appeal of the sport was not diminished. For some, it was theorized, Kim's high-profile death actually increased interest.[16] In reflecting upon the Mancini-Kim fight, journalist Fred Bruning ruminated that the typical fan "longs for an honest exchange in a world filled with deception."

> He craves the release that blood violence provides. He thrills to the raw courage on parade, to the sight of men better than himself settling the score in the way that scores were meant to be settled. Or he is among the enlightened. He appreciates the ballet, the drama, the exquisite timing, the lunge, the parry, the coup de grace. He admires the conditioning, the discipline, the determination. Or he is just somebody looking for excitement, a night out for a little harmless diversion. To him, the men in the ring are performers, vaudevillians hoofing across a roped-in stage, and he has paid the price of admission. He's entitled.[17]

The Four Horsemen

The death of Duk Koo Kim soon became old news. In the days and weeks following the tragedy, newspapers reported a spate of the usual lamentations from public officials to the effect that it was a shame, that Mancini was not to blame, that Kim had died a valorous death, that it was an unfortunate end to a great fight, that it was just one of those things, and so on. The American Medical Association (AMA), however, long silent on the subject of the dangers of boxing, issued a statement just two months after Kim's death, in which its journal editor Dr. George Lundberg argued that the sport should be made illegal because "the principal purpose of a boxing match is for one opponent to render the other injured, defenseless, incapacitated and unconscious." He even suggested, apparently for the sake of irony, that if boxing remained legal, then gun fighting should also be legalized! Boxing, he concluded, was "a throwback to uncivilized man [and] should not be sanctioned by any civilized society." In 1984 the AMA governing board officially went on record calling for the abolition of boxing. In Congress a series of hearings was conducted on the sport by the House Subcommittee on Commerce, Transportation, and Tourism that recommended legislation be passed establishing national standards to ensure that boxers did not enter the ring without proper medical clearance. That recommendation, which would have placed the federal government in a regulatory position superseding state commissions, never made it to the floor of the House of Representatives.[18]

In Las Vegas attention quickly shifted away from the death of Kim toward the nationally ranked UNLV Runnin' Rebels basketball team. Meanwhile, a steady parade of championship and high-profile fights continued. Attracting a substantial amount of the attention were four charismatic fighters—Thomas Hearns, Roberto Durán, Marvin Hagler, and Sugar Ray Leonard—who moved between the welterweight and middleweight classifications and became enmeshed in what seemed like a continuous round-robin of fights. Each man brought to the sport his own ring style, but the center of attention was the stylish Sugar Ray Leonard, whose handsome baby face, intelligence, and sunny personality made him a favorite of journalists and fans alike. Leonard had grown up near Washington, DC, and was thrust into the national spotlight when he captured the 1976 Gold Medal at the Montreal Olympics in the 140-pound division. He had a natural gift for working the media, and his winning smile made him a recognized television personality doing 7-UP commercials. He also packed a mean wallop and was occasionally referred to as "the baby-faced assassin."[19]

At the onset of his professional career, Leonard set himself apart from most fighters by refusing to sign a long-term contract with a promoter, reasoning that he could handle his own negotiations just fine. He famously spurned Don King's repeated efforts to sign him to a lifetime contract. Instead, Leonard hired a financial adviser from his hometown of Potomac, Maryland, who had no prior experience in prizefighting. Mike Trainer worked closely with Leonard throughout his career, and his guidance enabled Leonard to make big money and to invest it wisely. Leonard walked away with a record purse for his first professional fight: forty thousand dollars. And he did not have to turn over a goodly portion—the standard rate being 33 percent—to a promoter such as Don King! He paid off a twenty-thousand-dollar loan (plus the 8 percent interest) he had received from a group of twenty-four friends to launch his career and pocketed the rest. In November 1979, having compiled a 25-0 professional record, Leonard captured the World Boxing Council welterweight championship by dethroning champion Wilfred Benítez at Caesars Palace when the referee stopped the fight in the fifteenth and final round after a sharp left hook sent Benítez to the canvas.

After an easy defense against Dave Green, in June 1980 Leonard lost his title before a crowd of more than forty-seven thousand in Montreal's Olympic Stadium to Roberto Durán in a rugged fight that saw Durán winning narrowly on all three judges' cards. Durán, a street brawler who had grown up in the slums of Panama City, was uneducated, crude, and vulgar. He provided a stereotypical foil for the polished Leonard, and their rematch six months later in New Orleans became a media sensation. Unlike in Montreal, where Leonard attempted to outslug Durán, this time he returned to his normal style, frustrating his opponent with his foot speed and lightning-quick jabs. Leonard also worked on Durán's psyche, taunting him while slipping away from his bull rushes and wayward punches. In the seventh round, Leonard mocked Durán with showboating tactics that drew both laughter and catcalls from the crowd. Late in round 8, Durán stunned everyone, Leonard included, when he stopped fighting, turned away, his hand making a dismissive sign, and famously told the referee, "No más!" Although he was not hurt by Leonard's punches, he seemed frustrated by his inability to land his punches and angered by Leonard's mocking tactics. He later claimed he was suffering from stomach cramps from having consumed three steak dinners the day of the fight, but that excuse did not resonate with most observers. Obviously not physically wounded, Durán had simply quit for reasons unknown. It was a bizarre ending to a weird fight, but Leonard had regained the crown: "I made him quit," he crowed. "To make Roberto Durán quit is better than knocking him out."[20]

This set up what promoter Bob Arum touted as "the Showdown," with Leonard meeting undefeated Thomas Hearns, who possessed an impressive 32-0 record and held the World Boxing Association version of the welterweight title. Bob Arum announced that this fight would "unify" the division under one champion. Hearns had won all but two of his professional fights by knockout, earning the Detroit native the ominous nickname of "Hitman." Main Event Promotions sold out the huge outdoor arena at Caesars Palace four months in advance of the September 16, 1981, date. Fans poured into Las Vegas in the days before the fight, creating major traffic jams. Everywhere a person went along the Strip, there were crowded sidewalks, long waits at restaurants, and jammed casinos. The *Las Vegas Review-Journal* reported that "a huge drop" at the casino tables was anticipated. "It's been New Year's Eve for several days," Sands Casino executive Al Guzman enthused.[21] Arum announced that the fight was "too big for the networks" and optimistically announced that an estimated two hundred million fans around the world would watch on pay-per-view.

Leonard never professed a love of boxing and openly and repeatedly talked about his intent to quit the ring after he had amassed sufficient funds for a secure retirement. However, he also came to appreciate that he possessed public relations savvy that opened the door for one huge payday after another. Consequently, he would retire and unretire several times before finally quitting for good in 1997. For this much-hyped fight, he received a guarantee of eleven million dollars to Hearns's five million. The unprecedented purse (and it was not for heavyweights) added to the excitement that swept across Las Vegas in the days before the fight. Sports books reported a much larger betting handle than Ali-Holmes had produced.

The large crowd was treated to a classic fight. True fight fans were naturally attracted to the welterweight classification, because the athletes were quick on their feet but possessed sufficient heft to throw knockout punches. The lanky Hearns—one journalist suggested he looked like a preying mantis on his spindly legs—relentlessly stalked Leonard throughout the fight, using his long arms to great effect. Leonard responded by counterpunching effectively while constantly moving to avoid a knockout blow. By the fifth round, a swelling under Leonard's left eye blurred his vision, and Hearns racked up a substantial lead on the judges' cards. In the thirteenth round, aware that his title was slipping away, Leonard launched a furious assault, pinning Hearns on the ropes while he pounded away. Near the end of the round, Leonard knocked down the exhausted Hearns. A sportswriter at ringside said that Leonard had "overwhelmed" his opponent, who had never before gone beyond twelve rounds. As the fourteenth round began, Leonard staggered his opponent with a power right hand and followed up with a serious of combinations. Once more Hearns was trapped against the ropes, where he was rendered defenseless, prompting referee Davey Pearl to stop the fight. Headlines in the *Las Vegas Review-Journal* said it all: "Hit Man Hit Hard." There was no controversy when *Ring* magazine named it the "fight of the year."[22]

Journalist Tim Dahlberg later said of this epic battle, "Before an arena filled with overdressed high rollers, celebrities, hookers and their pimps and thousands of avid fans, Leonard and Hearns had put on a show for the ages. They fought an epic ebb-and-flow fight that ended as it did only because Leonard had something left when Hearns had expended his all." Casino executives were enthused. A newspaper reporter on the scene observed, "The fans have seen a fine fight. Five minutes after the fight, one must fight his way through the throng just to get inside the door at Caesars Palace. There's no doubt who the real winners will be on this warm Las Vegas night."[23]

In February 1982 Leonard defeated Bruce Finch in Reno. It was a rare event for the state's second-largest city to hold a championship fight during this era of domination by its much larger urban rival to the south. Seven thousand fans turned out at the Reno Convention Center on a cold northern Nevada evening to watch Leonard waltz through an easy payday. He battered his overmatched challenger to the canvas in the second and third rounds, at which point referee Mills

Lane stopped the fight. In April Leonard was in Buffalo, preparing for another easy payday against the pedestrian Roger Stafford at the time he was contemplating moving up to the middleweight division to take on "Marvelous Marvin" Hagler. Neither bout occurred as anticipated, because Leonard began seeing spots and bright lights in his left eye. An examination at the Johns Hopkins Hospital in Baltimore resulted in the diagnosis that Leonard had suffered a tear in the eye that resulted in a partially detached retina. After successful surgery Leonard tearfully announced his retirement from the ring.[24]

Much to the delight of boxing fans, however, Sugar Ray Leonard was not about to let his formidable adversaries earn all the big money. He later related in his autobiography that he not only wanted the money, but also missed the limelight, the thrill of being the center of attention. Thus, a year after announcing his retirement, Leonard returned to the ring with the intention of fighting in succession Durán, Hearns, and Hagler. But such was not to be, and after winning a tune-up fight with Kevin Howard, Leonard up and retired again, stating that he had lost his desire.

Leonard's departure from boxing (he said it was an irrevocable decision) set the stage for another Las Vegas match between popular middleweights. It would be memorable. Promoter Bob Arum publicized the match between Marvelous Marvin Hagler and Hearns simply as "The Fight." No understatement that. Both men had previously defeated Durán at Caesars Palace, Hagler by a unanimous decision and Hearns via one of his patented early-round knockouts. With the fight scheduled for April 15, 1985, and taking note of the big payday the two men would earn, pundits commented upon the irony that this was the deadline for the American people to file their income tax returns. Hearns broke his right hand when he bounced a blow off Hagler's bald head in the first round, as the two men stood toe to toe and relentlessly rained blows upon each other. The second round was almost as intense, and in the third Hearns ripped a large gash above Hagler's nose that prompted referee Richard Steele to temporarily halt the action to have the wound examined by the ringside physician. The bleeding was stanched and the fight resumed, and shortly thereafter Hagler crunched two strong rights to Hearns's jaw and followed up with a left hook that sent him to the canvas. When Hearns wobbled awkwardly to his feet, Steele stopped the fight. Boxing historians soon took to calling this classic "The War" and claimed it provided the "eight best minutes in boxing history."[25]

With Hagler the reigning middleweight champion, Leonard once more unretired, announcing that he had accepted a guarantee of eleven million dollars to challenge Hagler (who received twelve million). In making this match, promoter Bob Arum had scored big again and energetically went about hyping what he dubbed "The Super Fight." Once more the venue would be Caesars Palace. For those who loved plenty of fistic action, Arum's "Super Fight" promotion was borne out. In the early rounds Leonard displayed his famed speed and unleashed a series of sharp combinations. But his inactivity began to show—"Rest makes for rust," boxing insiders like to say—and as the rounds went by, he visibly tired. Hagler continued his dogged pursuit of the bobbing and weaving Leonard, who responded to the challenge by somehow finding the energy to assume the offensive in the final rounds.

When the fifteenth round ended, both men were still furiously exchanging blows as the crowd roared its approval. As the judges' scorecards were tallied, tension swept the pavilion because everyone knew it had been a very close fight. When Leonard was named the winner by a narrow split decision, the reaction was decidedly mixed. Veteran sportswriter Jim Murray approved with his usual hyperbole, writing that Leonard had "exposed" Hagler by making him "look like a guy chasing a bus . . . in snowshoes." Conversely, others saw Leonard as benefiting from his popular image: British journalist Hugh McIlvanney wrote that Leonard had won over the judges by his "few flashy moments," while it was Hagler who did the real scoring throughout the fight. Regardless, this was easily the "fight of the year," according to *Ring*. The official record indicated that Leonard had landed 306 blows to Hagler's 291 and that both men had launched more than 600 punches.[26]

His financial future secure, Leonard once again announced he was retiring, but, predictably, that changed yet again. He agreed to move up in the weight category to challenge Canadian Donny Lalonde, the reigning light-heavyweight champion, at Caesars in November 1988. Although knocked down in the fourth round, Leonard rallied and won on a TKO in the ninth round. In the process, with three separate international boxing agencies recognizing titleholders, he simultaneously claimed the newly created title of super middleweight. This set up a title-fight rematch with his old nemesis, "Hitman" Hearns, in June 1989 at his favorite stomping grounds at Caesars. This time Arum lured him with a guarantee of fourteen million dollars. Arum dubbed this renewal of an old rivalry as the "The War." Hearns lived up to his nickname, sending Leonard to the canvas twice with booming right hands, but Leonard responded both times with furious rallies. He controlled the twelfth and final round, which probably enabled him to squeak out a draw. Even Leonard's normally supportive fans disagreed and roundly booed the decision.[27]

Leonard's long and profitable run in Las Vegas ended on a positive note when he and Roberto Durán squared off for the third time. This time the fight was held on December 7, 1989, at Steve Wynn's sparkling new Mirage Hotel and Casino. Wynn wanted a high-profile fight to launch his new high-end venture and built a 16,305-seat temporary arena for the event, barely two weeks after the Mirage had opened. The response was enormous. With the casino and grounds jammed with people the afternoon of the fight, Wynn took the unprecedented step of limiting access to the property to hotel guests, ticket holders, and the nearly 1,000 members of the media who had secured credentials. True to Wynn's promotional genius, a host of celebrities added to the glamour of the evening, with Sylvester Stallone, Chevy Chase, Bo Derek, Jack Nicholson, Donald Trump, Billy Crystal, and Michael Jackson among the rich and famous spotted by reporters.

Arum and Top Rank Productions announced that the fight was to be called "Uno Más" (One More), but both men had lost speed and resilience with the passing of years. Durán was now thirty-eight, Leonard thirty-three, and both men had been boxing since their early teenage years. Arum would have been more accurate if he had called this the "Cold War," because when the sun went down over the western mountains, the desert air chilled rapidly and the temperature dipped below forty degrees. Both fighters came to the ring swathed in heavy blankets. "I've never been so cold," Leonard said afterward. "I didn't know it got that cold in Vegas. I thought this was the desert."[28]

Perhaps it was the cold December air. More likely it was that nearly a decade had passed since their first encounter, but the fight lacked the excitement of their earlier matches. It proved to be a listless twelve-round affair, with many fans leaving in disgust before it ended. Leonard's loyal fans insisted he had put on a classic demonstration of the art of boxing, but many in the audience simply said it was a dull fight. John Henderson in the *Las Vegas Review-Journal* concluded, "The performance was masterful. The performance was smart. The performance was dull." Late in round 11, Leonard suffered a large cut near his surgically repaired eye. Fifty stitches were later required to close the gash. Leonard hoped to get Durán to quit again, but this time Durán plodded onward, ignoring Leonard's trash talking and occasional mocking gestures. Leonard won decisively on all three judges' cards, and as the men departed the ring a spectacular fireworks display lit up the Las Vegas night above Steve Wynn's new trend-setting property. Not surprisingly, Leonard announced his fourth retirement, but few believed him. Leonard was named the "fighter of the decade" by *Ring* magazine. The fact that up to this point he had never fought in Madison Square Garden only served to establish the fact that Las Vegas had indeed become the capital of prizefighting.[29]

The third Durán-Leonard fight brought to a close the round-robin style battle of the welter- and middleweights that had done so much to make Las Vegas the fight capital of the world. Hagler retired in 1987 after his loss to Sugar Ray and moved to Italy, where he appeared in several Italian action motion pictures and did occasional boxing commentary in England. Hearns improbably continued fighting until he was fifty years of age, proud that over his thirty-two-year career he had held at various times six world titles. Like Hearns, Durán struggled with financial problems and prolonged his career that began in 1968 until he finally retired after losing the National Boxing Association's (NBA) version of the super-middleweight title to Héctor "Macho" Camacho in Denver in 2001. Leonard predictably retired after winning the lopsided decision over Durán in 1989, but he unretired twice more, losing to Terry Norris in Madison Square Garden in February 1991 and finally, like Durán, losing his last match by an early TKO in an embarrassing performance to Camacho six years later in Atlantic City. For a bright individual who understood the dangers of the ring and had long promised to retire early, his professional career stopped just short of twenty years. But he had become very wealthy.

Bob Arum, the man who made millions from the four men, later told a journalist, "It was a magical time. We had the four horsemen, Hagler, Leonard, Hearns, and Durán. Most of the fights with those guys fighting each other were in Las Vegas."[30]

Iron Mike

Despite the excitement that the four welter- and middleweights created, Don King understood that nothing draws a crowd like an awe-
inspiring heavyweight. The key to King's success was his ability to
ingratiate himself with black fighters, and despite various and repeated
charges of illegalities and irregularities that included grand jury investigations and inquiries by the Federal Communications Commission,
congressional committees, and television networks, King survived
admonitions, reprimands, and lawsuits, managing to thrive in a sport
long reputed for its underworld connections and ethical shortcomings.
As boxing historian Jeffrey T. Sammons wrote in 1990, King succeeded
by using "charm, devious persuasion, and outright coercion."[31]

One of the many fighters that King managed to control via carefully drafted contracts was a diligent but seemingly lackluster heavyweight from Easton, Pennsylvania. After working for several years as
a sparring partner for Muhammad Ali and dutifully doing King's bidding by fighting on many undercards, Larry Holmes finally got a shot
at the WBC heavyweight title in 1978 at Caesars Palace against Ken
Norton. After fourteen rounds that found the fight even on the judges'
cards, Holmes unleashed a blistering attack in the final round to win
a split decision. Their action-packed fight still resonates with boxing
fans possessing long memories. Probably no one was more surprised at
Holmes's victory than Don King, but he moved quickly to exploit this
unanticipated financial opportunity.

Holmes dominated the heavyweight division for the next seven
years, but he lacked the charisma of Muhammad Ali. A hardworking professional, Holmes defended his WBC title seventeen times
between 1978 and 1985. Ten of those fights occurred in Las Vegas at
Caesars Palace, the Dunes, and the Hilton. He defended his title successfully against the likes of Gerry Cooney, Trevor Berbick, Tim Witherspoon, and Leon Spinks, but also cashed paychecks after meeting
such unknowns that only a Don King could successfully promote as
a legitimate challenger: Scott LeDoux, Lorenzo Zanon, Randall Cobb,
and Marvis Frazier, the inexperienced son of the former champion.
Holmes's run of good fortune ended in a major upset on the Strip at the
Riviera Hotel and Casino when Michael Spinks won a unanimous decision on September 21, 1985.

By that time, however, Don King had latched onto an exciting nineteen-year-old he believed could become his newest moneymaking machine: Michael Gerard Tyson. Born in 1966, Mike Tyson grew up without the guidance of a father in an environment of poverty, drugs, and crime of the Bedford-Stuyvesant and Brownsville housing projects and had numerous brushes with law enforcement. By age twelve he had landed in an upstate New York juvenile detention center. It was there that he learned to box. He became a sensation in New York City's amateur ranks. After turning professional, he won twelve of his first nineteen victories by knockouts in the first or second round, displaying an impressive set of skills that included excellent hand speed, power, and timing. Under the tutelage of veteran trainer Cus D'Amato, he refined his skills. On November 22, 1986, with Tyson less than two years into his professional career but already owning a 27-0 record, Don King put him in the ring at the Las Vegas Hilton against defending WBC champion Trevor Berbick. Tyson displayed his strength and power by knocking Berbick around the ring and won with a TKO in the second round, the youngest fighter in history to claim the heavyweight crown. Sportswriters were stunned by Tyson's dominating performance, a *Las Vegas Review-Journal* writer proclaiming "the Dawn of a New Era." Columnist John L. Smith concluded a ringing endorsement of the twenty-year-old champion thusly: "Louis. Marciano. Ali. Now Tyson." Four months later in the same Hilton ring, he added the WBA title to his résumé with a unanimous decision over James "Bonecrusher" Smith, and in August 1987, once again at the Las Vegas Hilton, he "unified" all three heavyweight titles with a unanimous decision over Tony Tucker, who entered the fight with a sparkling 34-0 record. In the next two years, King promoted six successful Tyson title defenses that included awesome displays of power in a four-round TKO over Larry Holmes and a stunning first-round knockout over undefeated light-heavyweight champion Michael Spinks.[32]

In February 1990 King confidently booked Tyson into a tune-up match in Tokyo against an apparent easy mark, James "Buster" Douglas, with the intention of making millions by peddling the mismatch on pay-per-view. After Tyson defeated Douglas, or so King planned, there would be a blockbuster match with Evander Holyfield later in the year in Las Vegas. King's plans were derailed in shocking fashion when Tyson, after trailing badly on the judges' cards, knocked Douglas down in the eighth round. The challenger beat his fists on the canvas in disgust that he had gotten careless, but closely followed the referee's count and was back on his feet at the count of nine. In the next round he regained control of the fight, sending Tyson to the canvas for the first time in his career, and then ended the fight with a knockout punch in the tenth round. In the weeks leading up to Tokyo, the match had drawn derisive criticisms from all quarters, and most Las Vegas sports books refused to set a line. At the Mirage, however, bookmaker Jimmy Vaccaro accepted bets that made Tyson an outlandish forty-two-to-one favorite. Vaccaro got plenty of free publicity for his unconventional betting line, but few takers, although one intrepid soul reportedly put down $1,500 on Douglas and walked away with $52,500.[33]

For once, Don King seemed completely flummoxed and proceeded to make a fool of himself by attempting to get WBC commissioner José Sulaimán to declare Tyson the winner, claiming that the timekeeper's count had gone to thirteen when Douglas was knocked down in the eighth round. The rules, of course, are clear: only the referee's count is official, and the media had a field day excoriating King's ploy. For a time, Sulaimán seemed intimidated by King's profane demands and announced that the outcome of the fight would be investigated. King's attempt to snatch victory out of the jaws of an obvious defeat was roundly denounced by writers and television commentators, many of whom openly accused him of attempting to "steal" the fight. Mike Lupica's commentary in the sports newspaper the *National* was typical: "These people [King and his entourage] you wouldn't trust around the silverware."[34]

For once, Don King's well-laid plans had been overturned in what experts quickly dubbed "boxing's greatest upset." Don King Productions was already deeply engaged in planning a blockbuster fight at Caesars Palace in which Tyson would defend his title against popular light-heavyweight champion Evander Holyfield in November. The master manipulator had been caught unprepared; like everyone else, King had never anticipated that Douglas would unseat Tyson. Unwilling to deal with King for a rematch with Tyson, Douglas instead opted to defend his new title against Holyfield for a large payday dangled before him by Steve Wynn at the Mirage. Douglas, however, reverted to form. Enjoying the perks of being the heavyweight champion, he had ballooned to 246 pounds from the 208 pounds he weighed when he knocked out Tyson. Against Holyfield, he lasted only three rounds before being counted out after absorbing what most observers thought to be a soft punch to the jaw. Douglas thereupon retired, a one-fight wonder.

Tyson, in the meantime, began his march toward regaining the title with a series of fights in Las Vegas. However, King's plans for Tyson to meet Holyfield in Las Vegas were sidelined in February 1992 when Tyson was found guilty of raping an eighteen-year-old woman in his hotel room in Indianapolis, where she was a contestant in the Miss Black America beauty contest. Tyson's arrest came at a time when the issue of date rape was becoming part of the national dialogue, and the trial in Indianapolis received extensive—and divided—attention. He was convicted of the attack upon Desiree Washington and sentenced to six years in prison, thus scuttling King's grandiose plans. Even the famed "defense attorney of last resort," Harvard law professor Alan Dershowitz, could not convince the Indiana Court of Appeals to grant a new trial. Women's rights groups were delighted with the outcome, but other critics believed that Tyson was an innocent victim who had been "set up" by Washington. Some of his defenders suggested that his relationship with Don King had subconsciously swayed the jury and the appeals judges.[35]

Thus was the much-anticipated match between Tyson and Holyfield put on the shelf while the newly convicted felon served his time in an Indiana prison. With Iron Mike's absence, the heavyweight division lost much of its allure. Fortunately for the Las Vegas boxing culture, a series of dynamic young Hispanic fighters were coming to the fore that provided a new direction for prizefighting.

The Hispanic Surge

The history of prizefighting is replete with tales of impoverished young men facing a life without substance or hope turning to the ring as a means to escape the squalid conditions into which they were born. During the nineteenth century, many prominent fighters were products of the heavy immigration from northern Europe, especially Ireland, and in the early decades of the twentieth century substantial numbers representative of other ethnic and racial groups entered the profession, most notably Jews, African Americans, and Italians. In 1984 boxing journalist Bert Sugar published a book listing his version of the one hundred top fighters of all time.[36] Only two of those individuals were of Mexican heritage: bantamweight Carlos Zarate and featherweight Salvador Sánchez. Because fighters in these lower-weight divisions receive scant national attention, these two men were known only by boxing insiders. Although several Hispanics from the Caribbean islands and South America had gained widespread popularity in the earlier decades, they fought primarily on the East Coast. The presence of fighters from Mexico began to attract attention in Southern California and Nevada during the 1980s. The influx of Mexicans began slowly during the years before the Second World War, but even the best of these newcomers—Alberto Arizmendi, Enrique Bolanos, Kid Azteca— were denied the opportunity to maximize their potential due to pervasive discrimination.

It was not until 1979 that a fighter from Mexico was given the opportunity to test his mettle in a main event in Las Vegas when Carlos Zarate lost a controversial split decision to Lupe Pintor at Caesars Palace in 1979. Zarate was so upset with what he, and most in attendance, believed to be an egregious error on the part of one judge that he abruptly retired from boxing. His record, nonetheless, was a spectacular fifty-three knockouts in fifty-six fights with fifty-four victories and just two losses.

In Zarate's path there walked an increasing number of fighters from Mexico who came to the United States in search of greater opportunity and bigger purses. Foremost among these was Julio César Chávez, who had won thirty-three fights without a loss in Mexico before making his debut in the United States in 1982. In 1984 he won his first title when he captured the vacant WBC super-featherweight title in Los Angeles. He became popular among the growing Mexican American population of Southern California. He made his debut in Las Vegas at the Riviera in 1985 when he defeated Roger Mayweather in defense of his super-featherweight title. In subsequent years he moved up in weight classifications to win several championships, ultimately winning and repeatedly defending successfully the WBC light-welterweight title. Chávez was admired by his many fans for his powerful punches and ability to demoralize opponents with his attacks to the body. He also demonstrated an ability to take a punch and was often said to possess a "granite jaw." Chávez further ingratiated himself with his Mexican fans by frequently returning to his native Mexico for title bouts.

Chávez ran his record to 69-0 on March 17, 1990, at the Hilton in Las Vegas before an enthusiastic sellout crowd when he won an extraordinarily controversial TKO over the holder of the International Boxing Federation (IBF) championship in a bout to "unify" the super-featherweight championship. His opponent, Meldrick Taylor, came into the bout with a 24-0 record, but he was made a distinct underdog at the sports books. Nonetheless, the young man from Philadelphia took command of the fight in the early rounds. Although Taylor entered the final twelfth round well ahead on points on all judges' cards, Chávez's heavy punches had taken a severe toll. With only twenty-four seconds left in the round, Chávez stunned Taylor with a right hand to the jaw, and a few seconds later dropped him to the canvas. When Taylor staggered to his feet holding onto a rope, referee Richard Steele looked into his eyes and asked if he could continue. Taylor seemed disoriented and did not respond. Steele thereupon signaled the end of the fight. Just two seconds remained in the round.[37]

Steele was roundly criticized for his decision by many members of the media, who charged he had deprived Taylor of the title by ending the match with the final bell about to ring. Steele said that he had no way of knowing the amount of time remaining and that his primary responsibility was to protect a defenseless fighter from serious, if not permanent, injury. His judgment was confirmed after Taylor was treated at a hospital where he was found to have suffered a fractured orbital bone, was severely dehydrated, and had lost an estimated two pints of blood, much of which he had swallowed. Doctors affirmed that another powerful blow to the head could have caused permanent damage.

In 1991 the Mirage Hotel and Casino took a bold step toward recognizing the importance of Mexican fans by linking a Chávez title defense against Lonnie Smith to the weekend in September when Mexicans celebrate Mexican Independence. Chávez delighted his fans by taking a unanimous decision. The sellout crowd of predominantly Mexican American fans stimulated the scheduling of future fights featuring popular Mexican fighters on Cinco de Mayo and Mexican Independence Day. The growing popularity of Mexican fighters was evident when Chávez was selected to be the headliner for the first fight night at the lavish 16,800-seat MGM Grand Garden Arena in 1994. Don King, who had signed on Chávez to be his big-money ticket after

Mike Tyson had been jailed, matched the undefeated champion with the lesser-known Frankie Randall, a Tennessee resident who sported a 48-2-1 record. Randall surprised the wise guys by dominating the fight. In the eleventh round Randall knocked Chávez to the canvas for the first time in his long career, and Chávez was penalized for his second low blow. When the split decision was announced, Chávez had lost his first professional fight after eighty-nine victories and one draw.

Randall's upset victory, however, provided the MGM with the perfect opportunity to stage a rematch. It was scheduled for the upcoming Cinco de Mayo weekend and proved to be almost as controversial as his last-second TKO over Meldrick Taylor. For the first seven rounds, the bout was about even on the judges' scorecards, but as the round ended the fighters bumped heads and a large gash appeared over Chávez's eye. Referee Richard Steele was forced to halt action in the eighth round when the wound began bleeding profusely and the ring physician ordered the fight stopped. Randall was penalized one point for a head butt that gave Chávez an unusual victory officially called a "split technical decision." Chávez continued to fight frequently in defense of his light-welterweight title and by 1996 was talking about retirement. However, the opportunity of a large payday presented itself, and Chávez agreed to a June 6, 1997, bout at Caesars Palace against the newest sensation, the handsome and charismatic "Golden Boy," Oscar De La Hoya. Unlike Chávez and the great majority of Hispanic fighters, De La Hoya was an American citizen, having been born in 1973 in East Los Angeles to immigrants from Mexico. That proved to make a difference to many fans who had themselves emigrated from south of the border.

The Golden Boy

At stake in the fight was the WBC light-welterweight title that Chávez had held since 1987, except for the four-month hiatus imposed by Frankie Randall in 1994. De La Hoya was just entering his prime fighting years. Fully ten years younger than the thirty-three-year-old Chávez, he had crafted a 21-0 record as a professional after a lengthy apprenticeship that began in an East Los Angeles gym when he was just six years old. By age ten he was fighting as an amateur, and family records indicate that he amassed a spectacular record of 234-6 by the time he won a gold medal at the Barcelona Olympics in 1992 as a featherweight. After turning professional, he continued to develop as a skilled ring technician who also packed a formidable knockout punch. His quickness enabled him to outmaneuver his opponents and avoid serious punishment. He became a popular box-office draw by winning most of his fights by early-round knockouts. In just his twelfth fight he won the WBO super-featherweight title in 1994.[38]

Street-smart and handsome, his winsome smile his calling card, De La Hoya became a media sensation. His good looks and facility with the English language made him a favorite of reporters. His personality and handsome features hinted at a star quality not dissimilar from that of Sugar Ray Leonard. He signed on with promoter Bob Arum and Top Rank to guide his early career. Arum's right-hand man, Bruce Trampler, wasted no time advancing De La Hoya's career. Unlike many professional boxers, De La Hoya paid close attention to the money he was making and where it was going. After he pocketed his first one-million-dollar purse by defeating Jimmy Brendahl for the 130-pound super-featherweight title, he socked the money away. His frequent appearances on cable-network fights expanded his appeal and earning power. Under Arum's guidance, he became a multimillionaire long before he had even approached the crest of his boxing career.

His smiling face soon was seen on television and billboards endorsing various products, many of them pitched toward Mexican Americans. After hiring Richard Schaefer, a professional money manager who knew nothing of the financial intricacies of professional boxing, he developed a diversified investment portfolio of stocks, bonds, and real estate and then branched into founding his own individual "Golden Boy" enterprises. Soon De La Hoya had surrounded himself with a cluster of attorneys and tax accountants. By the time he retired from the ring in 2008, he had a net worth estimated in the high seven figures. The most visible parts of his business operations were Golden Boy Partners and Golden Boy Real Estate, and later there came Golden Boy Promotions to promote boxing and mixed martial arts (MMA). Typical of his enterprises was the creation of a line of men's clothing specifically tailored for the Hispanic American male. As he wrote in his autobiography, his success as a fighter and entrepreneur enabled him to live the American Dream. He had risen from his modest origins in the East Los Angeles barrio to live a life he boastfully described as "more fame, more fortune, more women, a life of limos and private jets."[39]

The Golden Boy's success, however, created a public relations problem for him within his own Mexican American community. It came to a head in the weeks leading up to his big fight in June 1996 with the boxing hero of the Mexican working class, Julio César Chávez. An American citizen and educated in Los Angeles schools, De La Hoya spoke both English and Spanish fluently. That created an identity issue for what should have been his natural fan base because he was not Mexican *enough*. The word *elitist* was frequently mentioned with a negative connotation. Chávez exacerbated the issue with his comment, "I'm an authentic Mexican. He's not a true Mexican. He has American nationality."[40] Chávez was a fighter whose proletarian roots in Mexico created instant credibility with Hispanic boxing fans. His hard-drinking, hard-living reputation also resonated with his natural fan base. Chávez's warrior image in the ring meshed well with his hard-living style outside it. At stops on a prefight tour that Arum arranged to promote closed-circuit ticket sales, De La Hoya was stunned when the crowds cheered his opponent and showered him with boos and catcalls. Such a reception even occurred on his home turf of East Los Angeles. The Golden Boy, it seemed, had become too much a mainstream American for those who maintained strong loyalties to their native Mexico. A number of threats that De La Hoya received prior to the fight prompted him to hire bodyguards.

While in San Antonio on a promotional tour stop, De La Hoya realized that he would be able to defeat the famed warrior when he encountered Chávez coming in from a hard night of partying as he was leaving the hotel for his normal early-morning roadwork. The fight drew a huge crowd to Las Vegas, and Arum cleaned up on pay-per-view. From the opening bell, De La Hoya used his speed and quick hands to take control of the fight, opening a large gash above Chávez's eye with a series of stinging jabs. By the fourth round Chávez was bleeding profusely, and the ringside doctor stopped the fight. De La Hoya had now won his third world title by taking the WBC 140-pound welterweight title away from a legendary fighter. This fight was also the end and the beginning of two boxing eras on the Strip, a place that was continually changing and reinventing itself. This was the last of the big outdoor fights held at Caesars Palace. The future of Las Vegas boxing now lay a few blocks south along the Strip, where sparkling new indoor arenas at the MGM and Mandalay Bay would become the locations for big fights.

The era of what cynics liked to call "parking-lot extravaganzas" had come to an end.

The Golden Boy—De La Hoya loved that nickname—proceeded to build his reputation as the biggest box-office draw in boxing by defending his welterweight title with decisions over the best fighters Arum could find to fill the house in Las Vegas: Pernell Wittaker, Hector "Macho" Camacho, and a rematch with Chávez. These victories set up a classic battle of Hispanics that was promoted jointly by Arum and King, who managed to sublimate their dislike for each other to generate the greatest payday for a nonheavyweight bout in history.

Félix Trinidad was a native of Puerto Rico and considered, pound for pound, the most challenging opponent De La Hoya had faced. De La Hoya took the fight seriously, training hard for three months before they met in September 1999 at the twelve-thousand-seat Events Center at Mandalay Bay. The enormous property had opened just a few months earlier, and this event marked its entry into the prizefight business. Billed as the "Fight of the Millennium," it set a record of more than two million "buys" on pay-per-view. It was hyped as a combustible dustup between a Puerto Rican and a Mexican American. As is often the case with prizefights that receive enormous prefight publicity, the actual contest did not provide much excitement. Cautious of Trinidad's power, De La Hoya followed a defensive strategy while relying upon winning points with his jabs and occasional combination punches. During the final three rounds, having been advised by his handlers that he was sufficiently ahead on points, he essentially went on the defensive and backpedaled while making little effort to land meaningful punches. This strategy backfired, as it enabled Trinidad to win the final rounds as the aggressor. He won on two judges' cards (115–113, 115–114), with the other scoring it a 114 draw. "I thought I had it in the bag. I swear. I really did," a deflated Golden Boy told the postfight press conference.[41] De La Hoya later blamed his first professional defeat upon bad advice, writing sarcastically in his autobiography, "It's difficult to fight both your opponent and your corner."[42] The anticipated rematch never occurred, with both men blaming the other for a failure to agree upon terms for such a bout. When Trinidad moved up in weight classification, the issue became moot.

Always interested in the bottom line, De La Hoya decided after he lost a split decision to Shane Mosley in Los Angeles in the autumn of

2000 that he would thereafter promote his own bouts. Upset that Arum and Top Rank were making millions while he was the one risking injury in the ring, he successfully made the break only after a nasty legal battle. His fights would now be handled by Golden Boy Promotions, but more often than not his company actually contracted with Arum's Top Rank Promotions for most of his remaining fights.

De La Hoya now was able to keep a larger percentage of the enormous revenues that his fights generated. In the ensuing years, he regained his WBC welterweight title by defeating Javier Castillejo at the MGM in June 2001 and recaptured the WBC light-middleweight title with an eleven-round TKO over Fernando Vargas in an exciting slugging contest at Mandalay Bay in September 2002. After a fifteen-month layoff, he lost all of his titles in September 2003 in a rematch with Shane Mosley by a unanimous decision. He moved up to the middleweight division in 2004 and won the title in a controversial decision over Felix Sturm, but by this time, at the age of thirty-two, the glitter began to disappear from the public image that was Golden Boy. He suffered a devastating knockout at the hands of Bernard Hopkins at the MGM in September 2004, and three years later he lost a split decision to Floyd Mayweather Jr. at the same venue.

His career came to a painful and humiliating end on December 6, 2008, at the MGM Grand Garden Arena against the younger Manny Pacquiao in what was promoted as a "Dream Match." The younger and stronger Filipino—now being proclaimed the "best pound-for-pound fighter in the world"—dominated the fight from the opening bell. It had now become apparent that De La Hoya no longer had the stamina or the quickness of his prime years. During the usual prefight dialogue, Pacquiao's veteran trainer, Freddie Roach, a former lightweight who had once fought for the world title and a longtime Las Vegan, commented that he believed, contrary to the betting public that had made De La Hoya the favorite, the Golden Boy no longer could "pull the trigger." He was correct, and De La Hoya understood that fact by retiring to manage his business enterprises. When he congratulated Roach and Pacquiao before leaving the ring, he said, "You were right, Freddie. I don't have it anymore." And he told reporters in the postfight press conference, "My heart still wants to fight, that's for sure. But when your physical [sic] doesn't respond, what can you do? I have to be smart and make sure I think about the future."[43]

The Golden Boy thus retired, but unlike so many top fighters at the end of the road, he did so an immensely wealthy individual. His decision to promote his own fights returned to him untold millions of dollars. The live gate for his final fight alone brought in an estimated $17 million, but pay-per-view had generated far greater revenues totaling $70 million. This bonanza came on top of the revenues for the earlier fight with Floyd Mayweather Jr., which had generated a live gate of $19 million and with nearly 2.5 million "buys" on HBO at $55 a pop an additional $120 million. This child of Mexican immigrants had truly lived the American Dream. His life was a modern-day example of the Horatio Alger myth of the self-made man. Unlike so many fighters, De La Hoya had a shrewd business sense. He took special interest in the work of his foundation that focused upon educational opportunities for Hispanic youth. Although his career after retirement was marred by some unsavory incidents and at one point he was forced to admit himself to the Betty Ford clinic for treatment for "certain personal issues," the native of the Mexican barrio of East Los Angeles had literally fought his way to the top of the American business world. He was, indeed, a Golden Boy.

The Decline of the Heavyweights

Oscar De La Hoya's career reached its zenith at a critical time for boxing. With boxing's heavyweight hope, Mike Tyson, having fallen from grace and with no quality heavyweight fighters on the horizon, prizefighting could have entered a period of sharp decline. De La Hoya and the cluster of talented fighters in the lightweight, welterweight, and middleweight divisions did their part to fill the void. Fight fans recognized that these fighters were quicker and often much more skilled in the "science" of the manly art. They invariably put on a good match that brought the fans back for the next bout. It was on the shoulders of this group of fighters, many of whom were Hispanic, that boxing managed to survive during the first decade of the twenty-first century. Nonetheless, the sport that had once shared center stage with baseball and football had entered a period of distinct decline. By the time of the arrival of the new millennium, the sport that had somehow once convinced the American people that it was a "sweet science" had lost much of its appeal and been pushed to the margins of the sporting world. This resulted in part from changes in American popular culture, but more significant were self-inflicted wounds. All of those problems came together in one shocking moment at the MGM Grand in Las Vegas on the evening of June 28, 1997, when the unexpected, the inexplicable, happened right before the disbelieving eyes of veteran referee Mills Lane.

Split Decision

Prizefighting on the Margins

As the twenty-first century approached, the public image of boxing took a decidedly downward trajectory. No longer were fights the center of casual conversation in offices and during the late-afternoon happy hour. Now, it seemed, no one really wanted to talk about boxing the way they once did; now the conversations revolved largely around football. The sport that had captured the nation's attention in the 1920s, and had continued to enjoy vast popularity during the days of such iconic figures as Jack Dempsey, Joe Louis, Rocky Marciano, Sugar Ray Robinson, Muhammad Ali, Sugar Ray Leonard, and for a time a young Mike Tyson, found itself by the mid-1990s suffering from a sharp decline in public interest that occurred amid a rising tide of criticism. It also faced an ominous new competitor in the rapidly growing popularity of mixed martial arts. Thus did prizefighting become a victim of its own excesses as well as from changes in the popular culture that had a distinct antiestablishment flavor and tended to embrace "extreme" sports.

The causes of boxing's decline are self-evident. Television continued to extract its toll upon the popularity of boxing by creating an environment in which only championship fights featuring boxers with high marquee appeal attracted a sizable viewing audience. The major networks had long since decided that boxing could not attract sufficient viewing audiences on a regularly scheduled basis and by the 1960s had moved on to other sports with greater appeal. The cost of accessing cable pay-per-view restricted the size of viewing audiences to only the most dedicated fans who were willing to spend upwards of fifty dollars to watch a single bout. In Las Vegas the emphasis was upon hosting high-profile championship fights, for which the price of a ticket tended to exclude the everyday working stiff. Unlike New York City before 1960, casino executives in Las Vegas did little to promote boxing from the bottom up, neglecting to provide opportunities for young boxers to develop their skills. The regular local cards once a mainstay at the Showboat and Silver Slipper were gone—as were the casinos themselves. The underlying intent of the casinos in sponsoring boxing was to attract large numbers of heavy-betting individuals, the much-sought-after high rollers. As such, boxing's structure in the late twentieth century did not encourage the recruitment of a new generation of fans.

Professional boxing had always suffered from cutthroat competition between rival promoters, many of whom were burdened with considerable negative baggage. In an age dominated by the larger than life personage of Don King, that problem was never resolved, but the image of boxing suffered also from the confusion created by three rival governing organizations and a maze of overlapping and confusing new weight classifications. In this way, and many others, boxing's worst enemies were the men to whom its stewardship was entrusted. In 1921, with professional boxing having achieved a newfound stature and receiving the blessing of state laws and newly created state boxing commissions, the National Boxing Association was set up to create an organization that would sanction title fights and recognize world champions. The NBA established itself as the recognized governing and sanctioning body when it crowned Jack Dempsey heavyweight champion after he defeated Frenchman Georges Carpentier in July 1921. The organization established eight weight classes based on historical precedent that remained unchanged for four decades. The most widely recognized divisions were heavyweight (unrestricted in weight), light-heavyweight (above 175 pounds and under 200 pounds), middleweight (above 160 pounds), welterweight (above 147 pounds), and lightweight (above 135 pounds). In 1962 the NBA, apparently in an attempt to distinguish itself from the National Basketball Association, renamed itself the World Boxing Association, although its primary focus remained the United States.

Growing interest in other countries led to the creation of the World Boxing Council in 1963. It eventually became the most prominent sanctioning body for bouts in the United States under José Sulaimán, who assumed the presidency in 1975. He became a powerful figure in international boxing and reputedly extended the WBC's influence into

161 countries. Despite competition from rival bodies, the WBC became dominant in the United States, primarily because of its close association with Don King. Critics repeatedly charged that Sulaimán not only did business regularly with King, but often seemed to be his most ardent booster. At age eighty-one in 2012, Sulaimán remained active. In 1983 former New Jersey boxing commission member Robert W. Lee Sr., who had founded the small United States Boxing Association in 1973 and focused its activities in New Jersey, attempted to replace Sulaimán as head of the WBC, but his bid was rejected at the annual meeting of the organization. This led to Lee renaming his organization the USBA-International. In 1988 the USBA-I took the name of the International Boxing Federation and sanctioned its own slate of championships. At any given time, an individual fighter might be recognized by all three bodies as the "unified" champion, but frequently more than one fighter would be simultaneously recognized by competing bodies as "world champion." The result was confusion on the part of the casual fan.

As if three governing bodies with similar names were not enough, beginning in 1959 a proliferation of weight classifications was instituted in an attempt to create more title bouts, and thereby sell more tickets. In that year the WBA established the class of super lightweight. This essentially sliced the weight divisions in half; in subsequent years there appeared a flood of new classes, such as super welterweight, super middleweight, and cruiserweight (200 pounds minimum to 220 pounds), which became an alternative heavyweight title. By 1984 there were too many different classifications, including such classification-splitting absurdities as "light flyweight," "junior flyweight," and "super flyweight," with no more than three pounds setting them apart. Many so-called world champions remained unrecognizable to the average sports fan. And so it went. The conflicts and the confusion created by three controlling organizations with nearly twenty different weight classes diluted interest among all but the most dedicated boxing fans.

This confusion stemmed in large part from the lack of a national commission to provide consistency and general oversight to the sport. Unlike the dominant team sports, there was no league structure to systematically identify champions and schedule competitions. Instead, promoters who were looking out for their own interests controlled the careers of individual fighters. No formal structure existed by which individual boxers were ranked fairly, and each match that a fighter entered became a single business deal controlled by managers and promoters. The stature of the three sanctioning bodies has always been suspect, their ratings and sanctioning of title bouts often believed to be the product of backroom politics. Financially, each boxer was on his own. During his fighting years he had no union to protect him or look after his interests, and oftentimes the manager to whom he entrusted his career had divided loyalties, or worse. And at the end of the boxer's career, the same story repeated itself over and over: he had no pension, lacked a meaningful career path, and was in debt.

The immensely popular 1976 motion picture *Rocky* created a patriotic, feel-good image of boxing with its story of the plucky underdog fighting against all odds in an attempt to capture the heavyweight title. That special feeling did not last for long. Competing narratives chronicling the fraud, deceit, and exploitation by those in charge of prizefighting overcame any happy sensations created by Sylvester Stallone's empathic portrayal of the likable Rocky Balboa. Studies by social scientists demonstrated that virtually all prizefighters came from poor socioeconomic backgrounds, having grown up in dysfunctional family situations. The typical professional boxer had little formal education and entered prizefighting because it seemed to be one of the few avenues available in which to earn a living. This even became the plight of such famous boxers as Joe Louis and Sugar Ray Robinson. Not only did they lack a marketable skill and find themselves in debt, but they also owed large sums in back taxes to the Internal Revenue Service. Lacking the knowledge or motivation to save and invest their income during their prime earning years, they had placed misguided trust in their managers and "friends."

Advances in medical research into the long-term damage to the brain from repetitive blows, and the decision by the leadership of the American Medical Association to publicize these dangers with specific reference to boxing, added to the growing public concerns about the sweet science. During the days of vaudeville and even well into the formative years of television, comedians could always get a good laugh from jokes and comedic routines mimicking "punch-drunk" fighters, but growing awareness of the devastation of chronic encephalopathy ended this line of humor. It was no longer a laughing matter, and that fact was driven home by public appearances of the popular former heavyweight champion Muhammad Ali. Not long after his defeat to Larry Holmes in 1980 and his retirement, he often seemed lethargic, complaining of a lack of energy. Friends noticed that he had uncontrollable tremors in his hands, and his speech had become slurred. He had trouble with muscle coordination, and his once-clever facial expressions were seldom seen. Between 1982 and 1984, Ali underwent comprehensive physical examinations and tests at the University of California at Los Angeles (UCLA) Medical Center. His attending physicians concluded that his condition resulted from "repeated blows to the head, over time."[1]

News reports indicted that Ali had been diagnosed with Parkinson's disease. But Parkinson's disease results from progressive neurological disorders produced by disease. In Ali's case, the diagnosis was Parkinsonism, which is damage to brain cells caused by trauma. It is a variant of the better-known Parkinson's, of course, but commonly found in former boxers. Ali faced a future armed only with a less than adequate high school education and a lack of marketable skills. At one point early in his retirement, Ali wistfully lamented, "Sometimes I wish I had gone to college. Those students don't know how lucky they are. I could have done more if I'd gotten a better education and gone to college."[2] Ali was fortunate that he had saved enough money to be self-supporting during his later years.

The result was that the image of boxing, never high among the general public, began a period of decline that can be traced to Duk Koo Kim's death in a Las Vegas ring in 1982 and the growing public awareness of Ali's postboxing physical difficulties. There remained the inescapable fact that boxing was violent and brutal, in the eyes of its critics a form of legalized physical assault posing as public entertainment. A "knockout"—the boxing term for a concussion sufficient to render the victim unconscious—was the most exciting part of a prizefight for most spectators. A "lust for cruelty" was one of prizefighting's most powerful attractions. Television sports commentator Joe Rogan agreed: "People love conflict, especially when it doesn't involve them and they get to be the voyeur. The bottom line is we enjoy violence, especially when it's in a controlled environment."[3] The tragedy was that Ali's physical condition was not all that out of the ordinary and that it had developed over many years while adoring fans cheered him on. Boxing historian Jeffrey Sammons concludes his classic study of the role of the sport in American society thusly: "Those people who are closest to the sport agree that a majority of boxers are in bad shape financially, mentally, and physically, and that those who make good are exceptions."[4]

Sports journalist Jimmy Cannon described professional boxing during the 1950s as "the red light district of sports."[5] He was referring to the influence of organized crime upon the sport in his native New York City. That influence during the 1950s led to congressional investigations and investigative journalist reports that severely damaged the popular image of the fight game. This significantly facilitated the rise of Las Vegas as a location for prizefights. That prizefighting transitioned to Las Vegas during the 1960s and 1970s, at a time when the Mob exerted extensive control and influence over the casinos, was not a mere coincidence. In the 1980s, the President's Commission on Organized Crime once again pointed toward the cozy relationship between prizefighting and organized crime syndicates. The commission at one point concluded, "If the same mob presence we have found in boxing existed, for example, in professional baseball or football, it would constitute a massive public scandal."[6] Why that scandal did not develop, critics hypothesized, was because the American people already perceived that boxing was inherently corrupt and that those who were negatively impacted the most, the boxers who risked all by entering the ring, came from the underclass whose welfare was of little consequence to affluent Americans.

The Tragedy of Mike Tyson

If any one individual can be identified as a symbol for prizefighting's demise, it would be Mike Tyson. His entire life and boxing career exemplified the problems plaguing prizefighting, from his troubled childhood to his sudden fame to the exploitation of his talents by Don King to his ultimate humiliation in a Las Vegas ring. Born into a dysfunctional single-parent family, he became a repeat offender as a juvenile, prone to violence well before he entered his teenage years. He became a feared figure on the crime-riddled streets of New York City's deteriorating housing projects, seemingly finding that inflicting pain upon others gave him a sense of pleasure. After repeated offenses and arrests, he was sent to an upstate New York juvenile detention facility where he learned to box and was taken under the wing of famed trainer Cus D'Amato. In 1985 at the age of nineteen, Tyson turned professional, becoming the youngest fighter in history to win the heavyweight championship two years later. In almost stereotypical fashion, he became the unwitting pawn of promoter Don King, who throughout his entire career walked a fine ethical line in his financial dealings and contractual relationships. In 1998, his career having spun out of control, Tyson accused King of bilking him of one hundred million dollars in a high-profile civil lawsuit. He was but one of many fighters who trusted King only to later believe that they had been duped.[7]

At the sordid end of his career, however, Tyson received little public sympathy because of his own self-inflicted problems. In 1992 Tyson was convicted and sentenced to six years in prison for raping an eighteen-year-old beauty-pageant contestant, eventually spending three years and three months of what should have been the best years of his boxing career in an Indiana prison before being paroled. He regained the WBC heavyweight title in 1995, but his life and career almost immediately began to spin terribly out of control as he struggled to contain the psychological demons that besieged him.

Tyson's personal problems and the dubious image of prizefighting merged in a Las Vegas casino boxing ring on June 28, 1997. Tyson's career would never recover from what happened that evening. Nor would the institution of boxing. His behavior that evening not only led to his sudden fall as a leading sports personality, but also came to symbolize the fact that in a rapidly changing America, prizefighting had lost much of its luster and was entering a period of undeniable decline.

The Fan Man Lands

In his autobiography, Mills Lane recalls heading off to catch an airplane for Las Vegas to referee a championship fight between Tyson and Holyfield. As he left the house, his wife, Kaye, said to him, "Mills, bizarre stuff happens when you are the referee. But you can handle it. You're like a cat. No matter what happens you land on your feet."[8]

Kaye's comments were probably based in part upon the bizarre episode that occurred on the cool evening of November 11, 1993, when her husband was refereeing a close title fight in which Riddick Bowe defended his WBA and IBF heavyweight crowns against Evander Holyfield in one of the last outdoor fights ever held at Caesars Palace. This was a rematch of their first meeting when Bowe had wrested the title in a rugged match from Holyfield in an eleventh-round TKO. After

six rounds the rematch was close, although to those at ringside Holyfield seemed to be slightly ahead. Early in the fight he had opened two
cuts on Bowe's forehead and in the fifth round had staggered him with
a left-right combination. At that juncture, while the two men were in a
clinch, out of the darkening evening sky the Fan Man made his unan-
nounced appearance.[9]

James Miller was a computer technician and small businessman from Henderson, Nevada, who had a passion for extreme aerial
activities. He became a skilled parachutist and took up paragliding in
Alaska before moving to Clark County. Not content with those adventurous avocations, he moved on to piloting a motorized fan-propelled
aircraft made of steel mesh in which he zoomed over the vast expanses
of southern Nevada desert. Miller was known among Las Vegas paragliding devotees as a daring, if not reckless, pilot, who was driven to set
personal records for altitude, speed, and distance.

According to eyewitnesses, Miller had been circling high above the
ring for an estimated ten minutes before he began a quick descent,
sweeping in over the hotel tower. His plan apparently was to land in
the middle of the ring to capture a few moments of fame, but as he
neared his target his parachute caught on a bank of lights suspended
above the ring. He and his flying contraption crashed on the ring apron,
man and machine becoming entangled in the ropes near Bowe's corner.
Within seconds Bowe's manager, Rock Newman, began to beat Miller
on his helmeted head with a large cellular phone before the unexpected
interloper was dragged into the crowd by angry fans who pummeled
him with their fists. Casino security personnel responded quickly, but
by the time they reached Miller through the milling crowd, he had
been knocked unconscious. Miller was rescued from his assailants and
whisked off to a hospital and then on to the Clark County Detention
Center, where he was booked for flying in a dangerous manner. He was
later released on two hundred dollars' bail. For reasons unknown—
some thought he had been inspired by the popular 1978 motion picture *Black Sunday*—Miller became obsessed with disrupting sporting
events from above. Two months later he landed another power glider
among a crowded section of the Los Angeles Coliseum during a Los
Angeles Raiders playoff game with the Denver Broncos and the following month similarly disrupted a World Cup soccer match in England,
leading to a stiff fine and permanent deportation. Commenting upon

his Las Vegas stunt, he later said, "It was a heavyweight fight, and I was the only guy who got knocked out."[10]

At the time of Miller's unexpected arrival, Mills Lane was attempting to break a clinch between Holyfield and Bowe on the opposite side of the ring. A video of the event suggests that he saw Miller crash into the ring apron out of the corner of his eye, and he immediately jumped between the two fighters and made a T with his hands, signaling a break in the action. After Lane conferred with Nevada Athletic Commission executive director Marc Ratner, the fight resumed after a delay of twenty-one minutes. Both fighters were obviously affected by the long break during the cool November evening, and Holyfield went on to win a close twelve-round decision. Bowe had lost for the first time of his career and bitterly blamed the Fan Man disruption for that defeat. Among the many distractions that Bowe identified was that his pregnant wife, who was seated near his corner, had fainted during the ruckus in which she had become engulfed.

The Fan Man Fight, as it came to be called, was a bizarre event that attracted national attention. Although completely unanticipated and beyond the control of Nevada authorities, the episode did nothing to enhance the image of the sport. The national media coverage and ensuing jokes that made the rounds of the late-night talk shows only exacerbated the negativity that was cast upon prizefighting. Fan Man served as a quasi-humorous escapade to a much more sobering event, one that also involved Mills Lane. But that episode, he wrote in his autobiography, "disgraced us all, boxers, every honest and hardworking trainer, cutman, manager, and promoter in the business, every boxing fan worldwide."[11] It was the Bite Fight.

The Bite of the Century

Mills Lane had made plans for a quiet weekend in Reno. A dedicated runner, he planned to get in some serious miles along the streets near his home in southwestern Reno. Running was a good way to stay in condition so that he could handle the big boys in the ring at the age of sixty-four. Besides, as he bounced along at his fast clip, he could review in his mind important details regarding his upcoming trial schedule as district court judge. Saturday, June 28, 1997, he mused, seemed to be a good time to drop by the card room at the Cal-Neva Casino for a few hours of his favorite form of relaxation, playing poker. Lane had already decided not to purchase pay-per-view to catch the big show in Las Vegas when Evander Holyfield defended his heavyweight title against Mike Tyson. After all, he had been in the ring with both men several times, and he was disgusted with the self-pity that Tyson had put on display during a prefight press conference on Monday. Instead of the usual macho claptrap that fighters express at such events, Tyson, perhaps now fully aware of the money that Don King had already siphoned off during his megamillion-dollar career, lamented, "I have no friends. . . . I've been taken advantage of my whole life. I've been abused, I've been dehumanized, I've been humiliated, and I've been betrayed."[12]

Lane's response to reading reports of Tyson's diatribe was predictable: "Bullshit! . . . Until you straighten yourself out, Mike, you're going to have problems." Lane wondered, however, "What in the hell was going through Mike's mind" because "I'd never before heard him wallowing in self-pity." However, he told himself, "It wasn't my problem [because] I was going to be several hundred miles away from the MGM Grand that Saturday night."[13]

Such was not to be. Lane's plans for a quiet weekend—indeed, his entire future—changed on Thursday when he received a call from an anxious Marc Ratner, NAC executive director. Don King was always looking for an angle, and this time his ploy was that seven months earlier, his fighter had lost the WBC title to Holyfield because referee Mitch Halpern had not protected him from illegal head butts. Because Ratner had assigned Halpern, considered one of his best referees, to the rematch, King vigorously protested in one of his typical prefight sideshows. With his usual hypertheatrical bombast, King charged that Halpern was biased against his man. Lane had watched films of that title fight, which Holyfield had won in an eleventh-round TKO, and, like Ratner and members of the Nevada Athletic Commission, had dismissed King's charges as unfounded. Ratner told Lane that he was determined to keep Halpern on the fight, but suggested Lane book a flight to Las Vegas for Saturday morning—just in case.

The next day newspapers reported that the commission had voted four to one to deny King's protest. At six on Saturday, Lane was awakened by a call telling him to be prepared to fly to Las Vegas because, as Ratner said, "things are changing here." Two hours later another call came, informing him that Halpern had decided to withdraw after concluding that he had been put into an impossible situation by King's outburst. Ratner reluctantly concurred. With just twelve hours to opening bell, Lane was 450 miles away, but he was going to be the third man in the ring that evening. He reassured himself that this would be his fifth time to referee a Tyson fight in Las Vegas and there had never been a problem before.[14]

Tyson had remained a big attraction after his release from an Indiana prison in March 1995. If anything, the rape conviction had added another sinister layer to his thuggish image that was an integral part of his box-office appeal. An eager Don King, in fact, had met him as he walked out the prison gate. It was time for both of them to make some big money.

And make millions they did. In September 1995 Tyson won back the WBA version of the heavyweight title with an impressive first-round knockout of Bruce Seldon, and he regained the WBC version when he overpowered Frank Bruno with a third-round TKO in March 1996. Now thirty years of age, Iron Mike had seemingly become his old self, dominant, intimidating, a menacing force of nature. Lane was the referee in this one-sided mismatch, his fourth time to officiate a Tyson championship bout.

Evander Holyfield had initially claimed the unified heavyweight crown when he easily defeated an overweight and seemingly uninterested Buster Douglas in October 1990. Before that he had held the WBC cruiserweight title for several years. He was initially prepared to defend his new title against Tyson in November 1991 in a much-anticipated megamillion-dollar fight, but Tyson withdrew due to an injury and ended up in prison before the fight could take place. Fans appreciated Holyfield as a skilled craftsman and a decent human being, but he lacked the lethal charisma that made Tyson such a box-office draw. Holyfield agreed to a fight with Tyson at the MGM Grand in November 1996, defending his recently regained title.

At age thirty-four, Holyfield was not given much chance, the experts having concluded that he was clearly past his prime. The opening betting line made Tyson a prohibitive twenty-five-to-one favorite. Thus, when Holyfield adeptly parried Tyson's punches and dominated the early rounds with sharp jabs and counterpunches, he surprised nearly everyone assembled in the packed MGM Grand Garden Arena. Especially Mike Tyson. Unable to bully and intimidate his opponent, Tyson seemed confused and became surprisingly cautious, then passive. By the tenth round he was losing badly on points, at which time Holyfield sent him reeling across the ring with a powerful right hand. Although he came out for the eleventh round, Tyson was dazed, and Holyfield pounced. Referee Mitch Halpern stopped the fight with Tyson apparently unconscious while still on his feet. It was not head butts that had caused Tyson's defeat.[15]

In the next seven months, Tyson devoted himself to a rigorous training regimen, seemingly determined to regain his title. Thus, when Mills Lane, the last-minute substitute referee, called the two fighters to the center of the ring for instructions, boxing fans were anticipating an epic battle. Such was not to be. It was, however, a blockbuster of a gate: the 16,300 fans in the Garden Arena and the 2 million watching on Showtime pay-per-view generated an estimated ninety-five million dollars in revenue. Tyson's guaranteed slice of the huge pie was thirty million, with Holyfield receiving thirty-five million. From the first bell, Tyson faced a confident defending champion who flicked away Tyson's punches as if he were swatting flies. Holyfield easily won the first round and continued to set the pace in the second; at one juncture, Holyfield ducked under a punch and butted heads with Tyson; Lane ruled it accidental and did not deduct any points. Lane later said that Tyson's behavior suggested he was frustrated and that at some point, he simply "went nuts."[16]

As the bell rang for round 3, Tyson came out without his mouthpiece, and Lane ordered him back to the corner to retrieve it. With forty seconds left in the round, for reasons that have never been adequately explained, while in a clinch, Tyson spit out his mouthpiece, and in one quick motion rolled his head onto Holyfield's shoulder and bit off the top part of the right ear. Holyfield jumped back in pain and screamed— he later said his initial thought was that a sniper had shot him— grabbing his ear with his gloved hand and seeing blood dripping from it. Meanwhile, Tyson contemptuously spit out a postage-stamp-size piece of cartilage onto the canvas. Sure enough, Lane's quick examination of Holyfield confirmed that a piece of the ear was missing; blood began seeping from the gash. Lane called a time-out as Holyfield's seconds attempted to stanch the bleeding. Facing a bizarre situation not covered in the guidelines, Lane consulted with Ratner, telling him that he was prepared to disqualify Tyson. According to Lane, Ratner simply replied, "Are you sure?" and so Lane conferred with ring doctor Flip Homansky, who confirmed that Holyfield could continue the fight. Aware of the huge audience who had paid good money to see the fight, and assured by a defiant Holyfield that he wanted to continue, Lane deducted two points from Tyson and ordered the round to resume.[17]

For his part, Holyfield was enraged and more than ready to continue. He nailed Tyson with a stiff right hand, but in an ensuing clinch just before the bell ended the round, Tyson bit again, this time on the left ear. Lane was partially blocked and did not clearly see the second bite, and a few seconds later the round ended. A Holyfield cornerman called Lane to the corner where he examined the left ear and saw clear tooth marks. "There's a limit to everything, including bites," he later remarked. "How many times do you want him to get bit?"[18]

Lane later recalled that this bizarre set of events infuriated him because he perceived it to be a gross violation of the rules of boxing and, more important, the spirit of the unwritten code that all boxers are expected to follow. "That's it, Mike," he said. "You're outta here. You're gone, you're done."[19] At that point, Tyson went berserk and in an uncontrollable rage charged across the ring in an attempt to attack Holyfield and his manager. Into the ring poured Ratner and other members of the Nevada Athletic Commission, several ringside spectators, an aroused and gesticulating Don King, a host of casino security, and who knows who else. It was absolute chaos in the ring. Tyson reportedly took a swing at a policeman but missed. Ratner and NAC commissioner Luther Mack confronted the seemingly berserk Tyson and ordered him to leave the ring, while a flying squadron of security personnel surrounded Lane and whisked him to the safety of his dressing room. After some semblance of order was restored, ring announcer Jimmy Lennon Jr. read the bizarre decision: "Referee Mills Lane has disqualified Mike Tyson for biting Evander Holyfield on both of his ears." The arena erupted in an angry wave of boos and shouts of protest as Tyson left the ring, headed for his dressing room. Still enraged, he had to be restrained from attacking some spectators who showered him with curses and beer.

In the aftermath of the near riot in the ring, MGM Grand employee Mitchell Libonati spotted the detached portion of Holyfield's ear that had somehow not been kicked away by the scuffling mob. A paramedic packed it in ice and delivered it to Holyfield's dressing room. Plastic surgery restored the ear to its original condition.

The public reaction was instantaneous and predictable. Tyson had managed to become a pariah. *Sports Illustrated* splashed a large headline across its cover showing the two fighters in the momentous clinch that shouted, *"Madman!"* Writers demanded that Tyson be suspended from boxing for a long time, some suggesting permanently. Comedians had a field day with Jeffrey Dahmer and Hannibal the Cannibal jokes, and pop psychologists did instant (and varying) analyses of Tyson's mental state. Veteran boxing writer Budd Schulberg, who was at ringside, described Tyson as a "rabid dog." Within minutes after the disqualification, jokes flew among ringside journalists, one suggesting that Holyfield's nickname the "Real Deal" be changed to the "Real Meal." Others concluded that Tyson had "bit off more than he could chew." They had just witnessed the "Bite of the Year." Bernie Lincicome of the *Chicago Tribune* weighed in with, "Tyson is the first fighter to lose because of gluttony."[20] And so on.

But dark humor aside, the Bite Fight greatly accelerated the already sagging image of prizefighting. Some suggested that boxing was fast approaching the level of professional wrestling, lurching from the status of a legitimate sport into a seamy burlesque. A few defenders rallied to Tyson, suggesting that his behavior merely reflected the essential violent nature of the blood sport of boxing. UCLA clinical psychiatrist Carole Lieberman suggested, "He acts on his impulses like a 6-year old would. He had a temper tantrum." But even these few defenders were essentially concurring with the conventional wisdom that boxing had been substantially diminished.

Las Vegas Review-Journal veteran boxing writer Royce Feour observed, "Boxing is a bizarre sport, but this ending had to be the most bizarre of all for any heavyweight championship fight." Even President Bill Clinton got in on the punditry with one word: "horrifying." Back in Reno, Mills Lane reflected on the episode. "Boxing has many black eyes. There are a lot of things that make you want to shake your head."[21]

The Nevada Athletic Commission wasted no time in fining Tyson three million dollars (according to its policies the largest fine it could levy) and suspending his license indefinitely. It could not, however, withhold payment of the rest of the purse, and so Tyson (and King) pocketed and somehow divided twenty-seven million dollars for Tyson's nine minutes of work. In his appearance before the commission in a room crowded with journalists and curious onlookers, Tyson was contrite and apologetic, reading a carefully written statement drafted on his behalf by former commission member Sig Rogich, a leading public relations expert who had been a close campaign adviser to Presidents Ronald Reagan and George H. W. Bush, along with many other prominent Republicans. "I snapped. I cannot tell you why, exactly, I acted the way I did. I snapped." In a later public statement, however, Tyson was more inclined to defend his action: "I would do it again under the same circumstances. Mills Lane was not protecting me from Holyfield's head butts. I would do it again if I see myself bloody and cut up."[22]

The Nevada Athletic Commission stipulated that as a condition for reinstatement, Tyson would have to submit to a complete psychological examination, citing its formal conclusion that he was suffering from a "constellation of neurobehavioral deficits." With other state commissions respecting the Nevada suspension, Tyson did not fight again for eighteen months. When he did return to the ring, he was but a shadow of his former self. Now into his midthirties, he had lost his intimidating edge, both physically and psychologically, and his career careened into oblivion. In 1999 he was sentenced to nine months in a Maryland jail for assaulting a motorist after a fender bender. Once more, in 2002, the NAC suspended his license due to repeated episodes of bizarre behavior, including his having become embroiled in a brawl during a New York City press conference.

Tyson's career, and the two chomps upon Holyfield's ears, provided an apt metaphor for the visible decline of the stature of prizefighting in American society. Beyond that, however, boxing's many excesses contributed to palpable declining public interest in boxing. Prizefighting seemed to have become a sick caricature of itself. Newspaper coverage declined substantially, and coverage of the sport by the unquestioned arbiter of the relevance of individual American sports, ESPN radio and television, only seldom made mention of boxing as it focused upon covering the three "major" sports of football, baseball, and basketball that had near-universal appeal to its large national audience.

Boxing's appeal had always hinged upon the popularity of the heavyweight division, and with Tyson's fall and Holyfield's retirement, the new crop of heavyweights did not resonate. A major pipeline for talented heavyweights ever since the 1930s had been the steady stream of black boxers coming out of the inner cities. In black communities, however, boxing had lost its attraction, and young men with the requisite physical tools were drawn instead to football and basketball. Instead of opting for learning the tools of the sweet science in a sweaty gym, young black athletes were instead drawn to college athletic scholarships with a sharp eye trained on the possibilities of a big payday from the National Basketball Association or National Football League. This route included not only the opportunity of obtaining a college education, but also the fame and glory of becoming a star who could perform on national television and maybe even hit the jackpot of a mainline professional sport if things worked out just right. And they would not have to earn a living subjecting themselves to the blows of another man's fists or deal with promoters. The role model for young black athletes no longer was a Joe Louis or Sugar Ray Leonard; it was Michael Jordan and LeBron James, Jerry Rice and Barry Sanders. Definitely not a Mike Tyson.

Anything Goes, Sort Of

It began innocently enough, with a simple question being asked: could a wrestler beat a boxer of equal quality, or vice versa? The new combat sport that evolved out of that intriguing question was originally called "ultimate fighting" because the techniques of the boxer, wrestler, karate expert, sumo wrestler, and even the simple barroom brawler were accepted. Soon the preferred name became mixed martial arts. The first such card was held in Denver in November 1993, and promoter Art Davie assumed it was probably a onetime thing, an experiment that might attract both boxing and wrestling fans. Advance publicity promised plenty of gore and mayhem in no-holds-barred contests, and Davie lined up fighters representative of several formats, including traditional boxing, kickboxing, wrestling, sumo wrestling, and jujitsu. A crowd of thirty-five hundred spectators filed into McNichols Arena, drawn as much by curiosity as anything. However, cable television generated more than eighty-five thousand "buys." By evening's end, entrepreneurs smelled a new pot of cash.[23]

It was an unusual evening. Senior writer Jon Wertheim of *Sports Illustrated* wryly described the assembled audience as "heavy-duty white trash, the curious and the bloodthirsty." More important, the crowd was also young, fitting the demographic most desired by television executives: those between the ages of nineteen and thirty-four. And as what became known as the sport of mixed martial arts matured, its appeal extended to all socioeconomic groups. But its appeal most definitely was directed at men and women under the age of forty.

Most of the matches that evening seemed lackluster, with combatants spending much of the time squirming around on the mat locked interminably in various wrestling holds, sometimes freeing an arm to throw a punch. The crowd responded to such dullness with catcalls and boos, but came to life when the action got frantic. A few bouts more than lived up to the promise of bloody action, especially when a kickboxer surprised his opponent with a powerful heel hook and broke an ankle; as the wounded warrior screamed in pain and floundered about on the floor, the crowd demanded the fight continue.

A new sport was born, and matches began to be held across the country. Several companies, including Semaphore Entertainment, which copyrighted the iconic label UFC (for Ultimate Fighting Championship), rushed in to capitalize. But the UFC had several copycats and competitors. Experimentation with various formats offered by promoters in different cities honed the sport and defined its commercial possibilities. Ultimately, MMA was inspired by the requirement of twenty-four-hour cable-television networks to find new forms of entertainment to fill the program day and attract new viewers. In 1995 Semaphore acquired the rights to the name UFC and the provided stability for the rapidly growing sport. For the newfound fans, a galaxy of new stars appeared on the horizon—Ken Shamrock, Royce Gracie, Oleg Taktarov, Pat Miletich, Georges St.-Pierre—who were completely unrecognizable to the uninitiated, including mainstream boxing folk.

During the first few years of MMA, blood flowed nearly as often as sweat. There was, for example, the occasion when a kickboxer launched a foot into the mouth of an opponent, leaving two teeth embedded in his foot. Wrestlers stunned boxers who found themselves unable to guard against a throwdown hold, or as jujitsu artists used leverage to bend and occasionally break opponents' body parts. In other bouts, however, the action was subdued as the two men grappled on the mat, seeking to gain a victory by "submission," perhaps by employing a "guillotine choke."

Individuals originally attracted to MMA came predominantly from those who as youngsters had embraced the new "extreme" activities such as in-line skating, snowboarding, and motocross. The popularity of MMA grew through their widespread use of the new social media. Spectators from Generation X were seeking a new sport to differentiate themselves from those of their parents and grandparents. Early on, to establish an image to separate MMA from boxing and especially the faux sport of professional wrestling, the eight-sided wire-enclosed cage was introduced to replace the traditional rope-encircled (square) ring. This was ostensibly to keep the fighters from falling off the mat, but the stark image of the octagon-shaped cage added an ominous, even sinister, touch to the new extreme sport.

For several years, promoters advertised, "There are no rules!" and that a contest would continue until, as one flyer put it, "knockout, submission, doctor's intervention, or death." American social historians were reminded of the savagery of the "rough-and-tumble" battles that were held over several generations in the sparsely populated Appalachian Mountain postrevolutionary frontier regions of Tennessee, Kentucky, and Virginia in which eye gouging and testicle extraction were primary objectives. Others saw in MMA a reversion to the primitive nineteenth-century bare-knuckle fights in mining camps and saloons. MMA promoters, however, emphasized that the new sport was not professional wrestling because it was a legitimate contest, not a contrived fake spectacle.

By 2000 MMA proved it could attract sizable crowds and surprisingly large cable-television audiences numbering in the several hundreds of thousands for high-profile matches. MMA also caught the eye of those who believed it to be dangerously "barbaric." Among those who became alarmed was US senator John McCain, a man closely connected to Las Vegas boxing. The future presidential candidate publicly denounced MMA as "human cockfighting" and sent letters to state athletic commissions demanding the sport be banned. Apparently, he took too literally the claims of promoters that the fights were "to the death." In response, state commissions established rules that toned down the sport's most egregious aspects. Small flexible gloves were required that protected the knuckles but permitted the fingers to be used. Weight classes were established, and the number and length of rounds were created, with varying lengths based upon the importance of the match. A lengthy list of fouls was established that included biting, eye gouging, hitting the groin area, head butting, rabbit punches, hair pulling, choking, kicking the head, and "fish-hooking" (pulling wide an opponent's mouth or nose). The rules were to be enforced by a trained referee, with three judges scoring the bout. These changes mollified the critics and prompted one prominent MMA executive to observe, not without some basis in fact, that the sport was actually less dangerous to the participants than boxing, football, and, yes, acrobatic cheerleading.[24]

With these changes, the sport went mainstream with only the New York athletic commission refusing to permit the fun. Gymnasiums that had long offered training for would-be boxers added instruction in the various fighting styles permitted under the new MMA rules, essentially cross-training students in several combat styles—jujitsu, kickboxing, wrestling, and boxing being the most prominent. To its devoted fans, the sport was much more realistic than boxing because, as one young fan told a reporter, "in a fight in the street, you throw your opponent to the ground, you know. You don't just stand up and duke it out, you know. It's realistic."[25] In 2001 UFC was purchased from Semaphore Entertainment by two wealthy Las Vegas brothers, major owners of the highly profitable Station Casinos that were strategically located across Las Vegas to appeal to the locals trade. Frank Fertitta III and Lorenzo Fertitta bought the rights for two million dollars. Essentially, they bought the well-recognized name of UFC and the contracts of a stable of fighters. They established their new investment under the unique name of Zuffa (an Italian word roughly translated as "scuffle") and formed it as a limited liability corporation. They immediately established good working relationships with the Nevada Athletic Commission, of which Lorenzo had been a commissioner. In 2005 Zuffa hired longtime NAC executive director Marc Ratner to become a vice president of regulatory affairs, with responsibilities focused upon working well with state athletic commissions. This was significant because Ratner had earlier aligned himself with Senator McCain's campaign to abolish MMA.

Most important, however, the Fertitta brothers hired a high school friend, Dana White, as president to direct the day-to-day affairs of Zuffa. White was street-smart, brash, and profane, a natural promoter who understood the necessary dynamics to promote UFC in an era of social media and satellite communications. His major business experience prior to assuming day-to-day control of this risky multimillion-dollar operation was managing a string of Las Vegas exercise studios, teaching neophytes the basics of MMA. His behavior was often outrageous, but it was not contrived and was a natural form of expression for this forty-year-old hustler. Within a few years, White's leadership turned Zuffa into an extraordinarily profitable company. He proved himself to be a shrewd businessman and promoter with a deft touch.[26]

White's informal motto was "Fighting in is our DNA." He believed combat is instinctive to the human species, which explained the rapid growth in popularity of MMA. "We get it, and we like it," he exuded. "It doesn't have to be explained." Not prone to proceed cautiously, White envisioned that by exploiting the potential of satellite communications, Zuffa could make the UFC brand of ultimate fighting popular worldwide: "I believe fighting was the first sport on earth. It works everywhere, and we're going to take it everywhere."[27]

White intuitively understood that while some bouts would be action packed, with plenty of knees, feet, elbows, and fists flying and blood splattering, others would become bogged down in interminable wrestling holds. To combat such dull moments, he brought to the staging of the bouts many of the trappings of rock concerts and professional wrestling. He copyrighted the name of "Octagon," used scantily clad young women to parade around the Octagon between rounds holding up the number of the upcoming round, and had the combatants enter the Octagon in a darkened arena drenched by intense light shows to the pounding beat of pulsating music. Perhaps White recalled the exciting moments at the Thomas and Mack Center when Jerry Tarkanian's UNLV Rebels basketball team took to the court amid raucous music, dazzling lights, and artificial smoke in a darkened arena. He deployed large screens to show close-up views of the action and naturally employed a hyperkinetic announcer for extra effect. Although UFC staged its bouts in major cities across the country, the Las Vegas influence was clearly on display.

Within a few years, White had made the UFC brand dominant in the still evolving sport, holding about a dozen major cards each year in large arenas across the United States, with pay-per-view television providing the bulk of the revenue. In Las Vegas, UFC events held at the Mandalay Bay or MGM Grand Garden Arena were sold out well before fight night. Over the years, Zuffa bought out rivals World Extreme Cagefighting, Pride Fighting Championships, and Strikeforce, consolidating its control. White, never one for modesty, said that these acquisitions were equal in significance to the 1966 merger of the National and American Football Leagues. He signed a lucrative sponsorship with Budweiser, making Bud Light the "official" beer of UFC, and moved aggressively into the Asian, South American, and European markets with television packages. He marketed apparel gear with the UFC logo and even produced a video game with UFC action figures. In 2012, as an indication that UFC had arrived, Zuffa and Fox television announced the signing of a seven-year contract that would put UFC on the major network four times a year and more frequently on the cable network FX. Finally, in a nod to the inevitable, but also in anticipation of another revenue stream, White announced that he had signed several female fighters.

Instant Replay

In less than twenty years, mixed martial arts had gone from being a onetime experiment to an established innovative sport that was reflective of the new trends in popular culture. That Zuffa had turned UFC into a profitable niche sport with plenty of upside potential was unquestioned. Whether it would be able to surpass boxing in the years to come remained uncertain, but it had become a definite possibility. What was certain, however, was that under Dana White's magical orchestration, UFC had staked a claim on the allegiance of a large number of younger Americans who are drawn to a blood sport.

Beyond question, a wide cultural and generational gap existed between the younger MMA adherents and older boxing traditionalists who had been raised in an era inspired by the likes of Joe Louis, Rocky Marciano, and Muhammad Ali, but perhaps most strikingly epitomized by the motion picture personage of Rocky Balboa. That boxing had lost its stature as one of the major American sports was readily evident by the lack of everyday interest that had once existed. Boxing news no longer appeared with regularity on the sports pages of daily newspapers, and it was almost never seen on the ultimate arbiter of what was important to the average American sports fan: ESPN's daily *SportsCenter* telecasts.

Only after UFC had consolidated its control over the sport in much the same way that NASCAR controls stock-car racing did the new sport begin to break through and receive coverage in the mainstream media.

As MMA gained momentum, newspapers began grudgingly including occasional reports on their sports pages, and in 2007 a UFC fight scene appeared for the first time on the cover of *Sports Illustrated.* But MMA nonetheless remained on the fringes of American popular culture, where boxing had long enjoyed a centrality that was now slipping away. Not until ESPN's *SportsCenter* highlights a spectacular moment of a UFC fight in its popular "Top-Ten Plays of the Day" segment will MMA enthusiasts be able to say that UFC has actually arrived as an equal contender with boxing.

Boxing's decline had many causative factors, but it is clear that casino managements had embraced boxing with an eye toward an immediate payback. This might have been profitable for the promoters, but it did little to create wider interest among potential new fans, leaving the door open for White and the UFC. Boxing promoters also took a short-term approach in their endeavors that did little to encourage the development of a new generation of boxing fans. When a major fight in Las Vegas neared, coverage crept back onto the nation's sports pages, but only temporarily. During the 2000s, Las Vegas casinos hosted markedly fewer fights that attracted substantive attention in the national media. The contrast with the last two decades of the twentieth century was striking. Of course, the motivation had always been short term, designed only to attract big spenders to the next prizefight. Will that special flurry of excitement that an Ali or Tyson fight once produced ever be replicated again along the streets of Las Vegas Boulevard South? Could it possibly be when the younger generation that has embraced MMA reaches their prime earning years in another decade or so that a new generation of entrepreneurial casino managers might reprise the big fight-night concept?

Many forces were—and remain—at work. As Las Vegas entered the second decade of the new millennium, it was in the midst of yet another makeover of its image, this time marketing itself as a "total entertainment experience." MMA meshed well with the expansion of the entertainment options offered in the city and seemed to be an imaginative way by which to connect with Gen Xers, many of whom had pioneered companies for the Internet age and had serious high-roller potential. Boxing remained, of course, but its appeal had now become more closely skewed to the growing purchasing power of Hispanics, which meant that the parade of heavyweights had been replaced by smaller, faster, and more exciting boxers in lower weight classes. That Oscar De La Hoya was the biggest draw in the city in recent years was an indication of this new trend.

Although the future of boxing remained murky following the downward spiral that consumed the sport at the onset of the twenty-first century, there can be no question that boxing has enjoyed a unique niche in the history of Nevada. Its initial popularity grew out of the dangerous and unpredictable masculine-dominated culture of the mining camps of the nineteenth century, but the state's business and political elite adopted it early in the twentieth century as a means of attracting tourists and potential investors in the state. Nevada's first prizefight promoter, Tex Rickard, was emblematic of the state's entrepreneurial spirit as he successfully promoted two major championship fights, both replete with strong racial overtones, that firmly entwined the sport of boxing with the state of Nevada in the national consciousness at the pivotal time when boxing was moving out of the shadows and into the mainstream of American sports. That Rickard moved from Nevada to become president of Madison Square Garden and a wildly successful fight promoter during the first "golden era" of American sports was no mere coincidence. In New York City, he became a dashing man-about-town, a successful entrepreneur who, among other things, capitalized upon the popularity of Jack Dempsey, whose own ties to Nevada were legendary.

Following the decline of boxing as a major sporting attraction in New York City in the 1950s, the sport returned to Nevada, which was in the midst of a gaming-induced economic boom and population expansion. Boxing became an important part of a much larger economic development strategy implemented by Nevada's gaming and tourist industry that quickly came to dominate the state's political and economic life. Heavy media coverage of championship fights publicized Las Vegas as the place where exciting action took place, and aspiring boxers knew they had arrived when they were signed for a main event on the Strip.

Sportswriters, heavily focused upon the details of the next big fight, failed to perceive the irony of the role played by Nevada casinos in luring boxing back to Nevada. Controlled by the most powerful organized crime families in the United States, the casinos seamlessly transferred boxing from New York City, where it had fallen out of favor due to Mob influence, to the Las Vegas Strip, where it would flourish. Casinos initially underwrote high-profile fights held at the Las Vegas Convention Center. By the 1980s, however, casinos began hosting the prizefights in cooperation with such leading promoters as Bob Arum and Don King. Several properties even built lavish arenas to accommodate large fight crowds as well as for concerts and other events. The fact that these venues also kept fight fans close to their casino floors was not overlooked.

Sportswriters and the television announcers who covered Nevada fights seldom pushed their coverage of boxing matches beyond the punches thrown and the championships won and lost to explore the underlying social issues that the fights so often revealed. The one obvious exception was Howard Cosell, who championed the cause of Muhammad Ali after he was injudiciously stripped of his heavyweight title by the Nevada Athletic Commission in 1967 without even the courtesy of a hearing. Ali's religious conversion to the Muslim faith and his struggles with the United States Selective Service were front and center in many articles and television reports, but the general decline in the number and prominence of white fighters and the rapid accession of black fighters to dominance were never seriously explored by the sports media. In a very real sense, however, the civil rights movement in the United States became the essential background for the understanding of the social and cultural significance of Nevada boxing.

The rapid growth in the Hispanic population in Nevada (it reached 28 percent in 2010) occurred simultaneously with the emergence of Hispanic boxers to prominence—most of them of Mexican nationality —especially in the lower weight classifications. Nevada's rapidly growing Hispanic population meant that charismatic Hispanic fighters had a ready and enthusiastic fan base, which at fight time would be substantially enlarged by an influx of fans from Arizona and Southern California. During the first decade of the new century, the presence of leading Hispanic fighters enabled the Las Vegas boxing economy to keep perking along. That reality became strikingly evident in the wake of the demise of Mike Tyson and the subsequent dearth of compelling heavyweight fighters of any race.

By the early 2000s, it became apparent that the stature of boxing had been severely diminished. The number of big fights in Las Vegas dwindled markedly. Boxing no longer appeared with regularity on the sports pages of the nation's newspapers, and coverage by television and radio likewise became minimal. Mixed martial arts was increasingly elbowing its way into the national consciousness, especially among those under the age of forty. Except for instances when a leading Hispanic fighter was in the ring, boxing's declining appeal seemed to replicate that occurring with another once very popular spectator sport: horse racing. Boxing and horse racing, it seemed, were drawing heavily upon a dwindling fan base composed primarily of older white males. Attendance at regular horse-race meets had been in a steady decline since the 1950s, and only a few races each year that had historical resonance as a special cultural celebration received media attention. Just as fans still pack the stands in Louisville for the annual Kentucky Derby, so too will high rollers show up in Las Vegas for the occasional big fight. But as the years passed in the new millennium, those occasions occurred with less and less frequency.

Another important change in public perception has the potential to reduce further the possibility that boxing will make a major comeback. In recent years, the American public has become sensitized to the long-term consequences of brain trauma resulting from the contact sport of football. Although the flurry of media attention focused almost exclusively upon the dangers posed for football players, the potential for collateral impact upon the future of boxing obviously exists. The dangers of boxing have long been well established, but concern for "punch-drunk" fighters who suffer severe postcareer dementia has never resonated with the general public as it has for famous former football players.

That lack of concern has meant that elected legislators have not been moved to take action. This apparently is because so few young men from outside the lower strata of society ever take up the sport. As Joyce Carol Oates has cogently explained: "One *plays* football, one doesn't *play* boxing." With its heavy reliance upon a pool of poor and uneducated young males to supply professional boxers, the sport has been able to survive the deaths of hundreds of fighters over the past century because the dangers posed do not threaten middle- and upper-class Americans. Therefore, the issue of brain trauma suffered by boxers has never resonated on the radar of elected lawmakers. Even efforts by the American Medical Association to ban boxing have not gained traction. Perhaps, if the crusade to reduce the dangers of brain damage caused by the popular game of football gains momentum, a side effect might result in meaningful legislative action regarding the future of boxing. It is instructive to recall the argument, seemingly persuasive, made by Dana White of the Ultimate Fighting Championship that mixed martial arts poses a substantially smaller danger of brain trauma than boxing.

Yet the long and tortured history of boxing reveals that the sport has surprising resiliency. As one of boxing's leading journalists, historians, and enthusiasts, Bert Sugar, wrote in 2006, boxing has managed to survive despite a long history replete with "more scandals, more scoundrels, and more skullduggery on its side of the ledger than any other sport."[28] Whether boxing can once more rebound and regain the vibrancy that it displayed in Nevada in the late twentieth century remains unanswered. But one thing is for certain: if a new generation of exciting boxers emerges, and if there are high rollers to be found and big fights to be fought, then there is no doubt that Nevada will find a way to make it happen.

Nonetheless, the decline of interest in boxing is real. It is significant that no other American city has demonstrated interest in wresting the "Fight Town" label away from Las Vegas. It just does not seem to matter that much anymore.

Notes

The Prelims

1. Randy Roberts, *Jack Dempsey: The Manassa Mauler* (1979; reprint, Urbana: University of Illinois Press, 2003), 219–35; Colleen Aycock and Mark Scott, *Tex Rickard: Boxing's Greatest Promoter* (Jefferson, NC: McFarland, 2012), 176–85.

2. Roberts, *Jack Dempsey,* 266–70.

3. Elliott Gorn, "'Gouge and Bite, Pull Hair and Scratch': The Social Significance of Fighting in the Southern Back Country," *American Historical Review* (February 1985): 18–43; Elliott Gorn, *The Manly Art: Bare-Knuckle Prize Fighting in America* (Ithaca, NY: Cornell University Press, 1986), 60–81.

4. Gorn, *Manly Art,* 65–68.

5. Kasia Boddy, *Boxing: A Cultural History* (London: Reaktion Books, 2008), 91–95.

6. H. W. Brands, *T. R.: The Last Romantic* (New York: Basic Books, 1997), 41–42, 565.

7. Gorn, *Manly Art,* 241–47.

8. Mary Murphy, *Mining Cultures: Men, Women, and the Leisure in Butte, 1914–41* (Urbana: University of Illinois Press, 1997); Sally Zanjani, *Goldfield: The Last Goldrush on the Western Frontier* (Athens: Ohio University Press, 1992).

9. Joyce Carol Oates, *On Boxing* (New York: Harper Perennial Books, 2006), 18–19.

Round 1. Fistic Carnival in Carson City

1. Official Fight Program, *Dan Stuart's Fistic Carnival,* Nevada Historical Society (NHS).

2. Leo N. Miletich, *Dan Stuart's Fistic Carnival* (College Station: Texas A&M University Press, 1994), 18–21.

3. Ibid., 18.

4. Ibid., 21–36.

5. Ibid., 31.

6. Ibid., 36–46.

7. Matt Donnellon, *The Irish Champion Peter Maher* (London: Trafford, 2008), 94–127.

8. Miletich, *Dan Stuart's Fistic Carnival,* 169–91.

9. *New York World,* February 22, 1896.

10. Official Fight Program, *Dan Stuart's Fistic Carnival,* 8; "Gambling Unlimited: Nevada, the Last Frontier State," n.d., Corbett-Fitzsimmons File, NHS.

11. John Marschall, *Jews in Nevada: A History* (Reno: University of Nevada Press, 2008), 142–44; "Portrait of Al Livingstone [*sic*]: Law Breaker, Law Maker, and Boxing Promoter" (John Marschall, working document).

12. Quoted in *Nevada Appeal,* November 4, 1979, print file, NHS.

13. *Chicago Tribune,* March 2, 1897.

14. Armond Fields, *James J. Corbett: A Biography of the Heavyweight Boxing Champion and Popular Theater Headliner* (Jefferson, NC: McFarland, 2001), 1–66.

15. Ibid., 94.

16. Ibid., 100–102.

17. Miletich, *Dan Stuart's Fistic Carnival,* 169–202; "The Fight of the Century" (San Francisco: H. S. Crocker, June 1, 1987), Corbett Fitzsimmons file, NHS.

18. "Women May See Fight," *New York Times,* February 25, 1897, 5; "The Prizefight and Equal Suffrage Going Hand in Hand with Great Hopes for the Future," *Nevada State Journal,* February 7, 1897, 3.

19. Quoted in Miletich, *Dan Stuart's Fistic Carnival,* 196.

20. "Ex-Senator John J. Ingalls Describes the Fight" and "Thomas T. Williams' Summary of the Fight," both detailed essays in "The Fight of the Century."

21. George Siler, "What Referee Siler Saw Within the Ropes," in "The Fight of the Century."

22. Fields, *James J. Corbett,* 103–6; Miletich, *Dan Stuart's Fistic Carnival,* 198–200.

23. "Williams' Summary of the Fight"; "Ingalls Describes the Fight."

24. Robert K. DeArment, *Bat Masterson: The Man and the Legend* (Norman: University of Oklahoma Press, 1979), 349.

25. *New York Times,* March 18, 1897; *Nevada Appeal,* March 18, 1897.

26. James J. Corbett, *The Roar of the Crowd: The True Tale of the Rise and Fall of a Champion* (Garden City, NY: Garden City, 1926), 262–66.

27. William A. Brady, *The Fighting Man* (Indianapolis: Bobbs-Merrill, 1916), 146–48.

28. Thomas T. Williams, "Scenes and Incidents"; "Detailed Account of the Fight by W. W. Naughton"; James J. Corbett, "Corbett's Account of the Fight of the Century," in "The Fight of the Century."

29. Boddy, *Boxing: A Cultural History,* 153 (see the introduction, n. 5).

30. For a technical analysis of the filming of the fight, see Dan Streible, *Fight Pictures: A History of Boxing and Early Cinema* (Berkeley: University of California Press, 2008), 52–95.

31. Miriam Hansen, *Babel and Babylon: Spectatorship in American Silent Film* (Cambridge, MA: Harvard University Press, 1991), 1.

32. Dan Streible, "Female Spectators and the Corbett-Fitzsimmons Fight," in *Out of Bounds: Sports, Media, and the Politics of Identity,* edited by Miriam Hansen (Bloomington: Indiana University Press, 1997), 16–47.

33. *Reno Evening Gazette,* March 19, 1897, 4.

Round 2. Low Blow in the Desert

1. For the definitive study of mining in twentieth-century Nevada, see Russell Elliott, *Nevada's Twentieth-Century Mining Boom: Tonopah-Goldfield-Ely* (Reno: University of Nevada Press, 1966). For Goldfield, see Zanjani, *Goldfield* (see the introduction, n. 8). For a rich collection of photographs and a perceptive interpretative commentary, see Sally Zanjani, *The Glory Days of Goldfield* (Reno: University of Nevada Press, 2002).

2. Charles Samuels's lively and episodic *The Magnificent Rube: The Life and Gaudy Times of Tex Rickard* (New York: McGraw-Hill, 1957) is useful, but it has been supplanted by Colleen Aycock and Mark Scott, *Tex Rickard: Boxing's Greatest Promoter* (Jefferson, NC: McFarland, 2012).

3. Samuels, *Magnificent Rube,* 12.

4. For the early life of Rickard from Texas until his departure from Alaska in 1904, see ibid., 1–86.

5. Aycock and Scott, *Tex Rickard,* 21–38 (see the introduction, n. 1).

6. Samuels, *Magnificent Rube,* 63; Michael K. Bohn, *Heroes and Ballyhoo: How the Golden Age of the 1920s Transformed American Sports* (Washington, DC: Potomac Books, 2009), 27.

7. George G. Rice, *My Adventures with Your Money* (Boston: Gorham Press, 1911), 61.

8. Ibid.; Samuels, *Magnificent Rube,* 95–96.

9. Samuels, *Magnificent Rube,* 96.

10. Ibid., 142.

11. Quoted in Elliott, *Nevada's Twentieth-Century Mining Boom,* 53–54.

12. Ibid., 90.

13. Quoted in Samuels, *Magnificent Rube,* 99; Richard G. Lillard, *Desert Challenge: An Interpretation of Nevada* (New York: Alfred A. Knopf, 1942), 262.

14. Zanjani, *Goldfield,* 168–80; Elliott, *Nevada's Twentieth-Century Mining Boom,* 91–96; Peter Goin and C. Elizabeth Raymond, *Changing Mines in America* (Santa Fe, NM: Center for American Places, 2004), 118–19. See also Rice's candid and humorous memoirs of his Goldfield adventures written in 1910 while in prison, *My Adventures with Your Money.*

15. Guy Louis Rocha and Eric N. Moody, "Hart vs. Root: The Heavyweight Title Fight That Time Forgot," *BoxingInsider.com,* April 15, 2008.

16. Samuels, *Magnificent Rube,* 100.

17. J. Dee Kille, "United by Gold and Glory: The Making of Mining Culture in Goldfield, Nevada, 1906–1908" (PhD diss., University of Nevada, Reno, 2008), 70–72; Aycock and Scott, *Tex Rickard,* 45–79.

18. Bert Sugar, *100 Years of Boxing* (New York: Routledge, 1982), 58–63; Colleen Aycock, "Joe Gans, World Lightweight Champion," in *The First Black Champions: Essays on Fighters of the 1800s to the 1920s,* edited by Colleen Aycock and Mark Scott (Jefferson, NC: McFarland, 2011), 79–101; Samuels, *Magnificent Rube,* 86–91.

19. Samuels, *Magnificent Rube,* 90–91.

20. Colleen Aycock and Mark Scott, *Joe Gans: A Biography of the First African American World Boxing Champion* (Jefferson, NC: McFarland, 2008), 152–79.

21. Sugar, *100 Years of Boxing,* 60.

22. Nat Fleischer, *Black Dynamite: The Story of the Negro in Boxing* (New York: O'Brien, 1938), 143.

23. The complex story of his alleged fixed fights is described, with multiple possible explanations, in Aycock and Scott, *Joe Gans,* 63–81, 109–24, with the authors weighing in on the version that Gans was the victim of the skullduggery of manager Al Herford.

24. Samuels, *Magnificent Rube,* 118.

25. Unknown journalist quoted in ibid., 108.

26. Aycock and Scott, *Joe Gans,* 156–57; Samuels, *Magnificent Rube,* 109–12.

27. Samuels, *Magnificent Rube,* 112.

28. Bohn, *Heroes and Ballyhoo,* 27; Samuels, *Magnificent Rube,* 112–13.

29. Quoted in Kille, "United by Gold and Glory," 74.

30. Ibid., 79.

31. Ibid., 66, 81–82; Murphy, *Mining Cultures,* 114–18 (see the introduction, n. 8).

32. Kille provides an analysis of the gender issue ("United by Gold and Glory," 75–77).

33. Streible, *Fight Pictures,* 174 (see chap. 1, n. 30).

34. Aycock and Scott, *Joe Gans,* 162.

35. For a detailed round-by-round description of the fight, see the *Tonopah Daily Sun,* clipping in Gans-Nelson File, Nevada Historical Society (NHS). See also Aycock and Scott, *Joe Gans,* 152–79.

36. Quoted in Eugene L. Conrotto, "Gans vs. Nelson," *Desert Magazine,* June 1959, clipping in Gans-Nelson File, NHS.

37. Ibid.

38. Aycock and Scott, *Joe Gans,* 73–75.

39. Rice, *My Adventures with Your Money,* 118.

40. Ibid., 113; Streible, *Fight Pictures,* 198–201.

41. Elliott, *Nevada's Twentieth-Century Mining Boom,* 103–44; C. Elizabeth Raymond, *George Winfield: Owner and Operator of Nevada* (Reno: University of Nevada Press, 1992), 87–146; Zanjani, *Goldfield,* 214–50.

42. Elliott, *Nevada's Twentieth-Century Mining Boom,* 159–60, states that had Goldfield not become the county seat of small, isolated Esmeralda County, it would have become a tourist attraction as a ghost town. In 1923 the majority of wooden buildings covering fifty blocks were leveled by a wind-driven fire. In 2010 the official population was recorded by the US Census at 285 citizens, but a 2012 report by the United States Post Office placed the number of active residents receiving mail service at 46.

43. Elliott, *Nevada's Twentieth-Century Mining Boom,* 90.

44. Aycock and Scott, *Tex Rickard,* 61 (see the introduction, n. 1).

Round 3. Reno, "Center of the Universe"

1. Randy Roberts, *Papa Jack: Jack Johnson and the Era of White Hopes* (New York: Free Press, 1983), 85.

2. Ray Hagar and Guy Clifton, *Johnson-Jeffries: Dateline Reno* (Battle Ground, WA: Pediment, 2010), 7.

3. Robert Greenwood, *Jack Johnson vs. James Jeffries: The Prize Fight of the Century* (Reno: Jack Bacon & Company and Baobab Books, 2004), 24.

4. Roberts, *Papa Jack,* 66.

5. Ibid., 69–82.

6. Sugar, *100 Years of Boxing,* 58–72 (see chap. 2, n. 18); Roberts, *Papa Jack,* 82–84.

7. Roberts, *Papa Jack,* 84.

8. Ibid., 66–67.

9. Lillard, *Desert Challenge,* 272–73 (see chap. 2, n. 13).

10. Samuels, *Magnificent Rube,* 135–41 (see chap. 2, n. 2).

11. Ibid., 137–46; Roberts, *Papa Jack,* 85–91; Aycock and Scott, *Tex Rickard,* 80–103 (see the introduction, n. 1).

12. Samuels, *Magnificent Rube,* 143.

13. Hagar and Clifton, *Johnson-Jeffries: Dateline Reno,* 27–31; Roberts, *Papa Jack,* 90.

14. Boddy, *Boxing: A Cultural History,* 182 (see the introduction, n. 5).

15. Greenwood, *Johnson vs. Jeffries,* 50.

16. Ibid., 48–49.

17. Roberts, *Papa Jack,* 97.

18. Hagar and Clifton, *Johnson-Jeffries: Dateline Reno,* 5–7; Greenwood, *Johnson vs. Jeffries,* 50–54; Sugar, *100 Years of Boxing,* 70.

19. Samuels, *Magnificent Rube,* 159.

20. Alicia Barber, *Reno's Big Gamble: Image and Reputation in the Biggest Little City* (Lawrence: University Press of Kansas, 2008), 76.

21. Hagar and Clifton, *Johnson-Jeffries: Dateline Reno,* 46.

22. Ibid., 45–50.

23. Greenwood, *Johnson vs. Jeffries,* 62–63.

24. Arthur Ruhl, "The Fight in the Desert," *Collier's,* July 23, 1910.

25. Roberts, *Papa Jack,* 101.

26. Greenwood, *Johnson vs. Jeffries,* 98.

27. In *Reno's Big Gamble,* 43–82, Alicia Barber provides an illuminating examination of the conflicting values that pervaded Reno during the early twentieth century and were exacerbated by the Johnson-Jeffries fight.

28. Greenwood cites a newspaper account in the *San Francisco Chronicle* of July 5 in which Rex Beach wrote, "A brass band climbed into the ring and it was rumored that with a true delicacy of feeling it was about to play, 'All Coons Look Alike to Me,' but racial feeling was too high, perhaps, and they favored us with a selection of national airs." Roberts (*Papa Jack,* 103), however, citing other sources, says that the song was played. At the very least, the fact that the band was even prepared to play the song is indicative of the racial mood in the arena.

29. Attell was publicly linked to the conspiracy to bribe several members of the Chicago White Sox to throw the 1919 World Series. He fled to Canada to avoid testifying before the federal court in Chicago in 1921 in the high-profile trial.

30. Greenwood, *Johnson vs. Jeffries,* 104–5.

31. Ibid., 109.

32. Samuels, *Magnificent Rube,* 171.

33. Greenwood, *Johnson vs. Jeffries,* 117.

34. Thomas Hietala, *The Fight of the Century: Jack Johnson, Joe Louis, and the Struggle for Racial Equality* (Armonk, NY: M. E. Sharpe, 2002), 46.

35. Etta would commit suicide in 1912, and Johnson would be forced to flee

the country to avoid prosecution for a contrived indictment for violation of the Mann Act.

36. Hagar and Clifton, *Johnson-Jeffries: Dateline Reno,* 91.

37. Patrick B. Miller and David K. Wiggins, eds., *Sport and the Colored Line: Black Athletes and Race Relations in Twentieth-Century America* (New York: Routledge, 2004), 74.

38. Greenwood, *Johnson vs. Jeffries,* 130–31.

39. Roberts, *Jack Dempsey,* 24 (see the introduction, n. 1).

40. Theodore Roosevelt, "The Recent Prize Fight," *Outlook,* July 16, 1910, 551.

41. Roberts, *Papa Jack,* 112.

42. Streible, *Fight Pictures,* 237 (see chap. 1, n. 30).

43. Roberts, *Papa Jack,* 113.

44. Barber, *Reno's Big Gamble,* 109–25.

Round 4. Nevada Loses Its Boxing Mojo

1. Samuels, *Magnificent Rube,* 185 (see chap. 2, n. 2).

2. Ibid., 204.

3. *Carson City Appeal,* February 3, 1919, 1.

4. Roberts, *Jack Dempsey,* 265 (see the introduction, n. 1); Roger Kahn, *A Flame of Pure Fire: Jack Dempsey and the Roaring '20s* (New York: Harcourt, 1999), 430–31; Jack Dempsey with Barbara Piattelli Dempsey, *Dempsey* (New York: Harper and Row, 1977), 225–33.

5. For two perspectives on this high-profile fight, see Guy Clifton, *Dempsey in Nevada* (Reno: Jack Bacon & Company and Baobab Books, 2007), 67–74; and Phillip Earl, "Blood, Sweat, and Leather: Jack Dempsey and the Baer-Uzcudun Fight, Reno, July 4, 1931," unpublished essay, n.d., Nevada Historical Society.

6. Although Graham and McKay played major roles in the development of Reno during the 1920s and 1930s and a broad outline of their careers is well established, details of their lives remain unclear. They left behind no documentary record, although various oral histories and newspaper accounts confirm their unsavory reputations. In 1939 they were convicted of conspiracy and mail fraud, sentenced to nine years in federal prison, and fined eleven thousand dollars, serving six years before returning to Reno and reassuming management of the Bank Club. In 1950 President Harry S. Truman granted both men a pardon, apparently as a favor to powerful Nevada politician US senator Patrick McCarran. See Dwayne Kling, *The Rise of the Biggest Little City: An Encyclopedic History of Reno* (Reno: University of Nevada Press, 2009), 4–6, 57–58, 106; Raymond, *George Wingfield,* 163–68 (see chap. 2, n. 41); Barber, *Reno's Big Gamble,* 105–11 (see chap. 3, n. 20); and William D. Rowley, *Reno: Hub of the Washoe Country* (Woodland Hills, CA: Windsor, 1984), 57.

7. Raymond, *George Winfield,* 1–217.

8. Clifton, *Dempsey in Nevada,* 68–74.

9. Baer's connection with Reno endured. During the 1990s, Baer's son Max Jr. became prominent in the Reno area in a highly publicized but futile attempt to open a casino based upon his popular role as Jethro in the popular, long-running (1961–72) television show *The Beverly Hillbillies.*

10. *Reno Evening Gazette,* May 26, 1931, 2; *Humboldt Star,* May 8, 1931, 1.

11. *Nevada State Journal,* May 7, 1931, 1; Clifton, *Dempsey in Nevada,* 78–79.

12. Clifton, *Dempsey in Nevada,* 79–81.

13. *Nevada State Journal,* June 5, 1931, 1; Robert Laxalt, "The Laxalts: Boxers in Spite of Themselves," in *Sierra Nevada Golden Gloves,* District Amateur Boxing Championships program, February 22–23, 1974; Clifton, *Dempsey in Nevada,* 79–85.

14. *Reno Evening Gazette,* June 15, 1931, 1.

15. *Humboldt Star,* June 24, 1931, 1

16. *Nevada State Journal,* June 14, 1931, 6.

17. *Nevada State Journal,* June 20, 1931, 1; Clifton, *Dempsey in Nevada,* 84–85.

18. *Official Program,* eighty-four pages, rare copy located in the University of Nevada Basque Library.

19. *Reno Evening Gazette,* June 22, 1931, 7; *Nevada State Journal,* June 15, 1931, 6.

20. *Nevada State Journal,* July 1, 1931, 4.

21. Earl, "Blood, Sweat, and Leather," 26.

22. Clifton, *Dempsey in Nevada,* 85–87.

23. *Nevada State Journal,* July 5, 1931, 1.

24. Ibid.

25. A detailed, round-by-round description by the Associated Press was published by both Reno newspapers on July 5, 1931. A rare copy of the film of the fight (perhaps the only one available) may be viewed in the University of Nevada Basque Library.

26. *Reno Evening Gazette,* July 4, 1931, 1.

27. Associated Press report, July 4, 1931.

28. *Reno Evening Gazette,* July 4, 1931, 10.

29. *Nevada State Journal,* July 5, 1931, 8.

30. *Nevada State Journal,* July 5, 1931, 4.

31. *Nevada State Journal,* July 5, 1931, 1.

32. Quoted in Earl, "Blood, Sweat and Leather," 49.

Round 5. When the Crowds Went Away

1. Murphy, *Mining Cultures*, 115 (see the introduction, n. 8).

2. Roberts, *Jack Dempsey*, 13–15 (see the introduction, n. 1).

3. Jack Dempsey, as told to Bob Considine and Bill Slocum, *Dempsey* (New York: Simon and Schuster, 1963), 30–55; Dempsey with Dempsey, *Dempsey*, 6–18 (see chap. 4, n. 4); Roberts, *Jack Dempsey*, 15–17.

4. Roberts, *Jack Dempsey*, 154–55.

5. Clifton, *Dempsey in Nevada*, 2–5 (see chap. 4, n. 5).

6. Ibid., 8–10; Dempsey with Considine and Slocum, *Dempsey*, 10; Dempsey with Dempsey, *Dempsey*, 35–37; Roberts, *Jack Dempsey*, 16.

7. Dempsey with Considine and Slocum, *Dempsey*, 10.

8. Clifton, *Dempsey in Nevada*, 11–15.

9. Ibid., 17–23; Roberts, *Jack Dempsey*, 32–39.

10. Roberts, *Jack Dempsey*, 37–66.

11. *Nevada State Journal*, December 1, 1921.

12. No relation to the famous baseball player of the same name, although the Nevada Cobb family had roots in Georgia, as did the Hall of Fame ballplayer who had a home at Lake Tahoe.

13. University of Nevada Oral History Project, "Jake Lawlor: Oral Autobiography of an Iowa Native, with a Close-Up View of Nevada Athletics, 1926–1970," 1971, 179.

14. Ty Cobb, "Inside Stuff," *Nevada State Journal*, February 26, 1939, 12.

15. Cobb, "Inside Stuff," *Nevada State Journal*, January 22, 1941, 8; Cobb, "Polishing Up a Tarnished Sport," *Nevada State Journal*, October 29, 1986.

16. *Nevada Revised Statutes*, 40th sess., March 13, 1941, 48.

17. Aycock and Scott, *Tex Rickard*, 170 (see the introduction, n. 1); Roberts, *Jack Dempsey*, 213–15.

18. *Nevada State Journal*, April 28, 1940, 14.

19. See the extensive coverage provided by Ty Cobb in the *Nevada State Journal*, May 13, 14, 15, 16, 17, 18, and 19, 1940.

20. Andrew McGregor, "Amateur Boxing and Assimilation at the Stewart Indian School, Carson City, Nevada, 1935–1948" (unpublished seminar paper, University of Nevada, Reno, December 10, 2010).

21. For an incisive analysis of Pratt's philosophy and its implementation, see Sally Jenkins, *The Real All Americans: The Team That Changed a Game, a People, a Nation* (New York: Doubleday, 2007), 19–41. See also Richard Henry Pratt, *Battlefield and Classroom: Four Decades with the American Indian* (Norman: University of Oklahoma Press, 2003).

22. Scott Riney, *The Rapid City Indian School, 1898–1933* (Norman: University of Oklahoma Press, 1999), 8, cited in McGregor, "Boxing and Assimilation."

23. McGregor, "Boxing and Assimilation."

24. Robert Laxalt, "The Laxalts: Boxers in Spite of Themselves," Robert Laxalt Papers, Special Collections, University of Nevada Library. See also Cheryll Glotfelty, "Robert Laxalt: Creating Culture in the Desert," in *The Maverick Spirit: Building the New Nevada,* edited by Richard O. Davies (Reno: University of Nevada Press, 1998), 114–32.

25. Lawlor, oral history, 177; David Hoy, interview with the author, Reno, June 9, 2012.

26. E. C. Wallenfeldt, *The Six-Minute Fraternity: The Rise and Fall of NCAA Tournament Boxing, 1932–60* (Westport, CT: Praeger, 1994).

27. "Bachelors of Boxing's Arts," *Sports Illustrated,* April 20, 1959, 34.

28. Jim Doherty, "Requiem for a Middleweight," *Smithsonian,* April 2000, 122–40.

29. Wallenfeldt, *Six-Minute Fraternity,* ix–xiii, 373–77; Martin Kane, "College Boxing's Last Round," *Sports Illustrated,* March 11, 1968, 22–23.

30. Robert H. Boyle, "It's That New College Try," *Sports Illustrated,* April 11, 1977.

31. Kevin Stott, "UNLV Boxing Club Leaves an Impact at Nationals," *Anthem View,* July 6, 2005; Damon Hodge, "Club Boxing Team Joins UNLV Roster," *Anthem View,* November 4, 1998; "Facility Gives UNLV Boxing a Head Start," *Anthem View,* February 17, 1999; Shane Bevell, "Packing a Punch: UNLV Boxers Upset Military Academies to Win National Title," *UNLV Magazine,* Fall 2006.

Round 6. "Let's Get It On!"

1. Mills Lane with Jedwin Smith, *Let's Get It On: Tough Talk from Boxing's Top Ref and Nevada's Most Outspoken Judge* (New York: Crown, 1998), 1.

2. Ibid., 83.

3. Ibid., 135–37.

4. Ibid., 54.

5. Ibid., 57.

6. Michael Sion, "Biting the Big Apple: Nevada's Favorite Son Hits Manhattan with His Own Brand of Justice," *Silver and Blue* (University of Nevada alumni magazine), September 1998, 6–11.

7. Lane with Smith, *Let's Get It On,* 62.

8. Mills Lane scrapbook, in possession of the Lane family. This source was instrumental in the writing of this chapter and covers the years 1957–72. It contains more than three hundred clippings of his boxing experience in the marines and as a college and professional boxer, and it ends with his early refereeing experiences.

9. Lane with Smith, *Let's Get It On,* 81.

10. "Bachelors of Boxing," *Sports Illustrated,* April 20, 1959, 34–35.

11. Lane with Smith, *Let's Get It On,* 82.

12. Lane scrapbook.

13. Ibid.

14. Ibid.; *Artemisia, 1960* (University of Nevada yearbook).

15. Lane scrapbook.

16. Ibid.; Lane with Smith, *Let's Get It On,* 154.

17. Lane scrapbook; Mike Sion, "Crimefighter with a Punch," *Silver and Blue* (University of Nevada alumni magazine), March 1994.

18. Lane scrapbook; Lane with Smith, *Let's Get It On,* 94–96.

19. Lane scrapbook.

20. Ibid.; Lane with Smith, *Let's Get It On,* 108–9; Rollan Melton, "Nevada Sports," *Reno Evening Gazette,* August 10, 1962.

21. Lane scrapbook; Lane with Smith, *Let's Get It On,* 110.

22. Bob Berry, interview with the author, Reno, May 30, 2012.

23. Lane with Smith, *Let's Get It On,* 111–12.

24. Ibid.

25. Lane scrapbook; Lane with Smith, *Let's Get It On,* 118–19.

26. Lane with Smith, *Let's Get It On,* 120.

27. Ibid., 119–31.

28. Ibid.; Lane scrapbook.

29. For a summary of his views on the status of criminal law in America, see Lane with Smith, *Let's Get It On,* 155–67.

30. Sion, "Crimefighter with a Punch."

31. Lane with Smith, *Let's Get It On,* 234–35.

32. *Oakland Tribune,* February 23, 1993.

33. Copy of letter, Lane to Bobby Hinds, February 25, 2000, Lane scrapbook.

34. *Las Vegas Review-Journal,* November 9, 2008.

Round 7. Las Vegas Embraces Prizefighting

1. Edward Hoagland, excerpt from *Compass Points: How I Lived* (2001), reprinted in *At the Fights: American Writers on Boxing,* edited by George Kimball and John Schulian (New York: Library of America, 2012), 480–83.

2. Randy Roberts and James Olson, *Winning Is the Only Thing* (Baltimore: Johns Hopkins University Press, 1989), 103–4.

3. Randy Roberts, *Joe Louis: Hard Time Man* (New Haven, CT: Yale University Press, 2010), 235.

4. Arthur Daley, "Boxing Is on the Ropes," *New York Times Magazine,* January 31, 1954, 19. See also John Lardner, "So You Think You See the Fight on TV!," *Saturday Evening Post,* May 2, 1954, 144–46.

5. Roberts and Olson, *Winning Is the Only Thing,* 104.

6. Jeffrey T. Sammons, *Beyond the Ring: The Role of Boxing in American Society* (Urbana: University of Illinois Press, 1990), 136–77; Roberts and Olson, *Winning Is the Only Thing,* 76–80.

7. Roberts and Olson, *Winning Is the Only Thing,* 79.

8. Sally Denton and Roger Morris, *The Money and the Power: The Making of Las Vegas and Its Hold on America* (New York: Vintage, 2001), 6.

9. Bob Miller, *Son of a Gambling Man: My Journey to the Governor's Mansion from a Casino Family* (New York: St. Martin's Press, 2013). Ironically, Governor Miller's rise to political power was as a district attorney with a reputation for his vigorous prosecution of those accused of major crimes.

10. Denton and Morris, *The Money and the Power;* John L. Smith, *Sharks in the Desert: The Founding Fathers and Current Kings of Las Vegas* (Fort Lee, NJ: Barricade Books, 2005); Geoff Schumacher, *Sun, Sin, and Suburbia: A History of Modern Las Vegas* (Las Vegas: Stephens Press, 2012); Eugene Moehring, *Resort City in the Sunbelt: Las Vegas, 1930–1970,* 2nd ed. (Reno: University of Nevada Press, 2000); Ed Reid and Ovid Demaris, *The Green Felt Jungle* (New York: Trident Press, 1963).

11. Ibid.

12. Russell R. Elliott, *History of Nevada,* 2nd ed. (Lincoln: University of Nebraska Press, 1987), 329–32. See also Davies, *Maverick Spirit,* 5–8 (see chap. 5, n. 24).

13. Arne Lang, *Prizefighting: An American History* (Jefferson, NC: McFarland, 2008), 144–46; Tim Dahlberg, *Fight Town: Las Vegas—Fight Capital of the World* (Las Vegas: Stephens Press, 2004), 40–51.

14. *Las Vegas Review-Journal,* May 1, 1955, 32; Dahlberg, *Fight Town,* 42.

15. *Las Vegas Review-Journal,* May 2, 1955, 16; Lang, *Prizefighting: An American History,* 145–47.

16. Kristen Peterson, "Johnny Tocco's Legendary Gym Still Thriving," *Las Vegas Weekly,* September 13, 2012.

17. Dahlberg, *Fight Town,* 57–65; Robert H. Boyle, "Sonny Slams Ahead," *Sports Illustrated,* July 29, 1963, 10–15.

18. Sammons, *Beyond the Ring,* 177–80.

19. Boyle, "Sonny Slams Ahead," 14.

20. Lang, *Prizefighting: An American History,* 149–50; Sammons, *Beyond the Ring,* 182–83.

21. Roberts, *Joe Louis,* 252–53.

22. Ibid., 247–59.

23. Ibid., 257. See also Chris Mead, *Champion: Joe Louis, Black Hero in White America* (New York: Scribner, 1985).

24. Dahlberg, *Fight Town;* John Trent, interview with the author, Reno,

October 17, 2012; "Parking Lot Paved with Gold," *Sports Illustrated,* October 13, 1980, 44–45.

25. Dahlberg, *Fight Town,* 27, 29.

26. Ibid., 69; Thomas Hauser, *Muhammad Ali: His Life and Times* (New York: Touchstone Books, 1991), 38–39; *Las Vegas Review-Journal,* June 25, 1961, 39.

27. Ibid., 39.

28. Muhammad Ali with Richard Durham, *The Greatest: My Own Story* (New York: Random House, 1975), 17–19; Hauser, *Muhammad Ali,* 53.

29. Hauser, *Muhammad Ali,* 56–112; Dahlberg, *Fight Town,* 69–93.

30. *Las Vegas Review-Journal,* July 23, 1963, 22; July 24, 1963, 32; Boyle, "Sonny Slams Ahead," 15.

31. Sammons, *Beyond the Ring,* 181–83.

32. Hauser, *Muhammad Ali,* 139; Roberts and Olson, *Winning Is the Only Thing,* 173–74.

33. Richard O. Davies, *America's Obsession: Sports and Society Since 1945* (Fort Worth, TX: Harcourt Brace, 1994), 224.

34. Dahlberg, *Fight Town,* 52.

35. Richard O. Davies, "The Bull and the Butterfly," in *Rivals! The Ten Greatest American Sports Rivalries of the 20th Century,* by Davies (Oxford: Wiley-Blackwell, 2010), 156–80.

36. Hauser, *Muhammad Ali,* 350–54.

37. *Las Vegas Review-Journal,* October 1, 1980, E1.

38. Hauser, *Muhammad Ali,* 395–421.

39. Ibid., 404; *Las Vegas Review-Journal,* October 2, 1980, E1.

40. "Doom in the Desert," *Sports Illustrated,* October 13, 1980, 36–44. See also Dave Anderson, "Muhammad Ali: Death of a Salesman," *New York Times,* October 3, 1980, 25; Hal Quinn, "Rolling with the Last Con," *Maclean's,* October 3, 1980, 38–39; and *Las Vegas Review-Journal,* October 3, 1980, A11.

41. *Las Vegas Review-Journal,* October 3, 1980, A11; Dahlberg, *Fight Town,* 87.

42. Hauser, *Muhammad Ali,* 409, 412–14.

43. Ibid., 413–18.

44. Dave Anderson, "The High Rollers Gather in Las Vegas," *New York Times,* October 3, 1980, 28.

Round 8. Las Vegas, "Boxing Capital of the World"

1. Ira Berkow, "Arum Is Proven Ringmaster," *New York Times,* April 7, 1987.

2. Budd Schulberg, *Ringside: A Treasury of Boxing Reportage* (Chicago: Ivan R. Dee, 2006), 124. Unlike Bob Arum, who has remained relatively

noncontroversial and therefore not the subject of journalistic probes, Don King has attracted considerable attention—and mostly sharp criticism—from journalists. Jack Newfield provides an extensive critical assessment in *The Life and Crimes of Don King: The Shame of Boxing in America* (New York: Harbor Electronics, 2003). See also Sammons, *Beyond the Ring,* 219–27 (see chap. 7, n. 6).

3. Newfield, *Life and Crimes of Don King,* 147.

4. Ibid., 141.

5. Ibid., 127–48.

6. *Las Vegas Review-Journal,* January 22, 1976, 22; January 26, 1976, 26.

7. "Doom in the Desert," *Sports Illustrated,* October 13, 1980, 35–44.

8. Dave Anderson, "The High Rollers Gather in Las Vegas," *New York Times,* October 3, 1980, 25.

9. *Las Vegas Review-Journal,* October 1, 1980, C1; October 2, 1980, 1; October 3, 1980, 16; Lang, *Prizefighting: An American History,* 162–65 (see chap. 7, n. 13).

10. Ralph Wiley, "Then All the Joy Turned to Sorrow," *Sports Illustrated,* November 22, 1982, 26–33; Mark Kriegel, *The Good Son: The Life of Ray "Boom Boom" Mancini* (New York: Free Press, 2012), 133–70.

11. "Boxing Shadows," *Time,* November 29, 1982, 84; Fred Bruning, "Shake Hands and Come Out Killing," *Maclean's,* December 13, 1982, 82–86. See especially a feature story published on the twentieth anniversary of the fight: Mark Kriegel, "A Step Back," *New York Times,* September 17, 2012, D1–6.

12. Sammons, *Beyond the Ring,* 249.

13. *Las Vegas Review-Journal,* November 14, 1982, 1; Wiley, "Then All the Joy Turned to Sorrow," 28.

14. *Las Vegas Review-Journal,* November 14, 1982, 1; Kriegel, "A Step Back."

15. Lang, *Prizefighting: An American History,* 171; Sammons, *Beyond the Ring,* 249–51.

16. Tom Callahan, "Boxing Shadows: The Bittersweet Science," *Maclean's,* November 29, 1982, 84.

17. Bruning, "Shake Hands," 13.

18. Sammons, *Beyond the Ring,* 249–50; David Noonan, "Boxing and the Brain," *New York Times,* June 12, 1983, 40ff.

19. Sugar Ray Leonard with Michael Arkush, *The Big Fight: My Life In and Out of the Ring* (New York: Viking Penguin, 2011), 1–70.

20. "No Más! No More! No More Box!," *Time,* December 8, 1980, 108ff; Leonard with Arkush, *Big Fight,* 147–67.

21. *Las Vegas Review-Journal,* September 16, 1981, C1.

22. Ibid.; Frank Deford, "Sportsman of the Year," *Sports Illustrated,* December 28, 1981, 34–41; "Clearing the Way for a Big Payday," *Sports Illustrated,*

June 6, 1981, 20ff; "Fist Full of Dollars," *New York Times Magazine,* September 13, 1981, 142ff; Lang, *Prizefighting: An American History,* 168–69.

23. *Las Vegas Review-Journal,* September 17, 1981, D2; Dahlberg, *Fight Town,* 95–113 (see chap. 7, n. 13).

24. Pat Putnam, "An Uncertain View of the Future," *Sports Illustrated,* May 24, 1982, 48–52; Leonard with Arkush, *Big Fight,* 196–212.

25. Pete Axthelm, "The Eight Great Minutes," *Newsweek,* April 29, 1987, 61; Lang, *Prizefighting: An American History,* 172–73; Dahlberg, *Fight Town,* 101–6.

26. William Nack, "Everything I Did Worked," *Sports Illustrated,* April 20, 1987, 50ff; Pete Axthelm, "Sugar's Sweet Confection," *Newsweek,* April 20, 1987, 67; Leonard with Arkush, *Big Fight,* 229–60; Lang, *Prizefighting: An American History,* 174–75; Dahlberg, *Fight Town,* 107–9.

27. Pat Putnam, "Another Classic," *Sports Illustrated,* June 19, 1989, 18–21.

28. Pat Putnam, "One for the Ages," *Sports Illustrated,* December 18, 1989, 24–25.

29. *Las Vegas Review-Journal,* December 8, 1989, D1; Leonard with Arkush, *Big Fight,* 261–75.

30. Dahlberg, *Fight Town,* 173–74.

31. Sammons, *Beyond the Ring,* 225.

32. *Las Vegas Review-Journal,* November 23, 1986, E1; William Plummer, "Cus D'Amato," in *Iron Mike: The Mike Tyson Reader,* edited by Daniel O'Connor (New York: Thunder's Mouth Press, 2002), 1–8; Lang, *Prizefighting: An American History,* 177–84.

33. Richard Hoffer, "He Got Up and . . . ," *Sports Illustrated,* February 10, 1990, 12–24; "Just Like in the Movies," *Time,* February 26, 1990, 62.

34. Newfield, *Life and Crimes of Don King,* 274; Rick Reilly, "Your Hair-Raising Gall," *Sports Illustrated,* February 19, 1990, 90.

35. Controversy about Tyson's treatment in the Indiana criminal justice system developed long before the initial trial and assessments remains divided. For example, see Randy Roberts with J. Gregory Garrison, *Heavy Justice: The Trial of Mike Tyson* (Fayetteville: University of Arkansas Press, 2000); Joyce Carol Oates, "Rape and the Boxing Ring," *Newsweek,* February 24, 1992; and Robert Lipsyte, "From Spark to Flame to a Roaring Blaze," *New York Times,* February 12, 1992, sec. 2, 13.

36. Bert Sugar, *The 100 Greatest Boxers of All Time* (New York: Bonanza Books, 1984).

37. William Nack, "The Brink," *Sports Illustrated,* March 26, 1990, 16–21; Lang, *Prizefighting: An American History,* 194–98.

38. Oscar De La Hoya with Steve Springer, *American Son: My Story* (New York: Harper, 2008).

39. Ibid., 177–91.

40. Dahlberg, *Fight Town,* 205–7.

41. Richard Hoffer, "Class Dismissed," *Sports Illustrated,* September 2, 1999, 56–58; Dahlberg, *Fight Town,* 207.

42. De La Hoya with Springer, *American Son,* 165; Lang, *Prizefighting: An American History,* 216–17.

43. ESPN.com (December 12, 2008).

Split Decision. Prizefighting on the Margins

1. Hauser, *Muhammad Ali,* 492 (see chap. 7, n. 26).

2. Ibid., 465.

3. Barry Bearak, "A Toehold in the Mainstream," *New York Times,* November 12, 2011, 10.

4. Sammons, *Beyond the Ring,* 353 (see chap. 7, n. 6).

5. Newfield, *Life and Crimes of Don King,* 325 (see chap. 8, n. 2).

6. Sammons, *Beyond the Ring,* 257.

7. Ellis Cashmore, *Tyson: Nature of the Beast* (Cambridge: Polity Press, 2005), 60–107.

8. Lane with Smith, *Let's Get It On,* 21 (see chap. 6, n. 1).

9. Dahlberg, *Fight Town,* 161–62 (see chap. 7, n. 13).

10. Lane with Smith, *Let's Get It On,* 36–37; Dahlberg, *Fight Town,* 62.

11. Lane with Smith, *Let's Get It On,* 21.

12. Ibid., 7–8.

13. Ibid., 8–9.

14. Ibid., 8–21.

15. Cashmore, *Tyson,* 60–81.

16. Dahlberg, *Fight Town,* 167–69; Lane with Smith, *Let's Get It On,* 16, 21.

17. Lane with Smith, *Let's Get It On,* 19.

18. Dahlberg, *Fight Town,* 168.

19. Lane with Smith, *Let's Get It On,* 20.

20. *Las Vegas Review-Journal,* June 30, 1997, C2; Schulberg, *Ringside,* 184–91 (see chap. 8, n. 2).

21. *Las Vegas Review-Journal,* June 29, 1997, C1; June 30, 1997, C2.

22. *Las Vegas Review-Journal,* July 1, 1997, C1; Dahlberg, *Fight Town,* 168; O'Connor, *Iron Mike,* 247–55 (see chap. 8, n. 32); Cashmore, *Tyson,* 81–82.

23. Jon Wertheim, *Blood in the Cage: Mixed Martial Arts, Pat Miletich, and the Furious Rise of the UFC* (Boston: Houghton Mifflin, 2009), 58. See also Erich Krauss and Bret Aita, *Brawl: A Behind the Scenes Look at Mixed Martial Arts Competition* (Chicago: ECW Press, 2002).

24. Wertheim, *Blood in the Cage,* 98–102.

25. *New York Times,* March 15, 2011.

26. Douglas Quenqua, "The Fight Club Generation," *New York Times,* March 15, 2011, E1, E10; Bearak, "Toehold in the Mainstream."

27. Bearak, "Toehold in the Mainstream."

28. Bert Sugar quoted in Thomas Myler, *The Sweet Science Goes Sour: How Boxing Scandal Brought Boxing to Its Knees* (Vancouver, BC: Greystone Books, 2006), 9, 13.

Bibliographic Essay

Of all American sports, only baseball and boxing have produced a substantial body of significant literature. The appeal of baseball is to the "national game," to pleasant memories of crucial games played decades ago, to the rich legacy of once-dominant teams and venerated players whose exploits have enlivened American life for more than 150 years. Whereas baseball evokes a flood of warm, nostalgic memories, the appeal of boxing is to the raw emotions that are released when two men enter the ring intent on inflicting serious damage upon the other and proceed to attempt to do just that. Boxing enthusiasts have long referred to this form of structured violence as "the sweet science," an ironic definition of a blood sport that places enormous physical and emotional demands upon the relatively few men who choose to become professional boxers.

To the dedicated boxing fan, no other sporting event can even come close to matching the sheer drama generated by a big fight. Many of the best sports motion pictures ever made have been those that have exploited the human dimensions of boxing. The attraction of the sport has been described in many ways, but it can often be viewed as embodying both physical artistry and unrestrained savagery. Ever since prizefighting captured the attention of Americans in the late nineteenth century, writers have found that a fight can evoke a wide range of emotions to tell dramatic stories of courage and redemption—as well as corruption and exploitation—that revolve around the likes of crooked gamblers, malevolent mobsters, conniving managers, aging trainers, and lovable underdog boxers inevitably seeking to escape a deprived childhood and multiple forms of hardship and adversity. In many instances, major prizefights can reflect transcendent political or social issues, as in the case of the Jeffries-Johnson fight that took place in 1910 in the small town of Reno and unleashed racial tensions and considerable violence across the United States. A prizefight can also become a metaphor for the conflicting forces engaged in international politics, as when a nervous world anxiously watched the gathering winds of war at the time Joe Louis and Max Schmeling met in a New York ring for the second time. Boxing, as encapsulated in the controversial career of Muhammad Ali, vividly accentuated the furious national debates raging in America over civil rights, religious diversity, and the Vietnam War during the divisive 1960s.

For even the most experienced boxing fan, witnessing the violence unleashed in the ring can be shocking. The fact that boxing evokes primeval emotions has long been recognized, and although it is seldom ever mentioned in the sports pages or the slick pages of literary magazines, death hovers over the ring every time the bell rings for the next round. That possibility tends to inspire the writer to dig down deep to find just the right words to describe the courage of boxers who willingly take that risk.

Not surprisingly, boxing has attracted many leading sports journalists. In fact, much of boxing history has been written by succeeding generations of journalists whose writings span the entire twentieth century. Among the most notable early sportswriting pioneers were Jack London, Heywood Broun, Paul Gallico, Grantland Rice, and Ring Lardner. During the midcentury, when boxing enjoyed an elevated status among sports fans, it was ably reported by such talented writers as A. J. Liebling, Red Smith, Arthur Daley, and Martin Kane, and during the latter decades of the century, when the national focus of boxing moved from New York City to Las Vegas, it was chronicled by such compelling writers as Frank Deford, Jim Murray, Thomas Hauser, Budd Schulberg, Norman Mailer, Richard Hoffer, Joyce Carol Oates, and Bert Sugar.

Academic historians have come only in recent years to appreciate the role that sports have played in the history of American life and culture. It has been only in the past few decades that historians have dared to consider the social and cultural significance of sports. It was not until 1973 that an academic organization was established—the North American Society for Sport History—and began publishing a refereed journal. In 1960 Harold Seymour, drawing upon his Cornell doctoral dissertation, published the first of several books detailing the formative years of baseball. Seymour's *Baseball: The Early Years* (New York: Oxford University Press) is generally considered the first serious academic book devoted to American sports, and during the next two decades several other histories of baseball appeared that carried the imprimatur of serious academic endeavors. It is readily apparent that those young scholars who dared undertake serious sports issues risked offending the traditional sensibilities of senior members of the faculty who sat on tenure and promotion committees. One of the first such scholars who as a graduate student at Yale dared write a serious dissertation on the formative years of baseball, Warren Goldstein, reports that his subject made his quest for a tenure-track position in higher education a long and frustrating experience.

Boxing had long enjoyed popularity with novelists and filmmakers, and it was only a matter of time before the growing academic interest in American social and cultural history would lead to a growing body of boxing histories. Not surprisingly, the emergence of such academic works coincided with the growing fascination in academic circles with themes revolving around race, gender, and class. Boxers came almost exclusively from the ranks of the poor and those ethnic and racial groups that had suffered the burdens of segregation and discrimination. What was more authentically emblematic of the traits of masculinity than those young men who sought to achieve the American Dream by becoming successful pugilists?

Taking note of the fact that organized sports attracted the involvement of a substantial portion of the American people, two leading scholars suggested that sports deserved the attention of a new generation of scholars. Writing in the *Chronicle of Higher Education* in 1994, Michael Oriard and Elliott J. Gorn (of Oregon State and Brown Universities, respectively) called upon scholars in such fields as sociology, anthropology, history, political science, psychology, and philosophy to put aside traditional assumptions about sports and to explore the many areas in American life where cultural studies intersected with competitive sports: "Where is there a cultural activity more freighted with constructions of masculinity than football, more deeply inscribed with race than boxing, more tied in the public mind to the hopes and hopelessness of inner-city youth than basketball?" And, with a nod to the current academic preoccupation with multiculturalism, Oriard and Gorn observed, "It is almost a cliché to mention that sports are the lingua franca of men talking across divisions of class and race. Sports can reveal just how interdependent particular subcultures and the larger consumer culture can be. Think, for example, of the symbiotic ties between inner-city playground basketball and the National Basketball Association."

Gorn himself had previously published a tradition-shattering history of prizefighting during the nineteenth century: *The Manly Art: Bare-Knuckle Fighting in America* (Ithaca, NY: Cornell University Press, 1986). Gorn's article describing the gruesome combat sport of "rough-and-tumble" that was prominent in the Appalachian Mountain regions in the nineteenth century drew considerable critical praise when it appeared in the prestigious *American Historical Review:* "'Gouge and Bite, Pull Hair and Scratch': The Social Significance of Fighting in the Southern Back Country" (February 1985). Three years later America's first bona fide sports "hero," the son of mid-nineteenth-century Irish immigrants, was the subject of a solid biography by Michael T. Isenberg: *John L. Sullivan and His America* (1988). It appeared in the new "Sport and Society" series being promoted by the University of Illinois Press. That same year Illinois published a penetrating critique of boxing by Jeffrey T. Sammons. One reviewer described *Beyond the Ring: The Role of Boxing in American Society* as documenting "the ruin waiting for almost all those ill advised to become professional boxers" and confirming "all the legends of crime, of swindling, and of the miserable economic rewards allotted to the vast majority of fighters. . . . No one reading Sammons can doubt that [boxing] is an evil." From these pioneering books, it was clear that boxing historiography would take a much different trajectory than that of baseball.

Sammons, a New York University historian, was especially powerful in his discussion of the racism that provides a compelling narrative of boxing history from Joe Gans and Jack Johnson to Muhammad Ali and Mike Tyson. However, for a detailed discussion of the pervasive racism that dominated the early history of boxing, the reader must consult three books written by Randy Roberts of Purdue University. He focuses upon the dynamics of racism in two important biographies, *Papa Jack: Jack Johnson and the Era of White Hopes* (New York: Free Press, 1983) and *Joe Louis: Hard Times Man* (New Haven, CT: Yale University Press, 2010). In 2000 Roberts collaborated with the prosecuting attorney in the rape trial of Mike Tyson, J. Gregory Garrison, producing *Heavy Justice: The Trial of Mike Tyson* (Fayetteville: University of Arkansas Press, 2000). Roberts is also the author of the definitive biography of the preeminent boxer of the 1920s: *Jack Dempsey: The Manassa Mauler* (Baton Rouge: Louisiana State University Press, 1979). Roberts's biography of Joe Louis is supplemented by the detailed monographs on the Louis-Schmeling fight by Lewis A. Erenberg, *Greatest Fight of Our Generation: Louis vs. Schmeling* (Oxford: Oxford University Press, 2006), and David Margolick, *Beyond Glory: Joe Louis vs. Max Schmeling, and a World on the Brink* (New York: Alfred A. Knopf, 2005). Also of importance to an understanding of racism and boxing are Thomas Hietala, *Fight of the Century: Jack Johnson, Joe Louis, and the Struggle for Racial Equality* (Armonk, NY: M. E. Sharpe, 2002), and Kasia Boddy, *Boxing: A Cultural History* (London: Reaktion Books, 2008).

I am indebted to the many scholars who have contributed to a large body of literature on the history of Nevada, several of which helped provide a frame of reference for this book. My debt to these many authors is great and will be found in the endnotes.

Index

Ferrell, Charles, 76

Fertitta, Frank and Lorenzo, 249

"The Fight," 214–15

"Fight of the Millennium," 227

film industry: controversy over the film of the Johnson-Jeffries match, 88–89; film of the Gans-Nelson match, 56, 58–59; film rights and the *Corbett vs. Fitzsimmons* movie, 30–32; film rights for the Johnson-Jeffries match, 68; Enoch Rector, 12, 17, 31

Finch, Bruce, 213–14

"finish fights," 11. *See also* Corbett-Fitzsimmons match; Gans-Nelson match

Fitzsimmons, Robert: antagonistic relationship with James Corbett, 22, 24; boxing career, 22–23; controversy with Wyatt Earp over the 1897 Sharkey match, 24–25; Jim Jeffries and, 65; match against James Corbett (*see* Corbett-Fitzsimmons match); matches against Peter Maher, 10, 16–18

Fitzsimmons, Rose, 28, 29

Fleischer, Nat, 47

Florida, 191

Florida Athletic Club, 11

Folley, Zora, 189

Foreman, George, 193–94, 202, 204

Foster, Bob, 162, 193

Fox, Billy, 174

Fox television, 251

Frawley Act (NY), 93–94, 99

Frazier, Joe, 190, 193, 194

Frias, Arturo, 206

Friday Night Fights (television show), 172

Frisch, Roy, 101

Fullmer, Gene, 181–82

Gallico, Paul, 120–21

gambling: legalization in Nevada, 99, 100; reform of gambling industry regulation, 177–78. *See also* casinos

Gammick, Johnny, 117, 125, 126–27

Gans, Joe: boxing career, 46–48; on Oscar Nelson's ability to absorb punishment, 50; Oscar Nelson's racism and, 54; reception in Goldfield, 48, 54. *See also* Gans-Nelson match

Gans-Nelson match: account of the fight, 56–58; background of the fighters, 46–50; betting on, 55; boxing as a metaphor for the mining life, 52–53; crowds drawn to Goldfield, 51, 55; the exploitation of racial attitudes and, 51, 53–54, 58; film made from, 58–59; final financial accounting, 55; Gans's weight and, 55; Goldfield's boosterism and, 52; Goldfield's decision to hold, 35, 42, 43; impact on Goldfield, 58, 60, 61; Billy Nolan and, 48; opposition to, 52; prefight publicity, 50–51; prelim fight, 55–56; George Rickard's promotion of, 3, 42, 43–46, 50–51; sale of speculative mining stocks and, 52; women spectators, 53

Gavilán, Kid, 172

Genasci, John, 138, 151

General Film Company, 89

Genovese crime family, 185

Gilfeather, Jack, 122

Gillett, James N., 72–73

Gillette Cavalcade of Sports (radio show), 170–71

Gilpin Airlines, 108–9

Gleason, Jack, 67, 87–88

"glove contests," 7

Goldberg, Rube, 51

Golden Boy Promotions, 225, 228

Golden Glove program, 129–31

Goldfield (NV): African Americans in,